SLATE QUARRYING IN WALES

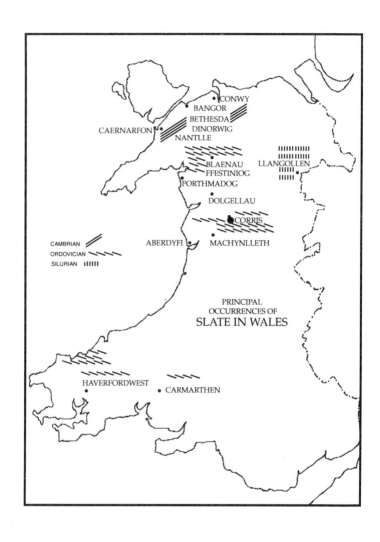

CONWY
BANGOR
BETHESDA
DINORWIG
CAERNARFON
NANTLLE

LLANGOLLEN

BLAENAU
FFESTINIOG
PORTHMADOG

DOLGELLAU

CORRIS

CAMBRIAN
ORDOVICIAN
SILURIAN

ABERDYFI
MACHYNLLETH

PRINCIPAL
OCCURRENCES OF
SLATE IN WALES

HAVERFORDWEST
CARMARTHEN

SLATE QUARRYING
IN WALES

by

ALUN JOHN RICHARDS

ISBN: 1-84527-026-6

Cover design: Sian Parri

First published in 2006 by
Gwasg Carreg Gwalch, 12 Iard yr Orsaf, Llanrwst,
Wales LL26 0EH.
Phone: 01492 642031 Fax: 01492 641502
e-mail: books@carreg-gwalch.co.uk
Website: www.carreg-gwalch.co.uk

Grateful thanks for research assistance are due to –

Meinir Coleman	Margaret Hughes
Mrs V. I. Cockroft	Rev. Martin Riley
Dr. David Gwyn	Dr. Dafydd Roberts
Griff R. Jones	Roger Symmonds
Gwynfor Pierce Jones	Jeremy Wilkinson
William T. Jones M.B.E.	Merfyn Williams
Dr. Michael Lewis	Richard Williams
John Lloyd	
Michael Freeman	The late Dr. Lewis Lloyd
Steffan ab Owain	The late Dafydd W. Price

The staff of the National Library of Wales

The staff of the Gwynedd Archives Service, Caernarfon and Dolgellau.

The members of Fforwm Tan y Bwlch.

For background material, my many friends involved or formerly involved in the industry.

For general help, encouragement and the use of the Snowdonia National Park Study Centre -

Peter Crew, Twm Elias, Robin Jones.

And for her tireless practical archival and fieldwork input and for proof reading, my wife
Delphine

Should this encourage the visiting of such sites to see the relics of a once great industry, it must be remembered that all are on private land and permission of the owner must be obtained before doing so, also the consent of the occupier of any ground, which has to be crossed to reach a site.

Abandoned slate quarries are dangerous. Rock is slippery, tips can move, falls can and do occur, portions of structures can collapse. There may be hidden and unguarded precipices and shafts. Underground workings should never be entered other than as a competently led and properly equipped.

Also by Alun John Richards published by Gwasg Carreg Gwalch

A Gazeteer of the Welsh Slate Industry
    IBSN 0-86381-196-5
Slate Quarrying at Corris
    IBSN 0-86381-279-1
Slate Quarrying in Wales
    IBSN 0-86381-319-4
Slate Quarrying in Pembrokeshire
    IBSN 0-86381-484-0
The Slate Regions of North& Mid Wales
    IBSN 0-86381-552-9
The Slate Railways of Wales
    IBSN 0-86381-689-4
Fragments of Mine and Mill
    IBSN 0-86381-812-9
Cwm Gwyrfai (With Gwynfor Pierce Jones)
    IBSN 0-86381-987-8
A Tale of Two Rivers (With Jean Napier)
    IBSN 0-86381-989-3
Welsh Slate Craft
    ISBN 1-84527-029-0
Crefftwyr Llechi
    ISBN 1-84527-034-7

CONTENTS

PREFACE

It has truly been said as we all must deplore,
That Grenville and Pitt have made peers by the score,
But now, 'tis asserted, unless I have blundered,
There's a man that makes peeresses here by the hundred,
He regards neither Portland, nor Grenville, nor Pitt,
But creates them at once without patent or writ;
By a stroke of a hammer without the King's aid,
A lady, a countess, or a duchess is made.
Yet high is the station from which they are sent,
And all their great titles are got by descent;
And where'er they are seen in palace or shop,
Their rank they preserve, and are still at the top.
Yet no merit they claim from their birth or connection,
But derive their chief worth from their native
complexion,
And all the best judges prefer, it is said,
A countess in blue to a duchess in red.
This countess or lady though crowds may be present,
Submits to be dressed by the hands of a peasant.
And you'll see, when her grace is but once in his clutches,
With how little respect he will handle a duchess.
Close united they seem, and yet all who have tried 'em
Soon discover how easy it is to divide 'em.
The countess wants life, and the duchess is flat,
No spirit they have – they're as thin as a lath;
No passion or warmth to the countess is known,
And here grace is as cold and as hard as a stone;
Yet I fear you will find, if you watch them a little,
That the countess is frail, and the duchess is brittle.
Too high for a trade, yet without any joke,
Though they never are bankrupt, they often are broke,
And though not a soul ever pilfers or cozens,
They are daily shipped off and transported by dozens.

In France, Jocobinical France, we have seen,
How Nobles have bled by the fierce Guillotine,
But's what the French engine of death to compare,
To the engine which Greenfield and Bramah prepare?
That democrat engine, by which we all know,
Ten thousand great duchesses fall at one blow.
And long may that engine its wonders display,
Long level with ease all rocks in its way,
Till the Vale of Nant Fracon its slates is bereft,
Nor Lady nor Countess nor Duchess is left.

Attributed to Judge Leycester
Greenfield and Bramah, were respectively Penrhyn manager
and the inventor of a machine for prising slate.

TRADITIONAL NAMES FOR SIZES
OF ROOFING SLATES
(Inches)

Typical Declared Weight per 1200 'Best' Quality Meirionnydd roofing slate. Caernarfon slates would tend to be heavier. Lower grades known euphemistically as 'Seconds' or 'Medium' or even 'Strong' would all be up to twice as heavy.

Empresses	26 x 16	4t	0c	0q
Princesses	24 x 14	3	5	0
Duchesses	24 x 12	2	15	0
Small Duchesses	22 x 12	2	10	0
Marchionesses	22 x 11	2	5	0
Broad Countesses	20 x 12	2	5	0
Countesses	20 x 10	1	15	0
Small Countesses	18 x 10	1	12	2
Viscountesses	18 x 9	1	7	2
Wide Ladies	16 x 10	1	7	2
Broad Ladies	16 x 9	1	5	0
Ladies	16 x 8	1	2	2
Small Ladies	14 x 8	1	0	1
Narrow Ladies	14 x 7	0	7	2
Doubles	12 x 6	0	14	0
Singles	10 x 5	0	9	3

These definitions varied a little from area to area and the names by no means covered all sizes, anything up to 30 being offered in the 1890s, by which time naming was falling out of use.

There was a semi-official Queen size which could be anything from 30 x 18 up to 36 x 26, and of course larger sizes were made to order Princesses were sometimes known as 'Fourteens', and the term 'Putts' was used for 14 x 12 and

'Ladies Putts' for 13 x 10, and 'Headers' for 14 x 12. 'Damp Course' slates came in many sizes from 20 x 9 down to 9 x $4\frac{1}{2}$.

Small low quality slates were classed as 'ton slates or 'randoms' and sold by weight, or in southwest Wales, (where they were rather numerous!), as 'locals'. Also in the southwest, the Langolman area produced igneous 'Green' slates that were smaller, thicker and sold in mixed sizes.

1. IN THE BEGINNING
To the late 18th century

In parts of Wales, particularly in the northwest, great mounds of slate waste, the detritus of a once great industry, glower over the landscape, silently reproachful of that industry's decline. On the skylines the walls of ruined drum houses stand like twinned cenotaphs commemorating its triumphs and tragedies. Slates cover the roof, and sometimes the sides, of every house. Slate block forms almost every building and wall. Slate slab is underfoot as steps and pavings, 'planks' of slate make fences. Almost every man-made artefact seems to be of the one, universal material.

Although its origins are ancient and its saga continues, slate quarrying was very much a Victorian industry. Apart from its greatest era almost exactly matching that monarch's reign, its bold, innovative development reflected the spirit of that age. It dominated the economy of the northwest of Wales, where, by the middle of the 19th century it accounted for almost half the total revenues from trade, industry and the professions and at that time in Wales as a whole, its output value compared with that of coal.

Slate quarrying has been described as the 'Welshest' of industries, for unlike mining or metal smelting and manufacture, its techniques were almost all locally devised. Dominating world output, it was manned almost exclusively by native Welshmen who sprang from the same soil as the stone they worked and it is said, have a temperament uniquely suited to the working of this recalcitrant rock. Paradoxically although the language of the quarry, its tools and its methods was, and still is, exclusively Welsh, there is no Welsh word for slate. Llech or Llechfaen can be applied to anything flat. For instance the Welsh Bible refers to Moses being ordered to hew two *'llechau cerrig'* (Exodus XXXIV, 1), this does not infer that slate outcropped on Mount Sinai, but is a literal translation of the Hebrew 'Flat Stone'. Furthermore any flooring flag regardless of its geology may be called 'llech'. Thus it may be difficult to distinguish between slate and other stone in historical records. Llechwedd, a not uncommon place name, may have a slate connotation but invariably denotes a flat hillside. Curiously, a tile in Welsh is 'Priddlech', literally an earth slate. The term 'slat' or 'slatten' is used for a roofing slate, but correctly means a writing slate.

The industry brought prosperity to Bangor and Caernarfon, it created towns such as Bethesda, Blaenau Ffestiniog, Llanberis and Porthmadog, and scores of biblically named hamlets such as Bethel, Carmel, Seion and Salem. It vitalised villages such as Corris, Dolwyddelan, Deiniolen, Penygroes and Talysarn. Above all, it created a whole new and proud way of life.

Most Welsh slate is a metamorphosed sedimentary rock, generally mudstone, which has been subjected by volcanic action and earth movements, to great pressures and temperatures. This has caused the rock to become grain orientated along parallel planes, which are independent of and at an angle to the bedding planes of the original rock This creates a cleavage plane allowing it to be divided into impervious, durable laminae of relatively great strength, which made and still makes it a valuable and unique material. Probably unique too, is the fact that, unlike other minerals slate is manufactured into a totally finished domestic product, on the, extraction site. The methods by which this is done has, mechanisation apart, remained substantially unchanged up to the present time.

Although 'Slate Grey' is a commonplace term, chemical inclusions produce a variety of colours. Protoxide of iron gives blue; peroxide of iron generates reddish and purple casts. Black slate contains iron sulphide and carbonaceous matter, green slate has a low iron content, but is high in magnesia. Highly undesirable is iron oxide, which causes early failure, particularly in acidic industrial atmospheres although its reddish-brown has decorative value. A total no-no is where iron sulphide joins with calcium carbonate to give self destruct properties in even the benignest of environments.

Slate is primarily regarded as a roofing material, yet flooring, fireplaces, cills, lintels, quoins and so on, eventually accounted for approaching half the output tonnage. Slate's imperviousness is ideal for brewery and chemical vats, and it was widely used for cisterns that were sold as 'Flat packs' of drilled and grooved pieces with appropriate rodding, like self-assembly furniture. It was also an ideal material for lining pigsties, cowsheds and so on, as well as those monuments to Victorian civilisation, the 'Gentlemen's'. Its high specific heat, made slate slab useful in dairies and larders. Later its dielectric properties would be exploited for switchboards. It is still used for billiards tables, although sadly, no longer sourced in Wales. Among slate's more bizarre uses was for the making of reusable coffins (Normally for pauper burials).

Most famously, slate was used for that inviolable Welsh tradition, slate gravestones. Originally they were just rough-hewn slab, laid flat on the ground bearing only initials and the date of death. During the 18th century serried ranks of epitaphed headstones began to sprout around every church and chapel, eventually becoming grander and more complex in an endeavour to reflect the status of the one memorialised.

Welsh slate occurs in 3 geological series; Cambrian, Ordovician & Silurian, being, respectively around 600, 500 & 400 million years old.

Slate occurs extensively in several parts of Wales, in veins which unlike say coal measures are highly discontinuous, and obviously can only be worked where they are reasonably accessible. The rock must exhibit clean, parallel cleavage, be free of jointing and other interruptions that would limit the size of block extracted. There needs to be a minimum of inclusions that could mar the appearance, integrity and durability of the product. It is also desirable that the plane of cleavage should be at the steepest possible angle to the bedding plane.

Some of the most important veins where the earliest commercial extraction took place are those Cambrian series that run southwest in a swathe from Conwy towards Pwllheli, the most abundant good cleavable rock being in the immediate hinterland of Bangor and Caernarfon. These gave rise to the 'superquarries' of Penrhyn, at what is now Bethesda, and Dinorwig on the northern shore of Llyn Padarn. These same veins attracted early quarrying on Mynydd y Cilgwyn to the east of Penygroes, which spread to eventually almost fill the Nantlle valley. Outcrops also occurred on Cefn Du, southwest of Llyn Padarn and in the Gwyrfai valley southeast of Waunfawr. Somewhat less desirable rock has been worked in the lower Conwy valley, though much, particularly to the east of the river, only makes rough building block. There are also isolated workable occurrences on the coast near Harlech, and inland at Trawsfynydd. The small quarries on Anglesey are also on Cambrian rock.

Ordovician veins run southwest from around Betws-y-Coed to Porthmadog, being at their richest and best around Blaenau Ffestiniog, tapering off on either side to less desirable material. Ordovician rock also occurs to a lesser extent in a broad, less continuous band, running parallel some miles further south, from Llangynog to Aberdyfi, with the best rock mainly around Corris. In fact these two occurrences, respectively north and south of the Harlech Dome, were once part of the same great anticline that arched over the Cambrian rock of central Meirionnydd. The relatively small and scattered occurrences of slate rock of southwest Wales are also Ordovician.

Silurian slate, is found to the north and south of the Dee

valley, in the Llangollen – Corwen area, in Glynceiriog to the east of Chirk and triflingly, in the Dulas valley north of Machynlleth.

Generally, it is the Cambrian series that provides the hardest and most durable slate, and the Silurian the least so, with the Ordovician in between. The Ordovician of Blaenau Ffestiniog, particularly the Old Vein, makes excellent roofing material and the Corris Narrow Vein, exceptionally good slab. The Silurian yielded (and still yields at Berwyn quarry) slab that is excellent, particularly for indoor use.

It is not possible to clearly define the beginning of the Welsh slate Industry. Some late Iron Age burial sites incorporated slate slabs, but since they were presumably used because they were handy flat stones and not because of intrinsic properties of the rock, this cannot be considered a true slate use. The Romans certainly recognised the properties of slate, as the surviving 3rd century flooring at Segontium (Caernarfon) testifies, this is of Cambrian series slate, clearly from a local source. The reason for the somewhat earlier use at Caer Llugwy, near Capel Curig, of Silurian material is less obvious, the adjacent Cambrian deposits cannot have been unknown, suggesting that hauling from Denbighshire may have been preferred to confronting the then unsubdued Ordorvices. A slate tanning tank from Brithdir near Dolgellau, of late Roman date, possibly suggests a source in the area, and if, as is just possible, some of the slate slabs present in the Sarn Helen road on the Migneint, are original surfacing, then Roman use of Ffestiniog slate is indicated.

In post-Roman times, slate blocks were used for building and for household objects such as bakestones and scrapers, but there is scant evidence of slate roofing until the 12th century. and then only for the most prestigious buildings close to sources of supply. In the 13th century, it was rather more widely employed, most notably by Edward 1 for his castles, although, even at Caernarfon, within sight of an abundant source of slate; timber and lead were the main roofing materials. When Edward 1 stayed at Nantlle, it is reported that he slept under a slate roof, suggesting that, (a), this was a sufficiently unusual happening to be worthy of record, and, (b), that slate quarrying was being carried out nearby, presumably at Cilgwyn.

In the 14th century repairs were made to Chester castle, reputedly with slate shipped coastwise from Aberogwen, near Bangor, presumably originating from Cae Hir, on the Penrhyn estate near what is now Bethesda. In 1399 a French poet, Creton, referred to the King (Richard II) arriving at Conwy *'where there is much slate'*. This slate may have come from one of the nearby early diggings such as Llechlan.

In the early 16th century repairs to Conwy castle were carried out with slate that probably came from Aberogwen despite Dyffryn Conwy being by that time well established as a slate area. One explanation is that it was wished to use the same source that had supplied the slate for its original 1280s construction. Alternatively the fact that a few years later Bishop Morgan (The translator of the Bible into Welsh), despite being a native of the Upper Conway slate area, specified this same material for the re-roofing of St. Asaph cathedral, suggests that its superiority was already acknowledged. This faith in what became to be known as 'Bangor' slate was vindicated in 1932 when during repairs to the cathedral these 400-year-old slates were found to be sound and re-useable.

The 16th century also saw an increase in permissions being granted for slates to be dug on the Penrhyn estate, and there are records of shipments from Aberogwen and Abercegin to Rhuddlan, Chester, Ireland and elsewhere. In fact this century increasingly saw houses across north Wales, several steps below mansion status, being roofed in slate, and slate working, at least on a small scale; becoming more widespread.

The mid 16th century total of 80 tons per annum being

shipped from Caernarfonshire to Ireland had trebled a century later and was accompanied by a considerable growth in the home trade. Certainly by the 17th century men in many locations were describing themselves as Slaters, a term which implied extracting and making slates as well as laying them.

The winning of slate was not confined to the northwest. Quarrying at Bryneglwys, in the Tywyn hinterland may date from the 14th century, and claims are made that at this time slate was being raised on the upper Dyfi. Certainly in the early 1500s Plas Aberllefenni, near Corris, was slate roofed, probably from Hen Gloddfa, later part of Aberllefenni quarry. A century later, John Leland remarked on the number of slate roofs to be found in Oswestry. These probably came either from Llangynog or from Glyn Ceiriog. Also, at that time, slate was being used in Wrexham, undoubtedly from quarries on Oernant, north of Llangollen, and from Llantisilio.

In south Wales too, there was early use. It has been suggested that the Romans used Pembrokeshire material at Caerleon, and famously several quarries on the Eastern Cleddau claimed to have supplied the roofing of Whitland Abbey. Slate used to repair Carmarthen Castle in 1338, presumably came from one of the small quarries near the town. In the 16th century several diggings in Pembrokeshire were dispatching through ports, such as Cardigan, Haverfordwest, Blackpool, St. Clears and possibly Carmarthen. By the end of the 17th century this had become a steady trade, with quarries such as Glogue being very much in business.

It must not be forgotten that well into the 18th century Wales, particularly northwest Wales was a remote region with poor communications. There was some trade with Ireland, but cattle droving apart, little with England. Wales was literally on the way to nowhere, and figuratively, going nowhere. The more mountainous areas were virtually devoid of roads, and even in the lowland areas, such roads as there were, were of doubtful utility in summer and almost impassable in winter. Turnpike Trusts were established in Caernarfonshire in 1769, but even villages of some size were inaccessible to wheeled vehicles until almost into the 19th century.

The maintenance of non-turnpike roads was a parish responsibility, inhabitants being theoretically obliged to participate in their maintenance. This obligation tended to be enforced only at the whim of the few big proprietors, who owned most of the land, and isolated from the seat of government, ran their fiefdoms with almost feudal authority. Moreover when a landlord demanded that tenants mended roads, it was more likely to be in the hope of exacting fines for non-compliance than any wish for improvement. It was not until 1827 that Parish Rates brought about 'professional' maintenance, but even then upkeep was minimal. The standard vehicle was the *llusg* or 2-wheeled sledge, possibly horse, but more likely ox-drawn or even the little wheel-less man-pulled slide car. On the farms much 'cartage' was done with stretcher-like 2-man wheel-less barrows. Thus no commodity, let alone one as heavy and breakable as slate, could be conveyed any great distance, save by water, the reaching of which called for the use of pack-horses or mules, failing which, product had to be carried away on the backs of the men who won it.

This meant that, other than right alongside where it was dug, slate was a material for the rich, and in Wales the rich were thin on the ground. Agriculture, much on unproductive acidic hillsides, was at subsistence level. Fishing served only very localised markets, woollen manufacture was carried out on home looms for pittances. In places metal mines provided some paid employment, but profits went to absentee landlords or distant proprietors. There was virtually no middle class. Few doctors could be afforded, few lawyers were needed, there was little coin to support shopkeepers and tiny tenant farms produced no surplus wealth. Contemporary accounts euphemistically described the Welsh diet as, *'abstemious'* with *'animal food* [i.e. meat] *and ale not among their usual fare'.* One-roomed hovels abounded, the better ones built of rough stones, some just 'mud and sod', the sparse accommodation frequently shared with a pig or a cow. Tenancies 'At Will' offered no security and thus no incentive for occupiers to make improvements. Roofs were thatched with straw or fern or at best wooden shingles, with an aperture for the smoke of the peat fire. Some of the larger, owner-occupied farmhouses were slated, but there was little chance of the roofs of tenanted properties being slated, as thatch maintenance was the occupier's responsibility whereas 'stone' roof repairs fell on the landlord.

Custom for slate being limited, and money for investment non-existent, Welsh slate for centuries remained a 'cottage' industry, little groups of men supplying the wants of the less indigent people of their immediate localities or the more affluent further afield. It was literally a cottage industry at Cwm y Glo, [Named not for coal; but for charcoal], at the northern end of Llyn Padarn, where slate blocks brought back by boat from where Glynrhonwy quarry would later be sited, was made into slates by the fireside.

The rock was mostly extracted by crowbarring or driving iron wedges into cracks or natural joints. Assisted if necessary by wetting wooden wedges or quicklime. (In the sea-cliff quarries of southwest Wales, the rising tide served to soak wedges). Fire-setting, i.e. heating rock then quenching to shatter it may also have been used but tales of this being employed in the 20thC are probably apocryphal. After discarding unsuitable rock, hammers were used to reduce good blocks to manageable size for splitting.

Methods in Pembrokeshire in the 16th century were described by Owen as *'The stone being digged in the quarry is cloven by iron bars to a thickness of a foot or half a foot and in length or breadth ii or iii foote and so carried for walling stones, or for tyle they cleave the same to what thines they thinke best, and so the self-same stone and quarry serveth to begin and end the house'*. Had this account been written 300 of 400 years earlier (or later!) would have differed little.

The smallness of scale up to the 18th century is illustrated by the continued use of the old units of 'Cant bach' (Small hundred) of 32 and the 'Cant mawr' (Big hundred) of 128 based on half and twice a pannier load of 64, respectively. It was well into the 18th century before the nominal thousand or 'Mille' (1200 slates to user, 1260 to merchants), came into full use.

During the 18th century things started to change, the Industrial Revolution was beginning, Britain was starting to move from agriculture to manufacture, trade was expanding and country dwellers were becoming townies, In the south and the north-east of Wales a measure of metallurgically-driven prosperity loomed, but in the remoter parts of Wales, apart from places such as Parys Mountain on Anglesey where copper mining flourished, these events were bad news. Woollen production was moving into factories in border towns such as Newtown and Llanidloes and arable agriculture was marginalised by the agrarian developments of eastern and southern England. Rural Wales, particularly in the northwest could well have slid into desperate want. Indeed in the 1730s there were disturbances in Bangor, protesting at the shortage and cost of basic necessities. Similar disturbances occurred at Pwllheli in 1751 and in 1766 mobs at Caernarfon tried to prevent a vessel being loaded with corn.

Paradoxically, this industrialisation, which could have been fatal to the frail barter economy of northwest Wales, was to provide its salvation. With the move from the country to the nascent industrial conurbations, houses were needed, and these houses called for roofs, lintels, fireplaces and the like. Thus, as the 18th century gathered pace, so did the demand for slate. It started to become something more than just a vernacular material of the poor or an exotic whim of the rich.

Activity increased particularly in north Caernarfonshire where individuals holding take notes from the landowners worked tiny diggings. These take notes were generally issued on an annual basis, almost always for a yearly rent of a few shillings plus a royalty either of say, an eighth or a tenth of the sale value, or a levy on tonnage or count. The terms usually specified that only one or perhaps two men could work, additional helpers being often permitted at an extra annual charge.

Almost all Gwynedd slate went to market by sea, having been carried by whatever means possible, to the nearest tiny navigable creek. Much went to Ireland, the rest to English ports, a little found its way to such places as Dunkirk or Rotterdam. By 1730 shipments totalled about 2500 tons per annum. As trade developed, so did the size of ships, demanding the use of proper ports, benefiting such places as Caernarfon, from where, in 1730, 101 vessels sailed with cargoes averaging 16 tons. In 1792, 237 vessels left carrying an average of 35 tons.

When, due to transport constraints, loadings were still made at the tiny creeks, it became usual to trans-ship into sea-going vessels at an adjacent port. Such was the case for slate dug on Cilgwyn common, where by 1762 8 of the diggings had developed into formal partnership quarries. Their product was carted to Foryd Bay, to be carried by tiny boats to Caernarfon. The fact that a saving of only about 3 miles on comparatively good roads (and avoiding one or two tolls) justified this double handling, illustrates the high cost of cartage.

The Conwy valley was feeling the limitations of Trefriw and the trans-shipments at Conwy, but the industrialisation of the Wrexham area, boosted the market for small diggings in north-east Wales, and some such as Craig y Orin were regularly sending several hundred tons a year to the expanding English midlands, but the heavy costs of road cartage restricted this trade. Indeed Thomas Pennant referring to slate quarrying at Llangynog in 1778 said *'The want of water carriage is a great loss to the work.'*

Although slate digging was becoming more widespread, the great thrust remained in the hinterland of Bangor and Caernarfon. This was still mainly at the head of the Ogwen valley on the Penrhyn estate, but also at Cilgwyn in the Nantlle valley, on the Faenol estate near the hamlet of Dinorwig and on the south side of Llyn Padarn on Cefn Du.

On these barren tracts, landowners were obtaining small but useful revenues from slaters take notes. Not that such dues were always paid. Periods of absence by the then owner of Faenol meant that royalties at Dinorwig were not always collected, and on Crown land such as at Cilgwyn, the slaters were quick to take advantage of the Surveyor General's slackness in pursuing his tribute, giving those diggers a resented competitive edge. Not that they invariably prospered, for in 1752, 2 men were killed during a riot when needy Cilgwyn slaters raided a granary.

From at least the beginning of the 15th century, the Penrhyn estate (including lands to which it had doubtful title) had been a predominant source of slate. Rents, royalties and the profits from any sales undertaken on the slaters behalf were an important part of its income. But a decade or two into the 18th century, Cilgwyn competition was causing takings to decline. The Cilgwyn slaters, apart from often paying no dues, had more easily worked rock and could make thinner, lighter and hence more cheaply transported slates. They marketed aggressively, developing a strong Irish as well as some Liverpool trade, where the reputation of their product was such that they could get a landed price of 14/- (70p) per Mille of 1200. Penrhyn product only fetched 13/- (65p), carriage and shipping costs would leave their diggers with less that 8/- (40p) out of which they had to pay around 2/8 (13.3p) royalty, leaving them with little more than half what the Cilgwyn men took home.

In 1738, Sir William Yonge and General Hugh Warburton, joint owners of the estate, alarmed at the fall in Penrhyn tonnage, due to diggers leaving to seek free pickings, halved royalties. This move failed and by 1746 Penrhyn output had fallen to a mere 250 tons, a tenth of the Cilgwyn total. With Penrhyn quarrymen now netting as little as 3/6 (17.5p) per mille, (a fair week's output per man), royalties were again reduced to 10d (4.17p).

Although Penrhyn's sales efforts were becoming increasingly ineffectual, they did make one decisive and far-reaching contribution to the marketing of Welsh slate, the standardisation of sizes.

Traditionally sizing had been very haphazard, such terms as tefyll (slices), ysglodion (chips) and ysgyrion (splinters) were used, apparently without any defined dimensions. By the mid sixteenth century, some slates were being sold, sized as 'Singles' (usually 10' x 5') and later, 'Doubles' (usually 12' x 6'), but consignments were more usually of random sizes. From a load, a roofer would first lay the largest, gradually going down to the smallest as he worked towards the ridge, giving rise to the graduation still to be seen on some old roofs. These early slates were fixed by a single oak peg and thus had a tapered top. They could be as much as $\frac{1}{2}'$ thick (up to six times the thickness of later slates). Since they were uneven and of trifling lap, moss packing was used to keep out rain, the term 'Moss Slates' persisting in use to describe very small slates long after this practice ceased.

With the need to establish standards for the increasing sizes of the rectangular 2 nail slates, that the market was

24

demanding, Warburton of Penrhyn, in 1738, devised the famous 'Female nobility' names. Already such was the influence of Penrhyn, that despite its then declining fortunes, this nomenclature soon became the Industry Standard, and with slight variations, remained so for almost two centuries.

Though there was some semblance of organisation emerging in Dyffryn Ogwen and Cilgwyn, most winning of slate remained a primitive operation of little gangs digging in holes wherever a promising outcrop presented itself, and transporting the make as best they could. Typical of these fragmented workings was Bron y Foel, where product was carried in baskets to be put on board boats at Ynys Cyngar, just west of Borth y Gest

Cae'n y Coed was within easy reach the little river port of Maentwrog, but further up valley at Ffestiniog transport was so difficult that the outcrops were only worked when slate was needed in the immediate vicinity. That is until one day, allegedly in 1765, that Methusalem Jones, an ex-Cilgwyn slate digger rented Gelli farm and commenced digging.

Gelli was a frontier post as it were on the desolate extremity of Meirionnydd high in a landscape carved by in an Ice Age that in winter does not seem to have yet entirely departed. Why Jones should have ventured here is unclear. Legend has it that guided by a dream; he drove his pickaxe, right plumb into the gleaming riches of the 'Old' vein.

The truth is probably more mundane, he was already a moderately successful entrepreneur, and a Damascene revelation is less likely than the overhearing of gossip in his Caernarfon pub, (which undoubtedly was the mainspring his modicum of prosperity). Alternatively, having lived and worked around Glynllifon estate of which Gelli was a remote outpost, he may well have received some kind of tip-off. What is undisputed is that he was the progenitor of the great Blaenau Ffestiniog slate industry.

He brought other ex-Cilgwyn men into partnership in

this Diffwys quarry and although he soon moved on to other things he must be also credited with creating the world's first slate quarrying firm.

These men faced a challenging task to get their product to market. Cae'n y Coed had already established the pattern of taking product down the river Dwyryd, but to reach the river involved a daunting packhorse journey down the quagmired mountainside and a fraught cartage along a washed-out parish road. But manage it they did, thus converting what had been an occasional back cargo for a boat bringing in supplies, to a dedicated fleet that eventually comprised some 50 vessels, manned by the 'Philistines'. This close-knit band of Penrhyndeudraeth based boatmen, would thread their way through the currents and sandbanks of the river to Ynys Cyngar, where hopefully the sea would be calm enough to manhandle the slate into a sea-going vessel.

Even when the slate was safely on board ship, the problems were not ended, as prior to the merchanting system being established, if a cargo was not bought outright by the ship's captain, the quarry owner had to personally arrange the selling of the slate at its destination. Until the early 19th century when bills of exchange became recognised, he had also to carry back the proceeds. One of the Diffwys partners, James Williams, is recorded as having walked to London in 1798, to arrange the sale of a cargo. Owing to wartime delays to shipping, he had to wait 3 months for the vessel to arrive, supporting himself by taking employment in a soap factory.

Thus as the 18th century passed its mid-point, the quarrying of slate was a burgeoning occupation, spreading out from its original north Caernarfonshire epicentre, but although signs of formal organisation were appearing, it had yet to become an industry. That development, and the great improvements in transport, communications and commerce that it created, and the prosperity it brought, still lay in the future.

2. THE GIANT STIRS
Late 18th century – early 19th century

There is some doubt as to whether it was precisely 1765, when Methusalem Jones' putative pick first pierced Blaenau rock, but it was certainly in that year when an event that was to have even greater significance to the industry took place. Susanna, only child of General Warburton, co-owner of the Penrhyn estate, married her kinsman, Richard Pennant MP, son of John Pennant, a wealthy merchant. This wealth derived in part from fashionable estates in Cheshire and elsewhere and from less fashionable but vastly more profitable estates in Jamaica. At the same time Pennant senior was in the process of buying out Sir William Yonge's heir, Sir George Yonge, now the other co-owner of the estate.

In contrast to other landowners who, according to contemporary accounts, devoted their energies to *'Drinking, Betting and Whoring'*, John Pennant and Warburton took a close interest in affairs at Penrhyn. In particular their slate revenues, which were being further, eroded by the efforts of the Cilgwyn men.

In 1768, they tackled the problem by cancelling all take notes and substituting 21-year dead-rent leases, with strict conditions under which slate was to be raised. A reeve was appointed to take charge of affairs at Abercegin and pay the slaters for whatever they raised. This seemingly shrewd move obviated all disputes about royalties, the 54 leases yielding a fixed annual income of £80.

When John Pennant died in 1781, Richard sought ways of augmenting his substantial inheritance, perhaps anticipating his ennoblement as Lord Penrhyn in 1783. Leasing might have seemed a good idea in 1768, but in the intervening years many of the tenants, freed of the burden of royalties, had prospered and were in many cases making serious money. For tenants to prosper was anathematic to Richard

Pennant, so in 1782 he bought out the leases and set about running things himself, offering employment to the dispossessed slaters.

It is impossible to exaggerate the importance of this event, for whatever view one may take of the subsequent history of the Penrhyn dynasty as owners and employers, from henceforward the working of slate in Wales could legitimately be called an industry. For the first time, slate was to be worked on a big scale, with adequate capital and with permanency of land tenure. Pennant's manager or agent was the able James Greenfield, who by the early 1790s had 500 men at Cae Braich y Cafn working about 70 bargains extending over about 500 yards on a NE/SW line near the present Penrhyn quarry main offices. They were raising a massive 15,000 tons a year, a good 50% more than the Cilgwyn/Nantlle men were putting out.

There was little difficulty in finding manpower for this spectacular expansion. Farm workers on £5 per year (plus keep), found quarry wages of 10d (4.2p), per day very attractive, particularly with the possibility of promotion to 'overlooker' on 1/- (5p), or even bargain Setter at 1/4 (6.7p). Despite being under the discipline of the clock and having to find their own food and shelter, few would want return to farm work.

Then in 1793, came the Napoleonic wars, which though mightily beneficial to industries such as iron smelting, was a body blow to slate quarrying. Building all but ceased, freight rates trebled, ships were captured by the French or their crews press-ganged and a heavy tax was imposed on coastwise shipments. On top of this there were seven consecutive years of bad harvests (1795-1801), which together with the sharp rise in living costs, brought much distress among quarrymen, leading to food riots in Caernarfon.

By 1800 Penrhyn's output and manning was a quarter of

what it had been. Pennant minimised his layoffs by deploying as many men as possible on improvements to the quarry and its transport arrangements. This foresighted benevolence enabled him to take full and prompt advantage of the recovery of trade that the new century brought. It is also to his credit that in 1798, aware of the hardships of his men, he provided a 100-acre site (But on poor ground it is said!), for them to plant potatoes.

At Dinorwig, on the other side of Mynydd Elidir, not dissimilar events to those at Penrhyn had taken place. Thomas Assheton on inheriting the Faenol estate in 1764 had tacked hyphen Smith onto his name and had taken up residence. In 1787, daunted by the task of organising his dozen or so take note diggers; he followed the Penrhyn example and put a stop to their individual workings. Unlike Pennant, Assheton-Smith did not take over himself, but granted a 21-year lease to the Dinorwig Slate Company, which was a partnership of two solicitors, Messrs Ellis and Wright and a Mr.Bridges, described as a merchant (undoubtedly a slate merchant). They did have problems as some of the doughty diggers, even in the face of force, continued to work on Dinorwig property. As late as 1809 'vagabonds' were still being reported, some allegedly tipping their waste after dark, into the company's workings. Expansion was less dramatic than Penrhyn's, the 1793 tonnage being less than 3000, but they seem to have been better able to maintain their output during the economic storms of the later 1790s.

In the Cilgwyn/Nantlle area and on Cefn Du, with no dominant private landlord and much of the ground being Crown land, the Penrhyn/Dinorwig pattern could not be followed. The first real organisation came in 1802 when John Evans, a prominent solicitor, John Price and Thomas Jones, both described as 'gentlemen', together with Richard Roberts a slate merchant, realised the potential offered by diggings mainly selling to Ireland, with just a short sea voyage comparatively safe from French raiders and exempt from the coastwise tax. Accordingly they formed the Cilgwyn & Cefn Du Slate Company, leased Crown lands at both places and set about the daunting task of ejecting the 'trespassers' (Allegedly 130 or more), and persuading them to accept employment. Other firms were also formed, such as the 1812 syndicate of 2 slate merchants, a quarryman, and, oddly, a stationer from Chester who took over Cook quarry near Cefn Du and who were soon raising 500 tons per year. Such firms reflected the emergence of a middle class of professional men and traders with funds to invest.

Prominent among these new men were the slate merchants, the successors to the reeves who had been arranging shipments and making sales. They became a formidable part of the slate trade, holding stocks for, and often advancing temporary finance to, quarry operators. Also they were able to take into stock sizes or varieties that were in poor demand, very valuable in an industry where the type of product had to be determined by the out-turn of the rock rather than by market needs. Ultimately, virtually all business was done through them. Penrhyn's success was to a great extent due to their pioneering the appointment of merchants, and their selection of able and active ones such as Worthington of Liverpool.

The reeves usual 18th century practice was to make a contract with an individual or partnership to take slate at a certain price, under certain conditions, for say, a 3-month period, this becoming the basis of the 'Bargain' system under which employed quarrymen invariably worked. This system had roots in the Copper and Lead mining industries, and was to remain in operation up to the mid 20th century. It entailed a gang making an agreement with the owner, or his letting steward, to work a particular stretch of rock for (usually) the next four weeks. A rate would be negotiated of so much per mille of each size of roofing slate or so much per ton of slab, with additional payments for opening and the working of dead rock. Later in a big quarry it would take the form of a single list throughout a quarry, the men being paid on this plus a payment or 'poundage' intended to reflect the difficulty or otherwise of working and clearing a particular stretch of rock.

Obviously the men would seek the highest rate of poundage whilst management would stand out for the lowest. With goodwill and understanding the system could work well, but these two virtues were not always in evidence when bargains were being set. Also there was scope for unfair practices; a measure of nepotic or chapel based favouritism was one thing, but the out and out corruption, which became rife in some of the larger quarries, was quite another. This, and ill-structured lists, could leave the bargainers payless or even in debt to the employer (for powder, fuse, blacksmith work etc.) at the end of the letting period. The bargain system was a perennial cause of dispute in all but the smallest family-run quarries, yet it was stoutly defended by the rockmen. This was partly because it gave an illusory feeling of independence, and partly because it distinguished the skilled men who won and reduced the rock, from men such as the rubblers who cleared away unusable material, and were paid on a daily or tonnage basis. Indeed also tradesmen such as blacksmiths, carpenters, masons and, later, mechanics who were regarded with some distain by 'real' quarrymen. When in 1823, Wyatt, the Penrhyn agent, concerned that some bargains were earning their teams £5 or £6 per 4 weeks others were, after deductions, sharing less than £1, offered to substitute a wage structure, he got a dusty answer. Even as late as 1876, at Hafod y Wern, moves to phase out the bargain system caused a riot, and an attempt at Foelgron to devise a fairer system met with failure.

Penrhyn experimented with gangs of anything from 2 to 12 men, but by the late 1780s, 4-6 was the norm. Interim payments were made every 4 weeks with a full settlement

(Tâl mawr) at the end of the 12-week bargain period. (Later on bargains were invariably of 4 weeks, with weekly intermediate 'subs'). A typical rate for Countesses, was 16/- (80p) per mille, Ladies half that and Doubles half that again. 'Ton' slates were rated at 8/- (40p) per ton. The quarry sold them at wharf for about twice those figures. The proprietor had of course to meet overheads such as the cost of breaking ground, clearing dead rock, installing plant, drainage and later on, fuel, but he could still end up with a considerable profit.

Serious quarrying activity was starting to spread. The small tonnages loaded at Aberdyfi and Derwenlas, (the port for Machynlleth), were becoming significant. By 1797 Barmouth harbour was including slate in its list of tariffs, and cartage from Llangynog to the canal at Llanymynech reached 2000 tons per year, and a little later, slate was regularly coming from the Bala & Corwen areas.

At Blaenau, Methusalem Jones' partnership, had expanded, employing about 20 men, but in 1799 their landlord sold out over their heads to a syndicate of Lakeland men, William Turner and brothers David & William Casson.

Turner, on the strength of having married a Wicklow girl, is assumed to have quarried in Ireland. The similarity of the 'Caverns' at Valentia in the south-west of Ireland to those at Pen y Ffridd and Clogwyn y Fuwch quarries in the Conwy valley allegedly links all three to Turner. Furthermore the Lake District practices such as corbelled tunnel adits seen at Clogwyn y Fuwch have been attributed to him. He may well have dabbled in the Conwy valley before coming to Blaenau, but his pre-Blaenau activities remain a matter of dispute.

Under Turner's leadership Diffwys had a great decade of development, starting with his turning the wartime conditions to advantage by obtaining contracts to roof military barracks. He built a road from the quarry to Cong-y-Wal, obviating the use of packhorses. They were amongst the first users of iron rails as opposed to wooden rails sheathed in iron (strapways). Despite the problems of trapped debris, they also used L section tramplates probably to 3'6' gauge, later conversion to edge-rail on the same sleepers left them with track of 3'3½' gauge. (This together with the 2'2' gauge of their original edge-rail was to present them with problems when 1'11½' was adopted by the Ffestiniog Railway).

Admittedly after Turner's time, but undoubtedly due to his innovative influence, the Cassons pioneered extraction from the steeply dipping veins by working underground, a practice which was to become the mainstay of all Blaenau operations. They also built further roads and would make a wider impact when they established Casson's Bank, which by the 1840s, had branches in Porthmadog, Blaenau Ffestiniog and Pwllheli. (It afterwards became part of the North and South Wales Bank, later absorbed by the Midland, now HSBC).

Alongside Diffwys, at Bowydd, some take note digging had commenced around 1780. In 1801, the landlord, Lord Newborough, emulating Lord Penrhyn, took over the management. Some roads were built but lack of access to a quay at Maentwrog contributed to the 1807 closure. Manod built a magnificent (and costly) road in 1801 but for the likes of Bwlch y Slaters, and Rhiwbach, transport was onerous.

At Dinorwig in 1809, following Ellis's death, Bridges dropped out and Hugh Jones a Dolgellau banker and Assheton-Smith himself joined Wright. Wisely, they lured William Turner from Diffwys with the offer of a partnership. This offer must have seemed attractive as Turner was well dug in at Blaenau, having for instance, established a family vault at Llan Ffestiniog church when a child died in infancy. Turner energetically set out to match the progress that had been made at Penrhyn quarry, beginning a rivalry that was to last a century and a half. Both quarries had already improved their shipment arrangements. In 1790 Penrhyn had overcome the 60-ton limitation on vessels using Aberogwen by establishing his own grandly named Port Penrhyn at Abercegin. Within three years Assheton-Smith had emulated him by building his own Port Dinorwig at Y Felinheli, making him independent of Caernarfon. Cartage had already been improved, with Dinorwig leading the way when in 1788 they made road improvements, slashing, their quarry to coast cartage costs from 10/- (50p) per ton, (more than the cost of production of the cheaper slates), to 6/6 (33p). Within two years Penrhyn had also completed roads, on which fleets of broad-wheeled wagons, each carrying up to 2½ tons, reduced cartage costs from 5/3 (27p) per ton to 4/- (20p), thus maintaining an edge on Dinorwig. In 1800 Lord Penrhyn also made a road to Capel Currig, where he built the Eagles Hotel (Now Plas y Brenin), partly to provide lodgings for acquaintances insufficiently eminent to be entertained personally.

However by the time the new partnership took over Dinorwig, all Penrhyn's road improvements were history, for in 1801 the Penrhyn Railroad had been completed. This tramway was a pioneer, since at that time it was considered that only a canal could economically handle the sort of tonnages that Penrhyn was planning. In fact, Thomas Dadford, the prominent canal engineer, had surveyed a canal route, but there would never have been the water for the 40 – 50 locks that the 600' fall would have entailed. Having wisely rejected the idea of 8 inclines on which barges would be carried on wheels, the canal idea was abandoned and a tramway laid out.

The tramway's initial oval rail with concave wagon wheels was a mistake, (the track had to be re-laid in edge-rail in the 1820s), as probably were the vertical drums used at the head of the 3 self-acting inclines, but it was in all other respects a model of its kind. Its lower end partly made use of the formation of an early line connecting a flint mill at Aberogwen with the new port at Abercegin. The equidistant spacing of the inclines, Cilgeraint near the quarry, Dinas, part way along, and Marchogion, just short of the port, was ideal. (The Marchogion incline had been, in horse-whim powered form been part of the old flint-mill line). Constant and easy gradients between the inclines whereby the horses could control the down going loads and readily haul back the empty wagons made for efficient working. The trackbed was well founded and the river Cegin was crossed and re-crossed by two fine stone bridges, one single, one triple arch, (which are still extant at SH593725 & SH722595). With trains of up to 24 wagons, pulled by 2 or 3 horses, each wagon carrying up to a ton (wagons were crewled down the inclines 3 at a time), it had a potential capacity well in excess of any then foreseeable tonnages. From the outset 16 horses and a dozen men did the work previously requiring up to 400 horses with some 140 drivers. Not only did the tramway reduce the cost of transport to the coast by some four-fifths to around 1/- (5p) per ton, but it also freed the quarry from dependence on the whims of highly independently minded farmers from whom most of the horses and carts were hired. Also horses were getting scarce and expensive, as apart from the wartime increase in feedstuff prices, a tax on them was imposed in 1797 to encourage their sale to the army.

Although the able manager Greenfield did do a lot of development, the terrace system often attributed to him originated in the early 1780s, a little before his time. These terraces at 65' – 70' vertical intervals, enabled a large number of men to work simultaneously and reduced breakages by restricting the distance rock fell. Rail lines in each gallery carried product in one direction and rubble for dumping the opposite way, the galleries being slightly graded to assist movement. Associated with this were some of the earliest self-acting inclines, whereby the weight of downgoing loaded wagons hauled up empty ones. This 1800s layout would remain in use, virtually unchanged until the 1960s.

By the time of his death in 1808 Richard Pennant, Baron

Penrhyn had not only more than recovered the lost business of the 90s, but had increased annual tonnage to 20,000, manning to over 600 and net profits to a reputed £7000 per year. (About £330,000 in 2006 terms) Moreover, he had consolidated his quarry as the dominant force in Welsh slate, and placed it in the forefront of innovation, his sandsaw mill being the first example of mechanisation on a serious scale. He enhanced profits with 'added value' enterprises such as the writing slate, chimneypiece and tombstone factories at Port Penrhyn. He also considerably expanded his land holding, although in some cases under circumstances of doubtful legality. This gave rise to the saying – *'Steal a sheep, they hang you, steal a mountain, they make you a lord'* He also laid down the 'model village' of Llandegai, anticipating the likes of Port Sunlight by almost a century. (This village of originally, 40 cottages had a church, but no tavern, and very definitely no non-conformist chapel!)

The Dinorwig Company, at first largely ignored the shortcomings of their roads, concentrating on technical improvements within the quarry. They put in galleries, on the Penrhyn pattern (but at slightly greater vertical intervals) and self-acting inclines which obviated the hazards described there by the Rev.W.Bingley in 1798.

The quarries are generally high up amongst the rocks, and the workmen, in conveying them down from thence, are obliged, as well as one horse before, to have another behind the carts, to prevent the whole, in some of the dangerous steeps in which these mountains abound, from being dashed headlong to the bottom, which must sometimes inevitably be the case without this contrivance. This seems a most inconvenient mode of conveyance: it appears that sledges, similar to those used in many parts of Westmoreland and Cumberland for conveying slates down the mountains, would not only be less expensive, but more safe and commodious'. (Actually some inclines were probably already in use at Dinorwig by this time).

The same year Bingley also graphically described similar problems at Craig Rhiwarth, near what he sourly called *'The small and dirty village of Llangynog'*

'The quarries are high in the mountain; and I observed that the mode here of conveying them down was different from, and apparently much more dangerous than, that practised in the slate works about, near Llanberis near Caernarvon. Here they are placed on a small sledge, which by a rope, is fastened to the shoulders of the man who has the care of conveying it down, which is done along paths made for the purpose, which wind along the side of the mountain. He then begins to descend his face towards it; and, having firm hold with his hands, the velocity which the sledge acquires in its descent is counteracted by the man's striking against the prominences with his feet, which since he goes backwards, and has at the same time to keep the sledge on its track, must be a very difficult task, and can only be acquired by practice. The danger attending this mode of conveyance I should think must be very great; but upon enquiry at the village, I was informed that serious accidents have been very seldom known to occur'. (This 600' descent was obviated by the construction of an incline).

Dinorwig further improved their cartage in 1812 by building a new road through Deiniolen, a slightly circuitous route enforced by hostile land ownership. This obviated the loading of boats on Llyn Peris, taking them through a narrow cut to Llyn Padarn and rowing to Cwm y Glo for reloading onto carts for Caernarfon. Although by 1821 they had scrapped all barrows and carts within the quarry, there seems to have been no thought of an external rail link.

The partnership was dissolved in 1820, Assheton-Smith taking sole ownership, retaining Turner as manager on an eighth share of the profits. With A-S nearing 70, it was probably his son Thomas Assheton-Smith Jnr. that caused the Dinorwig Railway to be built. Opening in 1824, it soon proved inferior to the Penrhyn line. Its 3 inclines were ill spaced, the Upper Cwm and the Lower Cwm inclines were only separated by an awkward loop and the long haul to the Garth incline, near the port, was unevenly graded. Its trackbed was not well founded and its slate sleepers broke. Poor though it was, it reduced carriage costs to something near the Penrhyn figure, giving both quarries a decisive competitive advantage over all other competitors. By 1826 Dinorwig was employing 800, a fourfold increase in only six years, and were sending 20,000 tons of product a year down their new tramway. In 1830 they built their first mill close to terminus of the new tramway. Although there would be many other mills, this level remained known as 'Mills level'.

In the Nantlle area, companies were being formed and quarries such as Penybryn, Gallt y Fedw, Tal y Sarn & Hafod Las, which had all opened at the turn of the century were now each sending four figure tonnages to the Caernarfon quays, where merchants such Richard Roberts, Robert Griffiths and Robert Williams were flourishing. Fresh openings there continued, including in 1816 Pen yr Orsedd, one of several quarries into which Turner was investing his earnings at Dinorwig. This quarry would soon have a hundred plus payroll.

In the meantime, at Penrhyn, George Hay Dawkins, who had in 1816 inherited the property (but not the title) from his cousin Richard Pennant, added Pennant to his name and set about managing affairs. He is perhaps best known for his want of both tact and taste in building Penrhyn Castle, and for causing the first ever strike in the industry in 1825 when Greenfield having tragically died, he put the unpopular William Williams in charge. However he did initiate direct shipments to America and made notable developments in the quarry such as the huge 16-sandsaw mill of 1816. By 1819 his payroll had risen from the 600 when he took over, to 800, producing annually over 24,000 tons, and before the 1820s were out, this was up to 40,000. Productivity had fallen from the excellent 33 tons per man-year of 1808, to 30 t/p/m/y, mainly due to more men being employed on 'added value' items such as gravestones, writing slates and so on, but it was still some 25% better than the best Dinorwig could do. With an average sale value in excess of £2 per ton, over twice the cost of production, Dawkins-Pennant was pocketing rather more than the £80 p.a. of less than 40 years before.

Dawkins-Pennant followed his predecessor's example of extending his land holdings, not always successfully, for instance he started work at Tan y Bwlch and at Bryn Hafod y Wern, but was evicted. As late as 1849 (10th August) a *Times* leader referred to the practice of landowners improperly seeking to enlarge their holdings, *'One common has been taken in without any shadow of right, which contains and is traversed by the most gigantic and valuable vein of slates that has ever been worked or discovered in any part of the world'*. D-P continued the practice of letting out leases for cottage building and making available building materials to 'good' workers. Usually the plot let was big enough to allow wages to be supplemented by vegetables, poultry, pigs or even a cow or two. Although the ground rents were modest, varying between 4/- (20p) and 10/- (50p) a year, the leases were short, so that after 30 years or so occupiers would see their property revert to the landlord and have to pay anything up to £4.pa to remain as tenants. Since this would cover rates and repairs, the terms were not onerous, but such tenants could and would be evicted if they ceased to be employed at the quarry, or if they pursued 'radical causes'.

Apart from the obvious problems of living in a home controlled by an employer, religion created difficulties. The majority of workers, were 'chapel', that is, they belonged to non-conformist sects such as Presbyterian, Methodist, Baptist and Congregationalist, all equally anathematic to Anglican owners. Thus they needed to live on non-quarry owned land, where they could build their biblically named places of worship, and establish schools under the 'British' schools movement rather than the Anglican Church 'National' schools dictated by the likes of the Pennants.

The eponymous naming of the villages that grew up around them illustrates the dominance of the chapels. S.G.Pattison, writing in 1869, clearly did not understand the fierce Non-Conformist Christianity of the Welsh slatemen when he questioned *'Why should this village on the river Ogwen where every sign and advertisement is in the Welsh language, derive its name from the pool by the Sheepgate of Jerusalem?'* He was of course referring to Bethesda where in 1820 the famous Congregational chapel was built on the Cenfaes estate, just outside the Penrhyn holding, and which, by 1871 would be one of 22 chapels in a settlement whose population of 6297 would almost equal that of Bangor, Conwy & Llandudno combined. (This chapel building fervour was not confined to quarrymen; in Wales as a whole from much of the 19th century, a new chapel opened every 8 days). This polarisation between Anglican, Tory management and Non-conformist, Liberal workers, would in future years exacerbate industrial relations particularly at Penrhyn and Dinorwig. Although it must be said that the Assheton-Smiths were less rigid in their Anglican stance than the Pennants, even on occasion, giving land for the building of chapels.

Also on land outside the Penrhyn holding, some independent quarrying was going on at Pant Dreiniog, and Moel Faban, and on a larger scale (and with proper leases!) at the ex Dawkins-Pennant openings at Tan y Bwlch and Bryn Hafod Y Wern. They all had a struggle to get their product to the coast, either to Aberogwen (where Dawkins-Pennant could not stop loading, but could and did stop waterside stacking) or to the less suitable Hirael jetty at Bangor.

Besides transport problems, marginal diggings on poor rock were at a further disadvantage. The war having increased the price of timber, there was a call for bigger sizes of slates that required fewer roof battens. Thus the steep price increases of the early 1800s were largely confined to the bigger sizes. Quarries such as Penrhyn could readily produce these and Dawkins-Pennant, undoubtedly pushed the rates for them to the maximum that the market would stand. With his profit secured on the premium products, he could afford to clear the smaller and poorer varieties at prices little above 18th century levels. Since it was the Penrhyn list which ruled the industry, returns were slim at quarries whose rock restricted them to smaller and rougher slates. For instance, in 1805, when Duchesses were fetching around £3. 2 0 (3.10) per mille, equalling £1.45 per ton, yet a mille of Doubles for which, you would be pushed to get 11/- (55p), represented £0.78 per ton. Over the next few years the gap widened even further.

As well as bigger sizes, the market was also demanding more choice, again favouring the larger producers. In 1788 Penrhyn offered 5 sizes in 2 qualities, by 1830 they listed 10 sizes in 3 qualities. This stock list was to progressively expand, until in 1880, 32 sizes each in various qualities were offered, even the humble Ton slates being available in 6 varieties. The likes of Penrhyn could finance such inventories, the smaller producers could not.

In Meirionnydd, (which then effectively meant Blaenau Ffestiniog) annual tonnage had gone from an insignificant 500 around the turn of the century to 12,000 by the early 1820s, mainly due to the export trade, boosted for instance, by the Boston city ordinance of 1816 that all roofs should be slate. Diffwys was very much the largest working, but Manod, right on the top of the eponymous mountain was not far behind and was tending to dominate the by now crowded wharves on the Dwyryd. Rothschild's old Moelwyn working was revived on a slightly different and more promising site. Workings to the east of Manod Mountain, such as Bwlch y Slaters and Rhiwbach, and those around Llan Ffestiniog, despite their cartage problems, were taking advantage of the by now more organised boating on the Dwyryd.

Their combined 1000 tons per month, would shortly look very small beer indeed, largely because of Samuel Holland, a. Liverpool merchant, whose enterprises included pottery manufacture, metal mining, quarrying on Cefn Du and elsewhere, and the merchanting of Penrhyn slate, (it was he who introduced Worthington to Penrhyn). In 1819 he speculated in a 3-year take note on Oakeley land at Rhiwbryfdir on the barren slopes at the head of Cwm Barlwyd, where some sporadic vernacular slate working had taken place. Results were encouraging, so when the take note expired he took a formal lease and in 1823 put his 19 year old son Samuel junior on a boat for Bagillt, to take the 3-day walk from there to Blaenau. Braving rat-infested lodgings on the way, young Sam sent the drunken quarry manager back to Liverpool for his father to sack, and set about running what would eventually become part of the great Oakeley quarry. The same year Bowydd (Lord Newborough's old working) was re-opened and copying Diffwys' underground methods, would in due time become a notable undertaking.

As in other areas, great technical improvements had been made in the larger quarries. Rails for internal transport became the norm, some mechanical sawing was being done and even dressing machines were being experimented with.

In Dyffryn Conwy, expansion was modest. Around 1830 something over 5000 tons was sent down river to Conwy each year. Some loaded at Tal y Cafn, but most from the two new quays at Trefriw capable of handling vessels of up to 50 tons. However although some tonnages would be raised in the Machno, Llugwy and Lledr valleys it would soon become apparent that the Conway area's contribution would remain modest.

Meanwhile at Nantlle, fortunes were mixed, there being

much activity but little prosperity. Pen yr Orsedd and Dorothea (opened in 1820), both found the going tough and in 1825 Talysarn failed. The Cilgwyn & Cefn Du Company languished, troubled by rock falls and the cost of the leases they had taken in Cwm Gwyrfai, Nantlle and Moel Tryfan with the aim of creating a chain of workings from Llanllyfni to Llanberis able to match Penrhyn and Dinorwig. In 1819 they tried to sell, described as being – *'with iron railways, whimseys and cars'*. Evans bringing in a friend, Poole, without consulting the other partners, caused friction, compounding their problems and there were allegations and counter-allegations of fraud. Shares valued at £101 in 1824 were sold at under £4 eight years later, their once 2,500 ton output was down to under 900 and their 1816 workforce of 60 bargainers and 40 rubbishers, was more than halved. When the company was wound up in 1831, wages were reputedly 9 months in arrears. Not that non-payment of wages was an isolated complaint, the 100 men at Hafod Las had similar problems and they were spoken of as seizing loads of slate to sell on their own account. In 1845, workers at neighbouring Ty'n y Weirglodd, like their neighbours at Hafod Las desperate for recompense, even offered to take payment in slate. As late as 1906, when the Braich Goch Company ceased trading, a testimonial from the men to the directors made particular mention of the fact that wages had always been paid on time!

There were also, increasing difficulties at Nantlle of rubbish disposal, lack of space or lack of foresight resulted in mounds of waste piling up on top of reserves of good rock. Waste was also a widespread problem, over at Llanberis by the mid 1820s, Cook quarry was choking to death on its own rubbish and was putting out barely half of the 1000 tons it had been making 2 or 3 years before. In contrast, neighbouring Glynrhonwy, with plenty of ground (and Llyn Padarn!) for tipping, was flourishing despite transport costs, and in 1826 was employing 126 men.

However by around 1810 Nantlle quarries had the benefit of roads so improved that most were carting to Caernarfon avoiding the Foryd transhipment, reducing their average transport costs from 11/- (55p) or more, per ton to 7/- (35p) or so, but each 2 or 3 workers in the quarry still required one man to cart. In the case of the cheaper slates, which represented most of their output, carriage almost equalled wage costs.

Costs for Hafod Las (Nantlle) quarry for August 1809, all per Mille or nominal thousand were (all decimalised) –

	'Raising' (wages)	Cartage	Price	Cartage as % of wages
Duchesses	£1.75	£0.90	£5.25	51%
Countesses	£1.25	£0.65	£3.15	52%
Small ditto	£0.90	£0.55	£2.15	61%
Large Ladies	£0.55	£0.50	£1.75	90%
Small Ditto	£0.4	£0.375	£1.30	91%
Doubles	£0.275	£0.25	£0.80	90%

This shows how even the reduced transport costs loomed large in the case of the smaller sizes and shows how recent rises were steepest on the bigger sizes, (In 1800 Doubles had been £0.70 and Countesses £2.00, thus the respective rises had been 15% and over 160%). With the economy of railed carriage proved, they needed a railway. Unfortunately unlike Penrhyn and Dinorwig, Nantlle with its numerous operators leasing small patches from several landowners, had no dominant and long-pocketed proprietor to provide one.

In a spirit of co-operation, not always manifest in slate quarrying, several of the larger lessees agreed on the idea of a collective railway. Just a year after the Dinorwig line opened, the Nantlle Railway Company was formed, opening for traffic in 1828. This was another notable event, as apart from its use not being confined to one quarry, it was intended for general traffic as well as slate, hence, it was, albeit horse-drawn, a full public and ultimately passenger carrying railway.

Unlike its two predecessors no great change of level was involved so inclines were not needed, and negligible gradients enabled the use of trains of 2-ton wagons of 3'6' gauge. These wagons, although quarry-owned, were all of similar with sheet-iron sides rather than the usual crate like pattern, which enabled them to readily carry freight of all kinds as return loads.

The route necessitated a big, single arch bridge and a short tunnel (Extant at SH479600 & SH481616 respectively) as well as a bridge, now demolished, across the Seiont near Caernarfon. Much better constructed than the Dinorwig line it ultimately gave direct connection to the Caernarfon quay to almost every quarry of consequence in the Nantlle area, and the endmost part of it remained in use, still horse drawn, and still with the same double-flanged wheeled wagons, until 1963.

The three tramways now in use opened a widening gap between those that had them and those that did not, particularly for those with inferior product. For instance in the 1820s, Ddol quarry near Llanberis, could only obtain an average 18/- (90p) per ton at wharf. Each ton cost them over 9/8 (48p), in wages to produce, loading cost 1/- (5p) and royalties $1/3\frac{1}{2}$ (6.5p). Paying 6/- (30p) for carriage left them no profit at all. Foresight was no guarantee, several quarries on the Glaslyn that had opened a 'slate's throw' from navigable water, found themselves high and dry when the completion of the Cob in 1814 drained the estuary. Yet, there were still new openings being made where the quality was mediocre and the transport problems appalling.

Penrhyn besides setting prices could also to an extent set the pace on wage rates which certainly failed to match the rise in slate prices during the early years of the century. Skilled men who might have got 1/6 (7.5p) per day in 1800 might find themselves getting around 2/6 (12.5p) a few years later, but the bad trade of 1814/15 soon forced pay down again. Wages rose a little in the brisk times of the mid 1820s but were back to near turn of the century levels in 1828 when Penrhyn laid off 100 men. This late '20s slackness, while not a recession did show the steam going out of the growth, which had brought Welsh tonnages of just over 20,000 in 1786, to five times that figure 40 years later.

This setback was largely because a great dead hand lay over the Welsh slate industry, the Slate Tax. A charge had been imposed on all slate carried coastwise in 1794 as a wartime measure, to help pay for naval escorts. Like other wartime taxes before and since, this tax stayed in force long after any need for it had passed. The Tax did not of course affect the quarries in northeast Wales, but it hit hard at those in Caernarfonshire and north Meirionnydd, who now accounted for most of the Welsh production.

Nantlle had its untaxed Irish trade, fine a few decades back when Dublin was the fastest growing city in Europe, but with the economy there moving into depression, that trade was in the doldrums. In fact with their home sales so bad, the Irish quarries were looking towards the British market, some such as the Imperial Slate Company of Killaloe, boasting that being on the Shannon, their transport costs were less than those of north Wales. Though the Irish quarries would never prove a rival to Wales, European countries, such as Belgium were also trumpeting their wares, and this certainly presaged problems that would arise in years to come.

The big market for slate was Lancashire whose population grew between 1800 and 1830 from 672,000 to 1,600,000, that of Liverpool alone rising from 77,000 to 165,000 in the same period. The small but threatening Leicestershire quarries, were reaching this market via the new canal network. More seriously, since the levy was on a head port to head port basis, the expanding Ulverston quarries in north Lancashire, could slip their cargoes along the coast tax free since the cargoes remained within the ambit of the Lancaster and Preston joint head port.

Then in 1830, the building trade started to really take off nationwide, but demand for Welsh slate did not. Prices already 20% below their 1827 peak, eased further in 1831. Penalised as they were by the Slate Tax, the quarries of Wales were losing out in the race to roof the new houses, factories and public buildings in the growing industrial cities of Britain.

3. THE GREAT LEAP FORWARD
The 1830s & 40s

A small, but to Wales, significant effect of the Napoleonic wars, was the interruption of the 'Grand Tours' of Europe. Persons of means had to forsake Switzerland and make do with the 'Welsh Alps'. Some such as Pennant, Bingley and Bennett when publishing accounts of their adventures made reference to slate quarrying. Thus they helped to direct the attention of influential Englishmen, not only to the beauties of Wales, but also to the investment opportunities it afforded.

As has been mentioned the prices of larger sizes of slates doubled during the first twenty years of the 19th century. Although some commodities had likewise risen, wages that accounted for up to 90% of quarrying costs, had not. This was a situation redolent of profit that did not escape the notice of financiers, including heavyweights such as N.M. Rothschild who formed the Royal Cambrian Company to take advantage of the situation.

Having had scant success with minerals and slate at Moelwyn, in 1825 Rothschild transmogrified his company into the Welsh Slate & Copper Mining Company and offered Holland £28,000 for his Rhiwbryfdir quarry. With only a few years to run on the lease, an offer worth a million and half in today's money was one he could not refuse. Although the Welsh Slate Company (Copper Mining was dropped from their title) ultimately became spectacularly successful, for the first 15 years it suffered heavy losses and was notorious for the late payment of wages.

However, besides failing to pay wages, W.S.C. also failed to pay dividends and Rothschild was replaced by Lord Palmerston as chairman of the company. The slate tax now impinged not just on the fortunes of financiers, adventurers and remote landowners, but also on those of His Majesty's

Barracks at Gelli quarry SH637463, 1990

*Empty trucks being loaded at Blaenau Ffestiniog GWR station for
return to Graig Ddu quarry SH724454, 1920s*

Bont Fawr Bridge Blaenau Ffestiniog, 1930s

Underground, Vanes Level Braich Goch quarry SH748078, 1980s

The original brine bath controllers for the electric haulage at Maenofferen quarry SH715467, 1995

Bwlch y Slaters quarry SH732455, 1990

*Cooke's level of Maenofferen quarry looking into Bowydd workings
1985*

Modern diamond saw Llechwedd quarry SH670087, 1990s

Drumhouse Gaerwen quarry SH745086, 1979

*Hand-wheel dressing machine c1860 in use 1990s Llechwedd quarry
SH670087*

Planing machine c1860 Llechwedd quarry SH670087, 1990s

Drumhouse main exit incline Llechwedd quarry SH670087, 1970s

Slate train, Glyn Valley Tramway early 20th century

Gorseddau Tramway, near Prince of Wales quarry SH549498, 1970s

Aerial view Gorseddau quarry SH 573453, 1988

Handling block c 1890 Llechwedd quarry SH670087

Glan y Pwll depot SH699469 where Llechwedd slate was loaded onto L&NWR, 1990s

Mill, probably Oakeley quarry SH690166. 1890s

Quarry wagons being carriers on transporter trucks Padarn Railway 1920s(?)

Posed early 20th century publicity picture Gilfach quarry SN128271

Foot of A3 incline Dinorwig quarry SH595603, 1980

Early (1850s?) saw Llechwedd Visitor Centre

Writing Slate factory probably Bangor 1890s

Water Wheel Wynne quarry SJ199379 c 1910

Enamelling Braich Goch quarry SH748078, 1960s

Llechwedd quarry SH700470, 1900s

Port Dinorwig SH524678 early 20th century

Handling block Bwlch y Slaters SH732455, 1960s

Wild Car Graig Ddu quarry SH724454 (1930s?)

Braich quarry SH510553, 1990s

Hafod y Llan Tramway formation, 1990

Slate splitting

Secretary of State for Foreign Affairs. Thus in 1831 the Tax, for so long lobbied against, vanished from the Statute Book.

The effects were immediate, prices firmed, outputs leapt. Penrhyn, for instance, re-employed the 100 previously sacked men and took on many more pushing their manning to 1500. By the early 1840s, with outputs almost double those of the 1820s, the great era of prosperity for the Welsh slate industry was under way.

The greatest growth was at Blaenau Ffestiniog. In the 1820s it was already a significant slate producing area, dominated by Diffwys's 6000 annual tonnages, but after 1831 things really let rip. By poaching Diffwys' customers, the aggressive Welsh Slate Company had already doubled their quarry's output to 4000 tons, but young Samuel Holland, obtained a new lease, at Cesail on the hill above his old working, and was soon matching WSC's figures. Landlord W.G.Oakeley aiming to maximize his royalties let the ground between W.S.C. and Holland's new outfit, to Nathaniel Mathew who was soon also in the four-figure bracket. (Confusingly he traded as the Rhiwbryfdir Slate Company, an anomaly ultimately resolved by changing the name to Gloddfa Ganol or Middle Quarry).

In 1834 Bowydd was taken on by Edwin Shelton and John Whitehead Greaves who had been working Glynrhonwy Upper and Fachwen quarries near Llanberis. They put in an extensive internal tramway network and their annual tonnage soon nudged 6000. The same year Fotty quarry was opened alongside Bowydd, (with which it would eventually amalgamate.

Holland had made road improvements, easing the journey to the Dwyryd at Maentwrog, but like all Blaenau product, his output still had to make the difficult, expensive and tide-dependent voyage down river. With Porthmadog having opened as a port in 1820, trans-shipment was less perilous than it had been when it was done in open water, but double handling and breakages were still involved. Romantic though it might appear in distant hindsight, the fleet of little boats, carrying tiny cargoes down the tideway already belonged to a by-gone age. By the mid 1830s, despite the opening of new quays, trying to ship almost 20,000 tons per year down the Dwyryd was looking increasingly ridiculous.

Proposals for a railway had stalled due to Rothschild's insistence that it should, Grand Old Duke of York–like, climb up Moelwyn to serve his workings before plunging headlong down to Porthmadog. With Rothschild off-stage, the way was clear for a more sensible route with direct access to Porthmadog that would put the Blaenau quarries on equal terms with Penrhyn, Dinorwig and Nantlle. Plus, equally importantly, ease the problems of supplying the burgeoning Blaenau Ffestiniog population.

It was largely Holland's initiative that got construction moving. In his Memoirs he recounts how, stopping for lunch at Penygroes, on one of his regular trips to the bank at Caernarfon, he fell into conversation with Henry Archer, who was investigating the leasing of the Nantlle Railway. He persuaded Archer to abandon his Nantlle intentions and to plan a railway from Blaenau, and to raise the capital from his native Dublin. Understandably the carters and boatmen were not best pleased, neither was W. G. Oakeley, concerned about loss of rents from the Dwyryd quays and the revenues of the Ffestiniog Turnpike of which he was a trustee. Indeed when the Ffestiniog Railway opened in 1836, the turnpike's revenues halved and the quays fell into disuse, but Oakeley having died in the year before, did not see his widow prosper handsomely on the enhanced royalties from the quarries and from sales of timber as the Porthmadog shipbuilding industry grew.

In spite of being in much more difficult terrain than previous slate tramways, a constant and moderate gradient allowed almost continuous running by gravity from Blaenau

Ffestiniog, nearly to Porthmadog. The one interruption being a hump requiring two short inclines, the up-going one waterwheel hauled, the down-going one, self-acting, (obviated in 1842 by the Moelwyn tunnel). The horses that hauled back the empty wagons, made the downhill journey as passengers in dandy cars. Like the Nantlle line, it was a public railway, and would survive as such long after the slate traffic ceased.

It had been costing up to 15/ (75p) per ton to get slate to Porthmadog, now it could be carried for 6/ (30p). The Welsh Slate Company almost immediately put in an incline connection, but it was three years before they would let Holland cross their land to do likewise. Shortly afterwards Mathew followed suit, but partly due to the carters and boatmen slashing their rates, other quarries were slow to connect. Llechwedd built their incline very shortly after their 1846 opening and Cwmorthin quarry built its magnificently engineered branch to the FR two years later. It was 1854s before Votty and Bowydd had incline connection via Duffws station, at the same time as Wrysgan was completing their sublime but sadly inefficient incline to Tanygrisiau.

Diffwys, possibly because they had to justify their considerable road expenditure and because of their different rail gauge, did not connect until 1865. In fact the siting of their 1845 Pant yr Ynn mill suggested that they had no plans to use the FR.

The expanding Rhiwbach and its neighbours sited east of the Manod Mountain still had to cart for shipment on the Dwyryd, but did derive a bonus from the reduced boating charges.

Important though it was, the FR's benefit to the Blaenau quarries was overshadowed by the aftermath of the Hamburg fire of 1842. Nathaniel Mathew's dash to take orders for re-roofing the city, resulted in Blaenau slate enjoying pre-eminence in European markets for three quarters of a century.

The FR. made the Dinorwig arrangements look very poor indeed. T. Assheton-Smith's son, (Thomas junior) had succeeded his father in 1827 and when Turner left the following year to pursue his other interests, he took over the quarry management. It did not take him long to realise that the tramway, that he must have bullied his father to install, would not do. Apart from its intrinsic shortcomings quarrying was now taking place well below its terminus, involving costly up-haulages.

The obvious lakeside route was blocked by Shelton and Greaves' Fachwen quarry, so a new route was planned and some formations cut 300' above Llyn Padarn, but Shelton and Greaves having unexpectedly vacated Fachwen, Dinorwig was able to buy it from its landowner, Lord Newborough (renaming it Faenol). Thus the track to be laid out along the lakeside partly using Fachwen's exit route (Which indeed may have been railed) and partly using a tipped-waste platform. Glan-y-Bala rock was tunnelled to enable the line to start from the southeastern end of the quarry.

The 4' gauge line followed an almost level cross-country route to the head of a big incline at Penscoins, near Port Dinorwig. The reason for the wide gauge and the avoidance of gradients was that it was planned for haulage by the cumbersome and low-powered locomotives of the time, and although for about 7 years horse-drawn, it was to be the first steam powered quarry railway, predating almost every other steam railway in Wales. The problem of mixed gauging was overcome by carrying the 2' gauge quarry wagons, four at a time on transporter trucks to Penscoins, where they were lowered by the incline to the port. Although this incline was later to prove something of a handicap, the Padarn Railway continued to serve the quarry until 1962. The only main change being in the 1870's when further tipping having provided a suitable platform, Gilfach Ddu workshops (Now the North Wales Slate Museum) were built. A new terminus was established here, the lower 'A' inclines which had terminated to the east of Glan y Bala were diverted direct to this new terminus, which also served Vivian quarry. The tunnel was re-laid in quarry-gauge and product from the eastern districts was brought through it by one of the new small locos that were then replacing horses within the quarry.

Later this line was re-laid around Glan y Bala on tipped rubbish. The abandoned tunnel becoming, successively, a workshop, wartime munitions factory, and now a cable tunnel for the pumped-storage station. The only other significant changes made during the whole of its life was one slight realignment at the foot of the Faenol (Nee Fachwen) quarry incline, and the 1920s abandonment of the chain and under-floor-sheave arrangements at Penscoins and the substitution of a conventional drum and wire-rope. (The section of track bed alongside Llyn Padarn now carries a narrow-gauge tourist railway, but sadly the great head-of-incline building has succumbed to the Port Dinorwig by-pass).

This, transport-wise at least, put Dinorwig firmly ahead of rival Penrhyn, where in 1840 Dawkins-Pennant having died, the dynasty took a further twist. The heir was Colonel Charles Edward Douglas, who had had the wisdom to marry Dawkins-Pennant's daughter Juliana. He followed tradition by changing his name to Douglas-Pennant, and as a military man, began to run the quarry on regimental lines. Not perhaps the best model for dealing with sensitive 'labour relations' matters, but the army was then one of the few professions providing experience in the control of a large workforce.

Nantlle quarries had the benefit of their new railway, but expansion was slowed by their dependence on the Irish trade. This connection had in earlier years forced Penrhyn and Dinorwig to seek the then less remunerative outlets in

England. Now with English building booming and the Irish depression becoming famine, the Nantlle producers had the task of breaking into the English market. Cilgwyn, after its problems, managed to move ahead in the mid 1840s, commencing a 40-year period of growth that would put its annual tonnages near 8000. Dorothea, wavered for some years, but when in 1848 a consortium of local people took it over, it was to prosper mightily, until by the 1870s, it was turning out 15,000 tons per year, or around a third of the Nantlle area total. What was also to become another great Nantlle quarry, Pen yr Orsedd, was still not doing well, but by 1864 it would have 400 men and rival Dorothea.

Expansion was not confined to the north Caernarfonshire and Blaenau areas. North of Llangollen, the Oernant, Moel y Faen and Clogau quarries were growing and when in the late 1850s they had a tramway (the Oernant) to the canal, they became quite significant producers. The Cambrian, in Glyn Ceiriog and some of its neighbours, were doing well despite cartage costs, as was also Craig Rhiwarth at Llangynog.

In the South of Meirionnydd, at Corris, new road building allowed access to promising locations, and in the mid 1830s quarries such as Braich Goch, developed out of small, vernacular workings. Just as Cilgwyn men had migrated to Blaenau, three-quarters of a century before, Caernarfonshire men now came to Corris. But unlike the Cilgwyn men they no longer came as entrepreneurs, but as workers. This reflected the changing sources of capital within the industry. Up to this time, apart from a few landowners and big financiers, investors for the most part had either quarrying experience or some local knowledge of the trade. Much of the Corris development was funded by investors of moderate substance, many from outside the area. As slate became more widely perceived as a source of profit, capital from such 'off territory' investors would became more usual.

As happened at Penrhyn and Dinorwig, the deep-pursed landowner could take the long view. Professional investors, with widely spread interests, could afford to wait for speculations to bear fruit. Businessmen with experience of slate understood the need to invest for the future. By contrast, the lay investor, perhaps lured by tales of untold wealth at Penrhyn, putting his savings into the latest quarry promotion, wanted immediate dividends. This short-term approach was to have profound and often disastrous effects on much of the industry. Good rock would be cast aside in favour of better rock, and sometimes badly framed wage-rates encouraged this. Rubble would be dumped on areas above good rock, so effectively constraining future development. Infrastructure would be skimped, collapses would occur due to lack of overburden clearance, or underground to lack of adequate pillaring. Profits which accrued in good times and which ought to have been retained for re-equipment or re-development, or as a nest-egg for hard times, were all too often disbursed as dividends.

Indeed in all fairness, if as was usually the case, a quarry was held on a lease of say, ten or twenty years, returns needed to be fairly immediate. Plant and machinery might ultimately be sold, but expenditure on buildings and civil work had to be recovered before it reverted to the landlord. Thus it was invariably only the freehold or very long-leased quarries that could contemplate big outlays on permanent structures.

The poor quality of managers was notorious, this often being due to a reluctance to put local men in charge. A man with scant knowledge, but who could be 'trusted', would be engaged rather than an 'unknown' no matter how great his experience and sound his record.

Unwisdom and incompetence apart, there was much outright fraud. A person finding himself the owner or lessee of a totally dud property would seek to unload it by floating a company and exhorting those *'Who were astute enough to avail themselves of a unique investment opportunity'*, to join him. His contribution was usually confined to making over the lease and the 'goodwill'. Invariably, the company would have 'agreed' to buy the plant and buildings for a generous sum and to have 'secured' his services as the (highly paid) Chairman or Managing Director. This 'pass the parcel', though less flagrant than it was in, say metal mining, was widespread and was to continue right into the 20th century. Such directors, having minimal equity themselves would, when it all fell apart, have no hesitation in putting the company into liquidation, buy back the assets at a knock-down price, and resume trading. (Or even float yet another company!).

Prior to the Companies Act of 1862, this was very bad news for the proverbial widows and orphans, since subscribers were responsible for the whole of the debts of a failed enterprise, not just the amount of their investment. Wise but unscrupulous investors sometimes put shares in relatives' names. An instance of this was the Merionethshire Slate Company, which failed in 1848, with heavy debts. Of the two subscribers who could actually be traced one had apparently surreptitiously transferred his holdings to his father and brother, both being reverend gentlemen, who denied all knowledge of the firm. Likewise the other having put everything in the names of his son and his brother picked up the plant and machinery at a bargain price and carried on trading under another name, leaving the relatives to meet the debts!

Companies with grand titles proliferated, promising the most optimistic returns from triflingly insignificant sites. The Prospectus would invariably include a report from an 'expert', who would declare it to be *'an unrivalled opportunity'*, the rock no matter how poor, would be pronounced *'excellent'*. If the term *'Another Penrhyn'* were not actually used, then there would invariably be a reference to

'The great profits, now being made at Penrhyn'. Many were merely erroneous, but others were totally dishonest. Some did not actually own the quarries they offered, presumably hoping to obtain them if and when the floatation succeeded.

Not untypical was the Great Welsh Union Slate Company's abortive £250,000 floatation of 1857. The properties offered were; Hillsborough quarry (Probably the small Corris quarry, Ty'n-y-Berth), Beaver Pool, an insignificant digging at Betws-y-coed, Ty'n-y-Ceunant, another small Corris working and 'St. Winifred's' of unknown location (possibly in Nantlle). Two years later the Union Slate Company was more modestly, seeking £30,000 for Hillsborough and two miniscule holes in Dyffryn Conwy, Penlan and Rowlin, which were such tiny scratchings that their locations are disputed. A year later the British Slate Company was looking for £75,000 for these latter two, plus Gaewern which though a bona-fide working was in difficulties. Research has failed to show that the promoters, some of whom were involved in all three offerings, had title to or even options on, any of these quarries.

Financial juggling apart, there were still men trying to make honest livings, usually against the odds. Despite the draining of Traeth Mawr having lost them their transport, men were still scratching at Brondanw Isaf in the 1820s and a few yards away at Brondanw Uchaf five optimists tried again in 1836. They at least had a nearby road, but reaching Llyn Llagi quarry called for a trek over bare mountain. Even worse placed was Arddu quarry, halfway up Snowdon, where much of the product hacked out of a couple of holes, remains stacked there to this day.

But in spite of error and fraud, the industry was moving forward. Although some small quarries stuck to their crowbars and wedges, increasing tonnages called for explosives, if only for tunnelling and for removing hard country rock. Some brave souls at Cilgwyn had used gunpowder to win rock since the end of the 17th century, and by 1800 limited use was made at Penrhyn, Dinorwig and elsewhere. The 1830 invention of the Bickford Safety Fuse enabled shot firing to become standard practice. This obviated the somewhat fraught procedures described by Rev W. Bingley at Parys Copper Mine in 1788.

'This process of blasting must frequently be attended with danger, as the men have been known to be so careless as not to be sufficiently distant when the explosion has taken place. The manner in which it was done was quite novel to me. They bore a hole in that part of the rock in which they wish to blast, about the width of a very wide gun barrel, and of a depth in proportion to the quantity to be thrown up. At the bottom of this they lodge their gunpowder, and then taking an iron rod, made about two feet in length, and tapered to quite a point, they place it in the hole, and fill it up on all sides with stones, clay etc. ramming it hard down with an iron, projecting at the bottom of which is made a nick, that it may pass freely round the rod. When it is filled up, and well hammered down, the rod is taken out, and a straw filled with gunpowder, substituted in its place. A match is then lighted and put to it with, as they express it, as much time in it as to permit them to get away, that is, of length sufficient before it burns through and lights the powder, to suffer them to escape out of the danger attendant upon the explosion'. (Until copper tampers came into use, sparks struck by iron ones were the cause of many premature explosions).

For blasting, shot holes skilfully positioned to move the maximum amount of rock with the minimum of damage (and least use of powder), were drilled with hammer and chisel or with a Jwmpah. This was a weighted iron rod upwards of 6' long, which by a repeated throwing action would produce a hole. Progression was 6' – 12' per exhausting hour. Black powder was and still is, always used, as high explosive would shatter slate. Frightening though it now seems, in the early days gunpowder was bought from the nearest grocer!

The greatest developments were in what we now call 'materials handling'. Rail systems were being put in to move block within the quarry, to handle finished product and more importantly to dispose of the waste. Apart from development waste of country rock and overburden, 10, 20 or more tons of actual slate waste was generated for each ton of product made. This waste was mainly rock unsuitable for use and the off-cuts from the dividing and squaring off of blocks. It all had to be taken away and tipped, hopefully on ground that would not be required for future working. Fine waste from hand dressing of roofing slates could be left where it lay, but with mechanical working, dressing waste and sawn ends would also require removal and disposal.

Even the smallest quarries usually had at least a length of track to a tipping point, or if underground, rails in the access tunnel. Eventually few workings were without rails of some kind, although Aber quarry, near Denbigh, which produced slabs of 6' x 4' and more, relied on hand barrows right up to its 1920s closure.

Permanent rails in the more affluent quarries were chaired. Temporary runs and those in smaller quarries tended to be flat-bar rail tenoned into wooden sleepers. Slate in spite of its abundance lacked the resilience of wood so was rarely used for sleepers. The stone block sleepers widely associated with coal and metal mining were almost unknown apart from the Nantlle Railway and the pre-steam Padarn Railway.

Later patent metal track was widely employed, an early variety, being the Thomas Hughes rail. This system, devised at Penrhyn, consisted of round iron bar 1' or so diameter, each length having turned down ends that slotted into cast-iron sleepers. It made a good, easily re-sited track, but unfortunately for Mr Hughes, any blacksmith could readily copy the rails, and a slab of scrap slate, with four suitably positioned holes, made an excellent sleeper.

Wagons became standardised mainly into three patterns. Flat wagons with wooden crossbars for carrying blocks. Iron bodied wagons open at one end for rubbish. Crate wagons for finished product. The wheels were often double-flanged, loose on the axle, to permit running on poor or makeshift track of variable gauge. Wagons were mostly hand-pushed, but for longer runs in the larger quarries horses or donkeys were used.

Blocks were loaded onto wagons by sheer legs. Underground, crab winches (which might be old sailing ship items) were used, lifting by reeving a cable through a pulley in the chamber roof. But even with good rail and lifting facilities, much of the 'materials handling' remained backbreaking work.

The layout of quarries tended to become more uniform as experience was gained, but scale, topography and the lie of the veins, meant that each one differed in detail. Hillside workings might be worked on just the one level, but increasingly the terrace system pioneered by Penrhyn and Dinorwig, was used. In Cwm Pennant, the little Dolgarth quarry and its famously unsuccessful neighbours, Prince of Wales and Gorseddau as well as Arthog, Abercwmeiddaw and Cambergi in Meirionnydd, would take this form. Later, before it went over to underground working, Penarth near Corwen had a fine array of terraces. Early workings at Craig Rhiwarth in the Tanat valley were terraced, but in a less orderly manner.

Other open-air quarries were pits. These might be hillside workings, which had followed the slate veins downwards. As work progressed cuttings, then tunnels, provided access and drainage. Quarries such as Cefn Ddu, Chwarel Fawr and several others near Llanberis developed in this way, as did parts of Dinorwig. Further south, the small and remote Gwanas and Darren quarries were to this pattern, as would be Maes y Gamfa, Golwern and many more. Cambrian at Glyn Ceiriog eventually had a tunnel accessing and draining 4 pits, as well as serving underground workings. Abercwmeiddaw also had such a tunnel but its utility was limited as block emerging from it still had to be up-hauled to the mill. Nearby Llwyngwern cut a similar tunnel, but although rail was laid in it, it only ever served as a drain. Rhos at Capel Curig cut a tunnel that eliminated pumping and the up hauling of waste, but the projected new mill that would have enabled it also to handle the output, was never built. Pen y Orsedd, Braich Rhyd and others at Nantlle, Llwynpiod, near Carmarthen, and on a grander scale Oakeley and Penrhyn all had dedicated drainage tunnels.

The big valley-floor pits at Nantlle faced serious water problems, a one time dream of a collective drain to the sea was never fulfilled so most had to be constantly pumped. Where there was a suitable water flow, self-acting injector pumps could be used, but powered pumps were usually required. Early ones were either rag and chain or bucket pumps but the standard pump, throughout the 19th century, was the lift pump, or in the case of deep pits, a series of lift pumps at perhaps 30' stages, operated by vertical rods. Water-wheel power was sometimes used, possibly with the wheel having to be sited some distance from the pump with flat-rods conveying motion. These rods, which could be several hundred yards in length, were supported by rollers, and moved to and fro by a crank on the water wheel. Rhiwbach and Rhosydd in the Ffestiniog area used this system, as did Glanrafon in Cwm Gwyrfai where the rods ran along a drainage tunnel that further downward working had rendered redundant.

A curious use of flat-rods was a pump at Graig Ddu at Blaenau, where a water wheel lifted water not to drain, but to fill the reservoir that supplied the mill water wheel.

A steam pump was used in 1807 at Gloddfa Coed at Nantlle, but that ended in disaster ten years later when injudiciously excavation caused the lot to topple into the pit.

Seeking a less expensive option in 1827, nearby Braich Rhyd put up a wind-powered pump, but a strong wind tore the canvas sails and then a very strong wind wrecked the whole caboodle. Expensive though they were to buy and run, steam engines would prove to be the only solution to dewatering problems in many Nantlle workings.

Besides pumping, pit workings required almost every piece of rock, be it waste or usable material, to be up hauled. In the earliest days hand windlasses were used, some like Cilgwyn and Hafod Las up-hauled by horse-whim, the latter quarry keeping 16 horses for the purpose. (The only known surviving example of a slate quarry horse-whim circle, where a horse walked around a vertical axle, which had a winding drum at its top, is at Hendre quarry near Dolwyddelan).

Where drainage was not a problem, a water-balance where the weight of a filled water tank could haul loaded wagons up an incline, was used. The earliest known water balance was installed at Tal y Sarn at Nantlle in 1827. Later Rhos as well as Cwt y Bugail, Bowydd and possibly Fron Boeth quarries at Blaenau would have them. One may have been used at Moelfre in Cwm Pennant. Others included Cwm Machno and Aberllefenni (Where remnants survive).

Normally the water tank ran on a track parallel to the load-carrying track but there are two interesting variations of this underground at Croesor. At Croesor quarry itself, at one time material was raised from underground workings below exit-adit level by a tank travelling vertically in a shaft above. At nearby Rhosydd the balance tank ran in its own inclined tunnel remotely sited above adit level so that the water discharge would be self-draining.

The very last water balance incline built in a slate quarrying ambiance was a double acting one opened in 1992 to carry visitors up to the Centre for Alternative Technology at Llyn Wern quarry near Machynlleth. The same principle was also used in vertical lifts, notably at. Penrhyn, where ultimately there were seven of unique and complex design.

Water wheels were also used to wind haulage inclines there being a magnificent example at Bryneglwys near Tywyn. Cefn Gam near Dolgellau, Cymerau near Corris, Llechwedd and possibly Moelfre, also raised material in this way. Rhos did so before the drainage tunnel allowed them to make more economical use of water with a water balance. Uniquely Hafodlas near Betws-y-coed connected the mill water wheel to their gravity incline drum to enable it to up haul. The equally unique horizontal haulage at Rhosydd was also water wheel powered. Unusually, Gwernor quarry at Nantlle used water-turbine haulage and Rhosydd used Pelton wheels.

Most up-haulages were on an inclined plane, but in a constantly deepening and possibly widening pit using a fixed ramp would be almost impossible, therefore material was invariably raised from pit workings by chain inclines. These carried loads hung from sheaves running on chain or rope catenaries. They were less efficient than conventional inclines, but having no fixed formation they could be moved as work progressed. The one known extant example of a fixed ramp in a pit is at Blaenycwm quarry near Blaenau, but this in fact was a gravity incline built in a worked-out pit to enable it to be used as a thoroughfare to connect other workings with the mill.

A later refinement of the chain incline, used at Nantlle, Dinorwig and Penrhyn was the 'Blondin'. This consisted of a wire rope stretched between two towers on either side of a pit. By means of a sheave running on this rope, loads could be lifted and transported, to be landed at the edge of the pit. They were thus more versatile than the chain incline, as loads could be picked up from anywhere beneath the carrying rope, rather than the one fixed point of the chain incline, particularly useful where a pit was being worked in several galleries. These Blondins used two coaxial winding drums, one (with a single rope) for lifting, the other (with two ropes) to move the sheave to and fro. Operating the lifting drum on its own raised or lowered the load hook. With the two coupled together the sheave could be moved, with the load height kept constant. They were criticised as being slow, as being difficult to maintain (freeing a jammed sheave meant a man had to crawl out along the wire!) and though theoretically moveable, doing so was not easy. They were powered by steam, or later, electricity.

In a few instances, such as Hafodlas near Betws-y-coed, Cae Abaty in the Dyfi valley and Llwyngwern near Corris, Scotch derricks were used to lift block from pits.

Fortunately, in most workings, materials movement was mainly downward, thus the double-acting balanced inclines pioneered in Penrhyn and Dinorwig proliferated, eventually upwards of 300 of them carried slate in Wales. The vast majority had a horizontal drum at the incline head, supported by two walls, joined by a roof. A down-going load of one, two or three loaded wagons unwound a rope on one half of the drum, causing another rope to be coiled onto the other half of the drum which up-hauled empty wagons. Great ingenuity was sometimes shown in raising heavy machinery by these inclines, exercises that were not always free of incident. Occasionally such inclines were single acting with a wheeled ballast truck acting as the counterbalance. In either case the operation was controlled by a brake, usually a strap acting on one end of the drum, operated with considerable skill by a brakeman via a long lever.

Normally the tracks passed straight through the drum house under the drum, but where space at the incline head was restricted, the drum might be remotely sited above and behind the top of the pitch. Sometimes where the head of the incline was on made ground too unstable to support a drum house, the drum would be in a pit under the tracks, this was done at Dinorwig and at some Nantlle quarries. Most inclines had sprags at the top to prevent wagons prematurely descending; these could be anything from simple hinged bars to complex chocking mechanisms controlled by a lever handy for the brakeman.

The earliest drums were entirely of wood, but after about 1840, they consisted of a wrought iron axle, cast iron spiders and a skin of wooden staves, or very occasionally sheet metal. A few inclines had instead of a drum a single rope running round iron sheave-wheels on vertical spindles. These were common in the Corwen area, doubtless due to the influence of the nearby Wrexham collieries, where this sort of gear was commonly used. Such sheaves could be in housings or in pits below the rails, although uniquely, the final incline on the Deeside tramway had horizontal sheaves overhead in a 'drum house'. Also uniquely, this structure was roofed in tiles since at the time of its construction Deedside quarry was concentrating on slab.

In most cases the wagons ran on their own wheels, but sometimes, particularly on steep pitches, they were carried on tables or 'truncs'. Some of these table inclines were substantial pieces of engineering, carrying two or even four wagons, with complicated geared brakes to cope with the considerable loads. Those at Vivian quarry at Llanberis were particularly fine. (One pitch has been restored and motorized by the Slate Museum to demonstrate its function).

At first fibre ropes restricted incline lengths, enforcing several pitches on long descents as at Moelwyn, but after the mid 19th century, wire ropes enabled such magnificent single-pitch inclines, dropping 700', as those at Rhosydd. These represented the limit of single-pitch working, since on greater lengths the weight and drag of the paid-out rope could not be overcome by the down-going load, necessitating the use of power as on the Ffridd incline at Llanberis.

The Blaenau method of underground working became almost universal in Meirionnydd but rare in Caernarfonshire only being used at Tan y Bwlch, Moel Faban and several smaller workings to the north of the Ogwen valley. In Denbigh Cambrian, Wynne, Penarth, Moel Ferna Craig Rhiwarth and Cwmmaengwynedd quarries were all similarly worked and in south Wales, Penceulan.

The 'cavern' style working at Clogwyn y Fuwch was not repeated in Wales except tentatively at Aberllefenni. Neither was the Pen y Ffridd stone-mining method of extracting on a wide face from a near horizontal vein, just leaving freestanding pillars to support the roof.

In the most basic form of underground working, a tunnel might be driven in search of a putative concealed vein, but a less speculative method was to prove the vein in an open working, then either chase it underground or drive a tunnel from a lower level to 'roof up' into the slate. This latter method might be repeated higher or lower down a hillside. The classic or Blaenau method of large-scale extraction pioneered by Diffwys and Bowydd around 1820, was to drive a level tunnel across a dipping vein, immediately below the overlying country rock. From this strike tunnel, sloping tunnels or 'roofing shafts' would be driven at say 80' intervals up though the slate vein keeping tight under the overlying rock so that it formed a roof. From these roofing shafts, slate would be extracted leftwards and downwards to create a chamber about 50' wide, leaving untouched a wall of slate (always referred to as a 'pillar'), perhaps 30' wide, to support the ground above. Thus all work was upward with material movement downward and with the opportunity to minimise rubbish haulage by backfilling worked-out chambers. To enable large numbers of men to simultaneously work, other strike tunnels above and/or below would be driven, with their roofing shafts and hence the chambers precisely aligned. Workings would eventually break through into those above leaving a continuous sloping cavern.

In the near vertical veins at Aberllefenni, a downward

variation of this method was used, which Sir Charles Foster, the Chief Inspector of Mines found sufficiently notable to merit publishing a descriptive paper.

Working underground usually meant water problems. As with pit workings a drainage tunnel was sometimes a possibility, the best example being Rhiwbach quarry's particularly fine one. Much of Maenofferen quarry at Blaenau was drained by Cooke's level, which in latter days served at the statutory escape route. Rhosydd considered a combined exit and drainage tunnel into the Orthin valley but cost apart, land ownership precluded it. There was a suggestion that the Blaenau workings could be collectively drained, as was often the case in lead mining, but co-operation on this scale was not a concept ready grasped by Blaenau proprietors.

Llechwedd was able to use a waterwheel pump (That uniquely was sited at Olwyn Goch some $\frac{1}{2}$ mile from the workings), and Oakeley did at one time make use of a water turbine to dewater chambers below drainage level, but until steam, and later electricity, was available work below the lowest adit level was severely constrained.

Underground working, in spite of the obvious difficulties, was often more productive than open working, as once the strike tunnels had been cut a minimum of non-slate material had to be removed, and block was always obtained from faces undegraded by extremes of weather. Indeed although there were the dangers and discomforts of working in near-darkness, the year-round 55°F spared men from summer heat and winter cold.

Permanent lighting underground was non-existent until the 20th century. and was rare until recent years. An exception was the gas lighting installed by Holland in 1842 in his 1000 yard long tunnel cut to enable material from the main workings to be brought to the mill. Since this was called the 'Horse Tunnel', it was said that the lamps were for the convenience of the horses, not the men. Other than the carbide lamps carried by supervisors, the sole illumination was by candles, which like gunpowder and other consumables, were paid for by the men themselves. Sometimes they bought the candles privately as shown when a widow of a man killed at Oakeley in the 1890s asked for her £10 compensation as a lump sum rather than in 10 monthly instalments, as she wished to open a shop selling candles to the quarrymen.

More usually they were issued by the quarry and deducted from wages, a remunerative exercise as instanced in 1877 when Braich Goch made enough profit on sales of powder, candles & fuse to cover their £200 royalty payment. Whatever the source, candles were a major expense. When underground working first started candles cost 1/ (5p) per pound, so a 2 lbs weeks' supply made a hole in a wage of 10/- (50p) and if a man had access to tallow, he would certainly make his own. Although by the end of the 19th century candles were down to 7d (3p) per pound, and wages had possibly quadrupled, the cost still loomed large in the family budget.

Clay was used to stick a candle to a rock or to a cap, the sole eventual 'modern' refinement being putting them into crude lanterns made out of one-gallon oil tins. It would be the 1950s before the Oldham electric cap-lamp completely ousted the candle.

Underground quarrying, particularly on a big scale, gave rise to much innovative engineering, especially in the transport of material. The horizontal tunnels, originally bored for access, formed ideal tramway routes. Where subsequent extraction interrupted these routes, bridges maintained continuity. These underground bridges were of up to about 50' span, typically comprising two baulks of pitch pine, 18' x 9', decked with 9' x 3' timbers. Each baulk would have two iron bars 2' diameter, projecting downwards a third of the way along. The bottoms of these bars would be joined by a 1' tie rod and braced at each end by 1' bars reaching to either end of the main baulks, where they were tensioned by nuts. Post and chain handrails were usual. In the case of longer spans, chains from the roof gave extra support. Inclines were crossed by hinged platforms.

The dip of the veins provided obvious paths for inclines to link the different levels. Underground inclines were frequently of the table type usually with the wagons riding on turntables (so that a long block coming in from a side tunnel could be turned to avoid fouling the walls of the incline tunnel). Also due to constrictions of tunnel width they were usually single acting, with the counterbalance weight running on a narrow track between the main rails, also due to lack of space, the headgear usually comprised sheaves on horizontal spindles, rather than the conventional drums used on the surface. Intermediate tunnels crossed these inclines by ingenious hinged bridges.

To enable men to move between levels underground, steps were sometimes provided, but commonly they had to scramble up and down hundreds of feet of waste, or use rickety iron or chain ladders to reach their workplaces. Not that those in open quarries were always better catered for. Pit workings, hundreds of feet deep, were accessed by slippery wooden ladders. Extensive hillside workings might have steps, which might be alongside inclines, or could zigzag dizzily and possibly perilously to vast heights. At least men in open workings were spared the reaching of roofs of underground chambers to inspect for loose rock or to fix pulley mountings. Portable ladders 60' or more in length were used, which according to an early specification had to be *British Larch grown on a plantation on a slope facing the north where the sun shines the least*. They were leaned against a wire stretched across the chamber and their erection took as much skill as it did nerve to climb them.

Whether open or underground, rockmen all had the danger and discomfort of working high on a working face.

They secured themselves by a rope (if underground, a chain) wrapped around one thigh. Although later when power drills were used, men stood on planks resting on iron bars driven into the rock, rope or chain working persisted into the mid 20th century.

Whilst some of the techniques of winning and moving the slate, were improved upon in detail later, the broad principles had, by the late 1840s, been firmly established. The industry could look forward to further progress, and play its part in Wales having by mid-century, more people in industry than agriculture, thus officially becoming the first Industrial Nation on earth.

4. SOMEWHERE TO DIG, SOMEWHERE TO LIVE
The 1850s –1860s

The promised profits drew more and more investors towards slate, but with most proved sites already being worked they had either to buy in paying over the odds, as Rothschild had done, or take a chance at an unproved location. The supreme example such chance taking was the Gorseddau quarry of 1855 where Lancashire men with no knowledge of slate made a most ambitious development in a wild and remote valley. Before the site was proved, terraces were laid out on 9 levels with a fine incline in the middle, planned so that extraction was done at one end of each terrace with dumping at the other.

Unusually these terraces had both 2′ and 3′ gauge track, the 2′ for internal movement and the 3′ connected via the incline to the line down to the magnificent cathedral-like Ynysypandy mill. This tramway, engineered to near main line standards continued on from the mill to Porthmadog by a route that avoided inclines, the one sharp gradient being overcome by a reversing loop. It was certainly the best constructed of all the horse tramways, 3′ gauge being specified to cope with huge expected output.

In addition Treforus, a village of some 40 pairs of 'semis' for the workers was planned, (although only 18 were completed) and Plas Llyn, the manager's house was of mansion proportions. Reputedly £50,000 was spent in 2 years. After 4 years work their 200 men could barely raise 1500 tons p.a., which at 7.5 tons per man-year must be an industry record for non-productivity. Even the peak output of 2000 tons p.a. would have scarcely met their wages bill let alone any other costs. Incredibly they persevered right up to 1867 when, their horses having been sold, the year's mere 25-ton output was hand-pushed to Porthmadog. On the site it can be seen how they abandoned their neat, disciplined layout, generating vast mounds of rubbish as they desperately and randomly sought good rock, even at one point trying underground. The dearth of dressing waste on the terraces and scarcity of sawn-ends on the mill-tip testifies to the smallness of the output.

Less spectacular, but equally typical of the madcap schemes was the 1859 Liverpool and Birkenhead Slate and Slab quarry Co Ltd, whose name was a great deal more impressive than their quarry, Braich Ddu at Trawsfynydd. With poor rock and even poorer transport prospects, they put in a mill and a costly Hunter saw and somehow stumbled on with a trifling output for over 20 years. Foel high on Moel Siabod, which had already proved something of a dud, was developed in the 1860s with a mill, 3 barracks and a multi-incline tramway. A second mill was put in at Pont Cyfyng at the foot of the tramway, which was soon in turn replaced by a third mill back at the quarry itself. More work was done on construction than ever was on slate making.

Another example of the 'slate mania', again in the 1860s, was when the McConnels, finding their Lancashire cotton interests hit by the American civil war, took over a couple of diggings at Bryneglwys where the excellent rock had not been fully exploited due to the output having to be pack horsed over the mountain to Pennal. They built the Talyllyn Railway and within 5 years had 260 men at work producing up to 8000 tons p.a., a handsome output but not enough to justify the great amount of capital (circa £100,000) expended.

Such businessmen-entrepreneurs had replaced the landed gentry as sources of capital, but by this mid-century time, the impact of the modest local investor was growing. The rise of waged employment in place of a barter economy created to an expanding middle class of shopkeepers, who increasingly put money into the industry. Directory entries such as the 1858 '*William Williams, Harlech. Draper, Grocer and*

Slate Quarry Owner' were becoming commonplace.

Regrettably such people were often seduced by the fact that shares were invariably sold part paid, with a tacit implication that by the time the there was a cash-call for the balance, the share price would have rocketed, generating a handsome profit. Almost inevitably they would face cash-call after cash-call on valueless shares. This was not necessarily due to fraud but the fact that occurrences of good readily accessible rock were very few indeed, and many of these only had potential in times of high prices and demand In fact it was almost impossible to recoup the full cost of laying out a quarry, success invariably depending on the failure of others. It was said that a quarry had to be developed, sold at a knock down price, redeveloped then again sold, leaving the third owner with some chance of a profit. Rhos quarry for example eventually prospered in this way, having been started in the 1850s, the third owners did well in the 1870s boom, and it in fact survived to the mid 20th century.

The other requirement for success was good transport. By the 1850s, the three rail lines took care of most of north Caernarfonshire and Blaenau had its Ffestiniog Railway, but other areas were less well served. Nearly 100 men were working in a dozen diggings around Beddgelert where for years railway connection was described as 'imminent'. Many schemes were mooted and in some cases land was bought and track bed built, but it was the 1930s before a train ever arrived. Without transport only Hafod y Llan got much beyond the hole-in-the-ground stage. They built a mill and put in a horrendously expensive incline system from high up on the slopes of Snowdon down to the valley floor in the confident expectation that they would be able to connect with the promised railway. The railway never came and they had to content themselves with carting from the foot of the incline to Porthmadog. This cost them 12/6 (62.5p) per ton, twice the sea-freight to Liverpool and almost as much as shipping to the Baltic. Inevitably they failed to survive.

To the north in Dyffryn Conwy despite the shortcomings of boating down river to Conwy, workings at Rhos, Cwm Machno and Dolwyddelan in tributary valleys, somehow coped and in the mid-century stampede to find sites, there was interest in the barren fastnesses of the Carneddau. In the 1860s, a 5-mile tramway was put in to bring material down to the river from the Cedryn and Cwm Eigiau quarries. This short-lived tramway had one incline partway along and a three-pitch incline down to the river at Dolgarrog. It was revived in the early 1900s in standard gauge on a slightly altered route, to facilitate the building of Llyn Eigiau hydroelectric reservoir for Dolgarrog Aluminium Works. The intermediate incline was by-passed and the 3-pitch, self-acting incline straightened into a single pitch haulage incline. This incline later also handled materials for the construction of the Colwyd reservoir, via the purpose built Colwyd tramway, remaining in use to service the reservoir until the 1970s. The incline formation still serves as a route for the hydroelectric feed-pipes.

Despite its shortcomings several small quarries also boated down river to a seaport, their rivers being reached by short tramways. Arthog and Tyddyn Shieffre used the Mawddach and Cwm Ebol and Fron Goch the Dyfi. The Cilgerran quarries used the Teify, but were mostly so close to the river that they had no need of tramways, being almost able to throw the slates into the barges. Regrettably they were also close enough to the river to throw their rubbish into it, eventually stopping navigation and silting up the port at Cardigan.

Just a few workings such as Cwm Machno managed to survive with long cartages, but more typical was Cefn Gam quarry, high in the Rhinogs that produced exceptionally strong and flexible roofing material in a fine, mechanised unit, but were eventually victims of elevation and isolation.

As was Gwanas perched defensively on Cribin Fach as if fearing assault from Visigoths or Vandals, or Darren, sheltering from the biting winds high under the Tarren y Gesail escarpment, where tens of thousands of untransportable slates still lie today.

Some opportunities were to be had at Blaenau infill sites such as Wrysgan, tucked up in a corner above Tanygrisiau. It operated for many years, its success only limited by the tightness of the site. Nearby Nyth y Gigfran squeezed in, also with precipitous access to the Ffestiniog Railway.

The most spectacularly successful infill site was Llechwedd. In 1845 Greaves and Shelton abandoned Bowydd, Greaves taking a lease on adjacent Newborough land but failed to find slate. For four years he tottered on the verge of ruin supported by handouts from his banker brother. It is said that when he could no longer pay his men they worked for nothing. According to legend he was roused in the night by a breathless horseman furiously pounding at his door to report that a pickaxe had penetrated that Holy Grail of slate, the Meirioneth Blue vein.

True or false he rapidly built Llechwedd into one of the great slate producers of the Blaenau. (Or indeed any) area, extracting from all five Blaenau veins. A particularly shrewd man, he did make incline connection to the Ffestiniog Railway, but only after browbeating them into carrying his slates at 3/3d (16p) per ton, little more than half the going rate. In fact he never relaxed his demands on the FR for ever-lower rates, which collaterally benefited all the users.

Rail connection was becoming increasingly important. The building of roads, good by the standards of the day, had encouraged the development of the ancient diggings at Corris, but it was the 1859 opening of the Corris, Machynlleth & River Dovey Tramway giving direct access to the river port of Derwenlas, enabled the area to become almost a 'Mini Blaenau Ffestiniog'. However with not much more than a tenth of the traffic of the FR, the Corris line was never able to match its Greaves-depressed charges, putting Corris at a slight but telling cost disadvantage.

Meanwhile to the west of Blaenau quarries such as Rhosydd were developing. Started as an open pit working in the 1830s, it had an easy route down Cwm Orthin to the Ffestiniog Railway. Unfortunately they found themselves cut off when Cwmorthin quarry barred all wheeled vehicles from crossing their land. The Croesor tramway of 1864 transformed Rhosydd's fortunes. It was a modest line, five miles long, dropping via three self-acting inclines, (Blaen y Cwm, Upper Parc and Lower Parc), from the head of Cwm Croesor to the Glaslyn flood plain and thence to Porthmadog. Though well constructed, it was not capable, nor was it called upon, to carry large tonnages. Entirely horse-drawn, (in later days locos did work to the foot of the lowest incline), it was virtually unstaffed, horses and drivers being hired as required. With minimal overheads, it was always able to at least match the F.R.'s charges. It enabled Rhosydd to grow from an insignificant digging to, by 1885, an annual tonnage of 6500 and over 200 men, making it one of the largest underground workings outside Blaenau Ffestiniog proper. Similarly the Croesor quarry itself, though not brought immediate success by the eponymous tramway, would, by the end of the century, under the great Moses Kellow's leadership, almost equal Rhosydd. Both these quarries were connected to the tramway by their spectacular, over 700' fall, single-pitch inclines.

Pant Mawr quarry was able to obviate a difficult packhorse journey, by linking onto the Croesor line via a 2-pitch incline plunging down into the Cwm Croesor. In 1886 when they merged with Fronboeth quarry and their operations were moved to a lower level, this link was abandoned and a tunnel bored through to Cwm Croesor, the lower pitch of the now redundant incline being extended to provide connection with the Croesor Tramway. Despite being augmented by the small open-air Cefn y Braich workings, and by slate actually extracted from within the tunnel itself, tonnages were never enough to justify the cost of this innovative development.

Parc quarry was also linked to the Croesor line, as were several smaller workings such as Croesor Bach, Llidiart yr Arian and the old Parc open quarry. The remote Gelli, and the ephemeral Bryngelynnen may have also used the line. The tiny, impossibly sited Cnicht that only a sheep could readily reach, may have used the Croesor if and when their trifling output succeeded in getting to it by a combination of near vertical sideway, ropeway and packhorse.

On the opposite side of Blaenau to the east of Mynydd Manod, Cwt y Bugail, Blaen y Cwm, Bwlch y Slaters and Rhiwbach quarries, remote from the FR, were still boating down the Dwyryd. This changed when, also in 1864, Rhiwbach built its tramway to Blaenau and offered the others connection to it. The tolls thus generated were in later and harder times, to prove vital to the Rhiwbach Company. It had been planned to continue the line down into the Machno valley, up hauling from Cwm Machno quarry by a water-balance, incline. Despite this never happening, Cwm Machno was able to survive into mid 20th century despite the handicap of carting first to the Conwy at Trefriw and later to the railway at Betws-y-coed.

This Rhiwbach Tramway arose out of one of the defining moments of the whole Slate Era, the steaming of the Ffestiniog Railway in 1866. No way could a clanking horse/gravity tramway have handled the tonnages that it would have to carry in the next decade. Neither could it have handled the supplies, particularly vegetables and dairy products, to support the population growth that accompanied the increased outputs. In 1868 the Ffestiniog and Blaenau (steam) Railway further augmented the FR's traffic by bringing in the output from the Llan Ffestiniog quarries and picking up the traffic that cascaded down the Graig Ddu inclines, a spectacular series of pitches that were matched across the valley by the equally spectacular zigzag of those of the revived Moelwyn quarry.

This all left the carters and the Dwyryd boatmen with only notional tonnages from Cae'n y Coed and Braich Ddu, which by 1869 ceased altogether, the Cambrian Railways bridge having all but stopped navigation on the Dwyryd. Penrhyndeudraeth was destroyed as a boating centre but the steaming of the Ffestiniog Railway with its public passenger services, gave it a new role as a 'dormitory town' for Blaenau Ffestiniog.

All this made the complex arrangements of the Padarn Railway obsolete, and caused the Penrhyn and Nantlle lines to seem medieval, and served notice that in future Blaenau rather than Bangor would be the slate capital of the world.

Four years prior to the FR steaming there had been no question of the Corris line being a steam railway, when the Talyllyn opened three years after it, there was no question of it not being steam.

Narrow gauge steam was now king of the hills and using FR technology its rule would extend from Bethesda to Burma and beyond.

Slab as opposed to roofing product, even when manufactured into finished items had been the poor relation of the trade epithetised as *'Can't make proper slates'*, but as an item in the Mining Journal for 25 April 1840 implies slab was being perceived as a product in its own right –

> *'Experiments have been made to ascertain the applicability of slate to other uses than the covering of houses. The result has been the discovery that, as a material for the paving of floors of warehouses, cellars, washhouses, barns etc. where great strength and durability are required. It is far superior to any known material. In the extensive warehouses of the London docks, it has been used on a large scale. The stones forming several of the old floors having become broken and decayed, have been replaced with slate 2' thick, and one wooden floor*

94

*which otherwise must have been relaid, has been cased with
slate 2' thick, the whole having been found to answer very
completely. The trucks used for removing the heaviest weights
are worked with fewer hands. The slates being sawn and
cemented closely together as they are laid down so they unite so
perfectly that molasses, oil, turpentine, or other commodity
which is spilt upon the floor is all saved; and as the slate is non-
absorbent, is so easily cleaned and dries so soon, that a floor on
which sugar in a moist condition has been spilled, may be ready
for the reception of the most delicate goods in a few hours.
Waggons or carts containing 4 or 5 tons of goods pass over
trackways of 2' slate without making the slightest impression.
In no one instance has it been found that a floor made of sawn
slate has given way; in point of durability, therefore, it may be
considered superior to every other commodity applied to such
uses. The consequences of the discovery have been that fullest
employment has been found in the quarries which produce the
slates and that additional employment has been given to British
shipping engaged in the coastal trade.'*

Certainly slab was finding more and more uses in bigger and
bigger sizes. Indeed by now men working slab were scornful
of those *'Only making tiles'* Slab demand revived quarries
such as some around Corwen and the upper Dyfi valley,
whose coarse roofing-slates could not compete with the
thinner product that the market was now demanding.
Indeed Corris roofing slate was only so-so whilst its slab was
world-class. Hafodlas, opened in 1854, with much money
spent during subsequent years, was saved from oblivion by
supplying slab for buildings when nearby Betws-y-coed
expanded as a tourist centre.

Slab workings had an advantage in that, generally, its
customers were more interested in the price and quality of
the product rather than in the perceived reputation of the
source. Thus a new and unknown quarry or district that
roofing-slate buyers distained, could break into the slab

market quite readily. Perhaps because it was a more prosaic, as well as a less valuable product than roofing slate, slab quarries were less subject to doubtful company promotions. Invariably when there was a questionable floatation of a quarry making both products, it was the roofing slate potential that was given prominence in the prospectus. Although a ton of slab sold for perhaps half the price of a ton of roofing slate, something like double the productivity could be achieved. If 'added value' items such as lintels, fireplaces, cisterns etc., were produced on site, even marginal quarries such as Maes y Gamfa and Ratgoed could be profitable. Later in the century, Parc with its Kellow's patent interlocking ridging and other specialities, would obtain an average of £4.00 per ton for its slab product, almost a record yield at the time.

Whatever product, the quarries were drawing more and more men into employment, all of whom needed accommodation. Some rented from their employer; at one time Penrhyn and Dinorwig owned respectively 1000 and 700 houses. Other large quarries such Rhos, Prince Llywelyn, Hafodlas, Cwm Machno and Pen yr Orsedd all owned houses, but large-scale lettings were not prevalent in Caernarfonshire. Self–build was more usual, avoiding the risk of the ejection on the whim of the quarry owner.

Some housing in the county was speculatively erected by builders for sale or let, but more typically, a landowner sympathetic to the Dissenting cause would be found who would allow a chapel to be erected that would be the nucleus for a (usually eponymous) settlement. As in the case of Bethesda, such settlements could become substantial.

Outside these chapel-centred hamlets, the cottages scattered across hillsides are very much part of the northern Caernarfonshire landscape. Often the owners emulated their betters by the unauthorised occupation of Crown or common land, undoubtedly invoking the ancient 'right' of

Tai Unos. This tradition was that if a house was commenced after sunset and was roofed with a smoking chimney, before sunrise, right of occupancy was established, together with land *'an axe throw from the door'*. (It is of course unlikely that this ever had any legal basis).

Most non-urban homes had at least some cultivatable ground, and town dwellers might grow say, potatoes or dig peat on a farmer's land in return for help at harvest time. Consequently, in accordance with the country tradition of exchange of labour, most quarrymen expected to absent themselves from work when their, or a neighbour's holding needed attention. Such unofficial time off was a constant source of friction right up to modern times Another perennial matter of dispute was leave to attend the quarterly Bangor fair, a necessary excursion since the custom of buying clothes and household durables from fairs and peddlers, resulted in a paucity of shops in rural Caernarfonshire. The matter was only resolved by adding fair days to Christmas Day, Easter & Whit Monday as official (unpaid!) holidays. Good Friday and Christmas Eve were regarded as half-days but oddly Ascension Day was a full public holiday until almost the end of the 20th century.

The costs of building or buying homes were met through Building Societies. These societies, among the first in Britain, were numerous in all the slate towns. Few were 'permanent' Building Societies in the modern sense, most comprising groups of men clubbing together to finance each others dwellings, the society being wound up when all had been housed.

In Caernarfonshire settlements nucleated around a quarry rather than a chapel were rare, an exception being Rhiwddolion alongside the little Bwlch Gwyn quarry, near Betws-y-coed. The community long survived the quarry's closure, the men obtaining work at Blaenau. Although by then there were trains, a daily walk of several miles to Pont

97

y Pant had to be made to catch them.

In Meirionnydd settlements tended to nucleate around the quarries rather than the chapels, the chapels following the settlements, a reversal of the Caernarfonshire practice. Blaenau Ffestiniog was the supreme example of this, and by mid century its original individual dwellings had been supplemented by teeming build-to-let terraces and multifarious chapels. Bursting at the seams, racked by epidemics, the provision of night-soil carts was considered the ultimate in municipal sanitation. Consequently, besides the one or two houses on site for 'on call' workers, such as smiths or enginemen, all the bigger quarries built and let dwellings. Cwmorthin, for instance, having no fewer than 53, some near the site, others at Tanygrisiau. Holland's built houses deliberately fronting onto the Ffestiniog Railway, with the intention providing doorstep delivery of coal and other supplies. Lord Newborough built unique 'one-chimney' houses *(Tŷ'r uncorn)* where a single storey dwelling had its 4 rooms disposed around a central fireplace block, somewhat in the Russian manner, which with the Siberian bite of Blaenau winters was not inappropriate.

There were of course smaller settlements. Rhiwbach quarry, in addition to its terrace in Cwmmachno, had a complete 'village' at the quarry itself with a chapel that served as a school and 'community centre' during the week. There was also a small shop, but main purchases were made in Blaenau on a Saturday, the 'shopping' being carried up the tramway on Monday morning's first rake of empty wagons. Generally shops even on quarry property were privately owned. There being no truck system that caused problems in other industries. The Welsh Slate Company briefly ran a shop, as did Dinorwig and Cilgwyn, but they were genuinely for the benefit, not the exploitation of, the workers.

Rhosydd also had its own community, complete with the

obligatory chapel. Even quarries as small as Foel Gron owned a few houses, in addition many quarries actively encouraged chapel building. This toleration, let alone provision, of non-conformist chapels, that would have been anathematic to the big north Caernarfonshire owners, illustrates the more liberal attitude towards to religion and indeed politics of the Meirionnydd owners.

In the south of the county, much of Corris belonged to Braich Goch quarry and the quarry at Aberllefenni owned virtually the entire village, where hood mouldings and other architectural detail contrasted with the more basic design of company houses elsewhere.

Ratgoed's row of four company houses, one a shop; plus a chapel with resident minister was a modest affair but Abergynolwyn was rather grander. Created out of two hamlets by the Bryneglwys quarry, rails connected to the Talyllyn Railway passed the back door of every house. Coal was delivered and night soil removed, for sale to neighbouring agriculturists.

In Denbighshire most of the dispersed quarries such as Penarth and Moel y Faen, built cottages for their employees. In south Wales, Fforest quarry near Cardigan had a self-contained settlement that, in spite of being almost inaccessible other than by river, outlasted the quarry by over 40 years. Rosebush's terrace was considered a model of worker's housing.

One thing all owners could agree on was the provision – or more accurately the non-provision – of public houses. Not a single instance is known of a public house on quarry-owned land. Many men from agricultural backgrounds had no experience of having money in their pockets, the work was thirst inducing, houses were crowded and alternative places of resort were non-existent. Besides, although the chapel/abstinence ethic was strong, it was not as all pervading as some historians would have us believe; therefore drunkenness was at least a potential problem.

Some owners made a positive contribution by opening 'Cocoa Rooms'. (Paradoxically Lady Newborough's Cocoa Room at Blaenau survives as the British Legion Club, not an institution one instinctively associates with the original beverage!)

Men living at a distance often stayed in barracks from Monday to Friday, a system that originated at the Parys Mountain copper mine in the 1740s. Some accommodation was just a doss-down in a quarry building or in the case of Croesor in a cowshed, but most were purpose built often designed on a 2 or 4 room basis so they could also be let as family accommodation. Barrackers would set out, perhaps as early as 3.00 a.m. on a Monday morning, carrying their provisions for the week arriving for a 7.00 a.m. start. They would then do a day's work, possibly soaked to the skin, hoping that in the evening there would be dry kindling in the barracks to start a fire to make a mug of tea. In winter they might be in wet clothes until they arrived back home on Saturday afternoon.

The author recalls the late Mr. Chris Hughes of Dolwyddelan telling him how, when a child, Sunday evenings after chapel would be occupied ensuring that his father's clothes and provisions were in order. And how he would hear in the small hours of Monday mornings, his father creeping downstairs to start his 5 mile walk (in winter in the dark, possibly in snow), over the trackless mountain to Rhiwbach quarry. Arduous though it was, this trip was easy compared with some Bethesda men's 10-mile walk, over a near 3000' bare mountain to reach Cwm Eigiau.

Barrackers might pay 1/- (5p) or so per week for a wooden bed, possibly shared between two, straw bedding and an infrequently washed sheet. Conditions were, even by the standards of the time, atrocious. Water for washing, drinking and cooking would be from a stream, which also served as a sewer for the lavatories (if any!). In the absence of a stream, barrackers had to buy water from enterprising pedlars.

There were no barracks at Penrhyn nor, except one mainly for the Anglesey men, at Dinorwig. There was a small barracks at Gorseddau and a larger one at Prince of Wales. Hendre Ddu (Pennant), Cedryn, Cwm Eigiau, Foel and Hafod y Llan, had barracks, as did the tiny workings at Cwm Bychan and Melynllyn. Cwt y Bugail barracks even had a library, but at Glanrafon and Ffridd Isaf accommodation was in a loft above the workshop.

Generally barracks were more widespread in Meirionnydd than Caernarfonshire. In addition to their tiny communities, Cwmorthin, Rhiwbach, Ratgoed and Rhosydd had barracks. Neither Rhiwbach nor Rhosydd's original barracks were the present ruins, the former first used an old farmhouse, the latter a building on floor 6. Rhosydd barracks was one of the most notorious in the industry, draughty, flea-ridden and damp, men ate, cooked and slept, each in as little as 200 cu/ft of space. (Equivalent to over 30 people in a modern semi) at over 1600' ASL. At Graig Ddu and Wrysgan conditions must have been equally inhospitable and Moelwyn barrackers and at one time families also, existed, snowbound in winter, close to the 2000' level. They at least had purpose built accommodation. At Blaen y Cwm they had to make do with a disused smithy and at Graig Ddu an old mill! Little Gelli quarry has a single all-purpose, house/barrack/office/workshop. When a quarry closed, men would take home their meagre barrack possessions, other than any personal bedding, this would be left on site to be part of a grand flea/louse/bed bug cremation!

Other isolated quarries such as Cefn Gam and Braich Ddu obviously needed barracks, but such was the shortage of accommodation in Blaenau Ffestiniog that even the quarries close to the town had to provide barracks. (Llechwedd's still exist as ruins behind and above the present offices). Even so, many men still had to make their own arrangements. Some found lodgings (up to 14 being taken in some quite modest houses); others had to sleep in stables and outbuildings in the town, (euphemistically called private barracks). Curiously, although Bryneglwys was no great distance from Abergynolwyn where most of the men lived, it had a barrack (above a workshop), older men being encouraged to use it to avoid the stiff climb to work each morning.

Some barracks were less horrific with perhaps each barracker paying a woman 2/- (10p) or so per month to clean and at Cwt y Bugail, a family lived rent-free in exchange for the wife keeping the barracks in order. Occasionally coal for heating and cooking was provided (at a charge!), but often they had to cut peat for a fire. In spite of the fearsome conditions, barracks nurtured choirs and poetry writing, and some, such as Cwt y Bugail had a library and night school. Where there was no other accommodation, lodging might be found on farms. Men who did so, usually helped out with the farm work, only going home on Tâl Mawr weekends, (the 12 weekly settlement of wages), very much typifying the quarrymen's commitment to the land.

Barracking tapered off during the 1930s, the Dinorwig Anglesey barracks being ordered to close as being 'unfit for habitation' in 1936, a daily bus service being arranged for the 200 lodgers. The last barracks to be occupied was Rhiwbach, where in 1952 just two men remained. Both could have gone home at night, one lived in Blaenau, and the other was from further away but had a car. Presumably the barracking habit was after many generations was too strong to break.

Even where there was no accommodation for the workers, there was invariably a house for the manager, usually sited well away from the noise and dust of the working area but with a full view of all comings and goings of the quarry. They were often large and impressive, with 'mod-cons' such as an icehouse for food storage, examples of which survive at Hafodlas and Cefn Gam. They were almost always closely screened by conifers, (which often still flourish long after the houses have been demolished). These trees gave privacy and dignity but as the late Arthur Jones, son of Edward Jones, the last manager of Votty & Bowydd to occupy 'Quarry Bank' recalled, they made the house dark and gardening difficult.

At even the smallest quarry, care was taken that the accommodation reflected the elevated status of the manager. At Gorseddau water was laid on, although regrettably via an open channel that must have had certain attractions to disaffected men. At Ratgoed the manager had his own earth closet, but the rest of the population, including the minister, had to take turns in the village 'two-seater. Communal toilet blocks were quite usual in isolated quarry settlements, particularly at height or on poor soil. Invariably sited over a watercourse well downstream from where drinking water would be drawn, they were sometimes a daunting distance from the homes they served. This of course was hygienic as far as the users were concerned, but not for the next settlement further down the valley!

In more cultivatable situations houses with gardens would, for obvious reasons, have earth closets. Interestingly, Blue cottages at Aberllefenni, the remnants of which are now restored as a house, originally had no contiguous gardens, but all had allotments some distance away, every one with its own 'fertiliser factory'.

5. METHODS & MECHANISATION

Obviously slates were once made entirely by hand. Rough blocks from the quarry face were reduced to a suitable size by skilfully striking them with a big African oak mallet, or by the use of hammer and chisel, or later, by drilling a hole and judiciously tapping in the expanding Plug and Feathers device. Roofing slates could then be made by splitting the block in half along the plane of cleavage, with a broad-bladed chisel, then 'halving the halves' until suitably thin laminae were produced. These would then be squared off to final size by resting the slate on a fixed iron blade and trimming each edge with an offset-handled knife.

For slab product separation along the plane of cleavage presents no problems to the skilled worked, other than the considerable weights sometimes involved but squaring off a slab 2' or more thick with a chisel is slow and laborious.

Although the Romans sawed stone by water-power, and slate graves markers were being sawn from at least the later 16th century in England (and in Vermont by Welsh immigrants), gravestones were still being cut in Wales by chiselling until well into the 18th century. When saws were eventually used they were hand-held frame saws with toothless blades up to 6'-8' long, cutting by introducing sand and water into the kerf. Such saws were still in use in some tiny quarries, such as Nantglyn near Denbigh and Berwyn on the Horseshoe Pass, well into the 20th century. Slabs were laid flat to be sawn, with the saw horizontal cutting along the length of the cut, not across it as a wooden plank is sawn, such hand-sawn edges can be recognised by the faint marks running along the length, with a ridge where the slab has been broken off to understandably avoid having to saw the full thickness. One of the earliest Welsh grave markers so cut is the 1746 Owen/Humphrey memorial at the tiny Llandanwg church possibly originating at Cae'n y coed.

Oddly in parts of southwest Wales, the slab was propped up vertically and sawn with a fine-toothed saw.

The 19th century expansion of the industry demanded the mechanisation of sawing, which was probably first done in 1802 at a timber sawmill at Rhyd y Sarn, near Maentwrog that had been taken over by Diffwys quarry who replaced the water-wheel driven timber saw with a sand saw. By 1805 Penrhyn was using such water-powered reciprocating saws that gradually gained acceptance throughout the industry, halving the cost of slab production. Power-sawn pieces are usually identifiable by the absence of any ridge on the sawn face. Lord Newborough's Glynrhonwy quarry on the southern shore of Llyn Padarn had a water-powered sand saw as early as 1823, but not strictly a sawmill since the saw was in the open air!

Despite of the development of more efficient circular saws, some reciprocating sand-saws remained in use for over a century. Moelfferna near Corwen actually installed them as late as 1911 and they were still being used at their associated Deeside mill in the 1920s. Tyn y Bryn at Dolwyddelan likewise retained them until about the same time. Shot saws widely used in stone quarries resemble sand saws, but use an indented blade and steel shot, they were never widely adopted for slatte, only Rhiwgoch at Dolwyddelan and Penarth at Corwen had them in the early 20th century. There was just one reciporcating diamond gang-saw, at Aberllefenni, late 20th century.

One of the first dateable examples of the characteristic curved marks of a circular saw is the 1805 Suwsana Pierce gravestone in Llan Ffestiniog churchyard. It was almost certainly cut in Diffwys quarry with a hand-cranked saw. These is at least one circular- saw cut gravestone in Llanidloes churchyard dated a year earlier, but the memorial may be much later than the burial. Hand cranked saws found little favour with proprietors (and certainly none with those certainly turning the cranks!), but did offer some advantage over hand sawing where no power was available. Gaewern at Corris, had at least two by the late 1840s, and nearby Darren had one or two in the 1850s. Bryn Llech (Bron Goronwy) near Ffestiniog and Gwanas high above Cross Foxes had one each. Cwmmaengwynedd in the Tanant valley had one underground, it presumably being cheaper to hack out an alcove in a tunnel than erect a building. Lighting costs did not figure in the reckoning as the men paid for their own candles!

The great step forward in speeding up sawing was the powering of circular saws. Diffwys are believed to have experimented at Rhyd y Sarn with one powered by a horse whim in about 1815. It was clearly not a success and it was only after powered circular saws had been thoroughly developed for timber and stone during the 1820s that slate producers took a serious interest in them. Bowydd was using them by 1830, with Penrhyn, Dinorwig and the larger Blaenau units installing them over the next ten years or so. Although some quarries, particularly those in Nantlle lagged in the adoption of this new technology, powered circular sawing was fairly general there by the 1850s.

There were many saw patents issued, including that of 1855 for the fearsome Hunter saw, whose replaceable teeth predated the general use of such items in engineering by almost a hundred years. Like some other early types (and modern diamond saws), the blade moved over the block being sawn. But it was the Greaves pattern of 1850, or variations of it, which became the industry standard. These had a moving table, with the toothed blade (revolving at about 30 rpm), protruding from underneath. Early versions advanced the table by a chain, but soon rack-drive became standard, usually driven by a double worm-gear train from the blade shaft. Although 2 & 3 speed devices were tried, normally the table feed rate could not be varied for different thicknesses and hardnesses of block. The best that might be done would be to change the gearing assembly or, to do as some big quarries did, set aside a few tables equipped with slow feed. De Winton, the great Caernarfon engineers, did make one batch of saws for Pen yr Orsedd in the 1880s with hydraulic table feed. These, by exerting a constant pressure, rather than a constant rate. of table travel gave automatic compensation for varying cutting conditions. Although these aroused much interest in the trade and remained in use for three-quarters of a century, only the one batch was produced.

Since at first saws were used only for slab production, quarries which dealt with both roofing slates and slab, only sent block destined for slab work to the saw-mill, continuing to produce roofing-slate entirely by hand in open-fronted *gwaliau*, close to the quarrying face or just outside an adit, This Welsh term literally means walls and indeed in early (and not so early) quarries if the slate makers had any shelter at all it would be by squatting down in the lee of a wall, In a big quarry the dressing sheds would be numerous, arranged in rows of a dozen or more, sometimes back-to-back, one side or the other being used according to the wind direction.

Thus, whilst quarries dealing exclusively in roofing slates, might not have powered saws, very shortly scarcely any slab quarries were without them. Even very modest workings such as Hafoty, near Croesor and Cwmcaeth at Namor, had their little mills with just one or two water-powered saws.

The idea of sawing in roofing slate production possibly came in as a result of writing slate experience, where blocks were sawn to size prior to splitting, in fact there was an attempt to sell roofing slate made in this way, i.e. with a sawn edge instead of a dressed edge (Mill Slates) However the market demanded a dressed edge so blocks were sawn oversize, with the split product being subsequently dressed to precise dimensions. Although this partly defeated the object of sawing, by giving the splitter rectangular blocks facilitated and speeded splitting and also eased the problems of trimming-waste disposal

This method was eagerly seized upon in Blaenau in the 1850s although some areas were reluctant to adopt it, particularly where hard Cambrian rock was being worked, Penrhyn did not saw all roofing slate until 1912, necessitating the commissioning of 100 extra saws.

Prior to the incorporation of sawing into the slate making process, mechanical dressers had come into use. These were rotative, with a skewed blade or blades, to give a lawn mower like shearing action. The earliest ones had a big, heavy-rimmed wheel that could be repeatedly tugged to build up a head of speed, so that before the inertia ran down, a number of slates could be trimmed. They were not much improvement over the traditional knife and trammel, but later ones treadle or pedal driven were dramatically faster.

Dressing machines sited in the *gwaliau* could not be powered, although it is said that in the 1870s at Rosebush quarry in Pembrokeshire, it was planned to drive them from a windmill! Putting them in the mill building to share power with the saws was the logical step giving rise to the Integrated Mill.

The typical integrated mill was a long building situated clear of foreseeable future quarrying or tipping and close to good, fast-running water. A water wheel (or other power source) in the middle of the building would drive, via overhead line-shafting and belts, a number of saws sited in pairs along the back wall. The line shafting would also drive, by horizontal belts, slave pulleys to serve the dressers, which would be sited along the opposite wall. The machines were controlled by the usual 'fast and loose' pulley system. Occasionally the line-shaft was under the floor, either in a slab-covered trench as at Aberdunant at Prenteg and Hafodlas near Betws-y-coed, or in a sort of cellar as at Cambergi near Corris and at Ynysypandy. Either arrangement cleared the working area of belts, and relieved the building of stress-loads, but a trench could get jammed with sawing dust.

Blocks intended for roofing slates would usually be coarse-split to 2'-2½' thick before being sawn, after which they would be passed to the splitters who were perched in the middle between the saws and the dressers. Then the split slates would be trimmed to size by the dressers.

The first mill to conform to this integrated layout was almost undoubtedly Diffwys No 6 mill, Blaenau Ffestiniog built around 1860, but the first quarry to put dressing machines in the saw building may have been Mathew's Middle Quarry at Blaenau or perhaps Minllyn in the upper Dyfi valley.

Diffwys No 6 used Mathew's type dressers that were fearsome 'French Revolution' guillotines whose knife, connected by a rod to an eccentric on the overhead line-shaft, thumped inexorably cropping slates and severing fingers with equal impartiality. Holland developed his own, but shortly the Greaves Rotative Dresser became, and with modifications remains, the industry standard.

There exists from an unknown late 19th century source, a somewhat poetic description of an Integrated Mill, almost certainly at Blaenau.

'The dressing shed and saw house was a long, lofty building, dull of light and air. Tramways ran into it from every side and conveyed the great blocks of raw slate to the millmen. Aloft, the beams of this workshop were whitewashed and a revolving rod from the giant steam engine of the works ran the length of the shed. Wheels spun from this rod at regular intervals and from them fell a system of endless bands to the machines beneath them. Some dropped to saw tables, some to the dressers sitting behind their guillotines. The main tramway separated these operations, and from time to time little tumbrils entered dragged by a horse. They brought fresh slate and removed the masses of splinters and debris. The air was misty with slate dust and through the haze whirled the endless straps, flashed the steel wheels from which they came and moved the drab

figures of a hundred men and boys. The prevalent colour of the shed and all therein was blue/grey, dim on dull days brightened from the glass roof on sunny ones. The golden light winnowed down through the dusty air, flashed on the faces of the saw-tables and struck brightly along the surfaces of the polished metal and the wet planes of the slate. Beside each saw-table stood the great masses of native rock as the men prepared them for the saw'.

Powered dressers were rare in Caernarfonshire, the knife and trammel remaining in use until the 1960s, but where machines were used, they tended to be of the Francis pedal-operated pattern. Invented by a manager at Penrhyn, they had swinging shears like a paper trimmer, and were considered more suitable for the brittle Cambrian rock than the Greaves machines. In later Caernarfonshire mills even where all dressing was done by hand, the layout tended to resemble the Blaenau integrated mills, but in place of dressing machines, there might be alcoves where the hand dressing was done. Modern automatic dressing machines are complicated bits of kit that can handle any slate, but most rely on the Greaves principle.

Waste disposal was a constant problem, other than in precipitously sited workings such as Nyth y Gigfran at Blaenau or Graig Rhiwarth in the Tanat valley who could allow their waste to skitter down hundreds of feet of mountainside, ton after ton had to be hand-loaded into wagons and trundled to the tip. The intensity of integrated mill working exacerbated the task and means had to be devised to clear the sawn ends and saw-fines as well as trimming waste Some mills had chutes directed to wagons on a track alongside and at a lower level than the mill. Croesor had rubbish wagons running below the mill floor itself, an arrangement that may have been intended at Ynysypandy. The shallow under-floor tunnel of Rhiwbach mill may have been intended for sawing-fines, the disposal of which was an on-going problem. Attempts were made to use belt conveyors for the removal of mill-waste, but it is only in recent years that the problems of jamming and wear have been overcome.

With the sole exception of Ynysypandy, all mill buildings were single storey. In fact it was unusual for any quarry building, other than a dwelling to have an upper floor. Mills had few if any windows, depending for light on ever open doors (even in winter!), and skylights. The latter's vulnerability to injudicious blasting accounting for the large stocks of glass that appeared on quarry inventories.

Apart from the obvious, mechanisation had two effects. The cost of plant and of structures to house them made work more capital intensive. It also physically separated the gangs. A bargain-gang would still work as such, two men in the mill, with the other two or three extracting block which was sent to the mill chalk-marked to identify 'ownership'. But the differing working conditions tended to produce a demarcation. For instance, other than in the smaller quarries, the gang would no longer meet at mid-day in the same *caban* or meal-room. The *caban* was much more than just a place where meal-breaks were taken, it was the focus of a fervent mutual loyalty. After eating, programmes of study, debate and self-education were held; all proceedings being presided over by an elected chairman. When the author had the honour of being a guest in a *caban*, he found the rigid etiquette, more appropriate to the most formal of banquets rather than a scratch snack in the barest of surroundings.

Despite this physical separation, the 'gang' system persisted well into the 20th century. It was not until 1920 that Penrhyn adopted the modern system of paying rockmen for the good rock they sent to the mill, and the millmen for the rock they reduced, regardless of from whom it originated. At the time opponents of this practice alleged that the rockmen in the quarry would be less careful of the quality of rock they sent to the mill, if their remuneration was unaffected by its eventual out-turn. This had been proved to be untrue by Moses Kellow at both Parc and Croesor in the 1900s, where he claimed a 25% increase in productivity, resulted from abandoning the old system.

There were other and deadly results of mechanisation. Although any working of rock, even splitting, can produce hazardous dust. Mechanical sawing in the confines of a mill greatly increased the incidence of pulmonary disease until fan extraction and later all-wet working were introduced. And working with chill winds howling through the unheated sheds was scarcely less unhealthy than crouching in a *gwal*. Plus, of course, working with machinery coupled with the general increase in the pace of work it imposed, brought additional possibilities of accidents.

Mill machinery was not confined to saws and dressers. Planers were used to smooth slab product, the earliest probably being the Hunter (patent 6794 of 1835), which was a massive double-acting, moving bridge machine, roughing on the forward stroke, finishing on the return. Later planers were invariably single-acting, moving table machines similar to those used in engineering. At first planed slab was a premium product, but by the 1880s almost all slab was planed, only the cheapest 'common flagging', being offered with riven surfaces.

Save for the tiniest workings, all quarrying called for buildings and with the increased scale of mechanised working these proliferated. Besides the *gwaliau* for slate dressing, there could be, particularly in Denbigh, also larger *gwaliau* near the mill where blocks for slab were split, and possibly other open-fronted sheds to store blocks under damp sacking to preserve or increase their moisture content whilst awaiting splitting. An office was inevitable and a powder house of some kind. This latter would be located out of harm's way, generally built with substantial walls but a flimsy roof (to direct any explosion upwards) and lined and floored with wood to keep the explosives dry. There might also be stables, fodder stores and sheds for holding fern for the packing of slates, and for other supplies. Except in the smallest partnership workings, there would be weighbridges to weigh rubbish to calculate rubblers' pay (and in some cases because the landlord imposed a tonnage levy on tipping). There would be one or more *cabanau* and certainly at least one smithy, where the most frequent job was tool sharpening, the cost being debited against the user's pay. (Occasionally smithing was a franchise operation, with a self-employed smith charging for his services).

Machinery needed to be maintained, demanding at the very least a saw-sharpening machine. Commonly these were automatic filing machines. Later machines, such as the Glaslyn Patent Sharpener, operated by a punching action, clipping an 'L' out of each tooth-root to re-form it, this enabled plain steel discs to be bought, costing perhaps £1 each, against the £1.50 of a toothed saw (Mid 19th century prices). A larger quarry might also have say, a drill and lathe, powered off the mill drive. The largest quarries had substantial engineering departments, the Gilfach Ddu workshops at Dinorwig, (which now houses the National Slate Museum), being an outstanding example. It had 6 lathes, and other machine tools powered by an 85 hp Pelton wheel, which replaced a 50' 80 hp water wheel. This also powered the foundry and smithy blowers, as well as the timber sawmill. Other than steel castings, every quarry requirement could be produced on site. There was even a tinsmith occupied full-time in the making and repair of the canisters in which men's pay was put up. Penrhyn had a similar complex at Coed y Parc, powered by two inverted siphon-fed water wheels. Most ambitious work could be carried out in these shops, making them independent of outside resources. It is believed that even saw tables may have been made, 'pirating' proprietary machines. Even the great Pen y Bont viaduct of 1854 was entirely designed and built by the Welsh Slate Company's own carpenters, probably copying the viaducts that Brunel had erected for the Great Western Railway.

Later structures would include engine houses, loco sheds and coal and oil stores. Later still there would be compressor houses as well as electricity plants and sub-stations.

Initially, buildings were made of country rock, often in huge sizes, but those built after sawing commenced would be made of sawn-ends. Whatever the material, they were frequently much more ornate than mere utility required. Even when they were devoid of the sort of elaborate embellishment as in the Hafodlas mill or the Vivian drum houses, they frequently showed an elegance that reflected great skill and pride of workmanship. Further buildings and machinery might be required if specialities such as mantel sets or ridging were produced on site.

Almost all machinery was driven by water wheel. Normally of cast-iron with wooden buckets driving line shafting via a ring-gear, they could be upwards of 50' in diameter. Revolving at 3-4 rpm, many produced over 50 hp, and were usually of the more efficient overshot type. In very exposed locations, where they were not shrouded by the mill structure, a wall would prevent high winds from blowing the water out of the buckets Occasionally the were completely inside a building as were the wheels for the Coed y Parc workshops of Penrhyn quarry and the Clwt y Bont factory. Some ingenuity was called for to make the best use of water, Votty & Bowydd had 3 big integrated mills tandemed; the tailrace of one feeding the next. At Pen yr Orsedd, one wheel served two mills, the power being transmitted to the second by a lengthy belt.

To reach water, a mill sometimes needed to be some distance away, early examples being Diffwys' 1846 Pant yr Ynn mill at Blaenau, (which still survives complete with wheel) and the long-gone Glyndwr mill of Moeltryfan quarry, erected in the 1850s. There are still traces of the mills at Lefel Dŵr Oer several hundred feet below the Craig Ddu quarry that they served. Penarth quarry near Corwen had a small, short-lived mill right down near the railway and the nearby Deeside quarry had to site its mill almost a mile away at Nant y Pandy and the Horseshoe Pass quarries sent their block some 4 miles down the Oernant Tramway to a mill on the canal at Pentrefelin. In Cwm Pennant, Prince of Wales quarry mill was reached by a fine tramway, as more famously, was the Gorseddau's Ynysypandy mill. Anecdotally Mathew's and later Nyth y Gigfran used a mill powered from the incline-winding wheel made redundant when the FR's Moelwyn tunnel was completed.

Usually with the typical fast-flowing Welsh streams there was little difficulty in devising by leat (a channel in the ground) and launder (a raised trough), a head of water to drive an overshot wheel conveniently sited with its lower half in a wheel pit and its upper half above ground Where this was not possible, advantage might be taken of a fall in the ground to mount the wheel at a lower level and drive by a belt. Abercwmeiddaw and Cambergi, in the Corris area, Cwm Ebol near Pennal and Penrhyngwyn on the northern flanks of Cader Idris, all used this artifice. Maes y Gamfa in the upper Dyfi valley could not do this and had to have deeply excavated wheel pit that resulted in the top of the wheel almost at ground level. Ynysypandy mill had the water wheel in a basement and one mill at Lefel Dŵr Oer had its wheel totally underground below the mill floor.

Actually these deep wheel pits, watercourses etc beneath mills were not necessarily excavated but were made by leaving voids in rubbish tips, anticipating the building of mills on them when they had reached full height. Both at Rhos and Rhosydd unused wheel-pit walls may be seen on tips that were never fully filled. In fact building on tips accounts for the early collapse of so many structures.

Occasionally, the mill wheel did a double duty, such as at

Hafodlas where deepening of the working called for up-haulage. A gear train and clutch from the mill line-shaft was used to power the adjacent drum of the main exit self-acting incline, enabling it to also raise blocks to the mill. Aberdunant, Abercwmeiddaw and Llwynpiod all had similar arrangements.

Where a good head of water could be piped in, more efficient Pelton wheels where used instead of water wheels. Where water head was restricted, axial flow turbines were sometimes used instead of the nozzle and cup Pelton wheels, but confusingly any sort of enclosed device was referred to as turbine.

'Turbines' drove mills at Cymerau, Foel and Ratgoed; at Gwernor besides powering their three saws one also hauled and pumped. Hendre Ddu in the Pennant valley had a turbine that, after closure, it is said, earned some boys 10/- (50p) for helping it 'find its way' to a nearby farm to drive an electric generator. Others were retrofitted to replace an inadequate water wheel, as at Gilfach Ddu workshops, at Hafodlas mill and at Cwmorthin's London mill.

Due to their high speed, turbines and/or Peltons commonly drove the air-compressors that came into use towards the end of the 19th century, and later and notably electric generators. Compressed air transformed the drilling of shot holes. Using chisel or Jwmpah, a foot per hour was good, hand cranked drills such as the fearsome 3-man Dixon two or three times faster, but with a power drill a foot per minute was commonplace.

Besides drilling, compressed air was also used to run winches, sometimes purpose-built units, but often adaptations of old marine steam donkey engines. Aberllefenni put in a fine water-turbine driven compressor in 1897, which involved the rebuilding of the then disused Cambergi reservoir, others such as Cwm Machno had similar but smaller installations. Croesor put in an elaborate hydro-compressor layout solely to serve an abortive development scheme. Unusually, at Rhos the compressor was driven by a large water wheel fed by the mill tailrace. Actually by the time compressed air was generally adopted, oil-engines were becoming available, so they were a more common source of compressor power as well as for other uses. Penrhyn put in a 350hp unit to power a compressor in 1912.

Whether for wheel or turbine, great ingenuity was shown in obtaining a supply of water. Obviously a dam was needed to store it, invariably of three-ply construction (Two stone walls with clay between), but Rhos used slate slabs and one of Rhosydd's many dams was of timber. Worked out pits were used as reservoirs, as at Rhiwbach and Cambrian at Glyn Ceiriog. At Rhosydd and at Penarth abandoned chambers were employed.

Reservoirs were fed by leats, sometimes several miles long. Further leats, frequently lined and covered with slate slabs, brought it to the wheels, the last few yards usually being by wooden launders on stone pillars. Turbines of course required a piped supply to maintain delivery pressure.

Following closure, quarry reservoirs or even the quarries themselves, were frequently used for public water supply, or occasionally for hydro-electric generation, as at Golwern quarry where the picturesque 'Blue Lagoon' was created for a hydro-electric supply for Fairbourne village, also at Moelfre farm (using the 'gone walkabout' turbine mentioned above) for a farm and at Cletwr for Pale House.

Although by the time powered working became general, steam engines were readily available, however they were expensive to buy and to run, (the delivered cost of coal could be treble the pit-head price), the boiler size, and hence coal consumption, was determined by maximum demand, whereas in a mill only a few machines might be actually working at any one time. Plus a driver/fireman had to be in attendance, from about two hours before work began to raise steam. Anyway since 1807 when the costly steam engine toppled terminally into the pit at Gloddfa'r Coed, steam had been viewed with caution.

At Blaenau, water shortage enforced the widespread use of steam. Welsh Slate at Rhiwbryfdir and Mathews' used steam for mill drive as early as the 1850s. Diffwys built the Pant yr Ynn mill off-site to use the Afon Bowydd, but subsequent on-site mills had to be steam driven and by 1873 they were using steam for all power.

Fortunately for many small mechanised quarries, such as Cwm Brechiau and Rhaeadr, they worked exposures in narrow valleys where a stream provided enough power for their modest needs, but for those lacking water catchment, such as Minllyn, Portreuddyn, Frongoch and little Cae Madoc, with its 2 saws and 2 planers; the cost of feeding their boilers must have been a burden. Tan y Bwlch's profits were almost wiped out by its 80 hp, multi-purpose engine devouring a ton of coal per day.

Like Blaenau, Nantlle, and Cefn Ddu were intensively worked with very little water, so many quarries there had to make extensive use of steam, the cost of which loomed large in their budgets.

For haulage, steam could be a proposition as its intermittent operation might allow a small boiler and firebox to be used, although this could be overdone, Wrysgan's incline often ground to a stop in mid-pitch waiting for the boiler to recover steam pressure. For pumping, reliability and flexibility of siting could make steam worthwhile, despite the fuel and labour costs of 24/7 working. Thus any quarry with restricted water supply used it primarily for mill drive. For instance, Llechwedd's first steam engine, in the 1850s was solely for incline haulage, and in 1864 Dorothea's 3 steam engines were all for haulage. Cwmorthin used steam for haulage and pumping but water for the mills. Croesor, before electrification, used steam for pumping and haulage but for the mill only as a standby in times of water shortage. Due to the use of steam underground, Croesor quarry used forced draught ventilation one of the very few underground workings not to rely on natural air circulation.

Some quarries used steam for mill drive, but later reverted to water. Rhosydd powered their No 2 mill of 1855 by steam, but although they continued to use steam for pumping, subsequent mills were water-powered. Similarly Prince Llywelyn's 1850 mill was steam driven but by the mid 1860s this had been converted to water-wheel drive and the new mill they built in the 1890s was water-turbine powered.

It is curious that well into the 20th century with steam, oil, producer gas and electricity able to efficiently provide poser, water wheels despite their high maintenance costs, were often retained. Possibly because fuel showed up on the balance sheet whilst the cost of keeping wheels turning was lost in general outgoings.

The larger steam engines were invariably horizontal units, usually with a separate boiler house alongside. The one big engine would sometimes do several duties, as at Rhiwbach where the same engine powered the mill, up hauled to it and powered the exit incline. Interestingly, the similarly laid out Blaen y Cwm used their engine for both their inclines, but only as a standby for the water-powered mill. Towards the end of the 19th century 'portable' engines were available as standard catalogue items. These self-contained engines were based on a standard traction engine fire-box/boiler unit with cylinders mounted either above or below the boiler. They were handy as a main drive in smaller quarries, or as readily moveable power-sources in larger ones. At Cwt y Bugail, an actual traction engine was stripped down and used directly for rubbish haulage and via a pulley system, also raised block from underground. Curiously, many years later when the quarry was being worked on a small scale, tractors were similarly used.

Because of the dearth of fast-flowing streams, some very small south Wales quarries, such as Sealyham used steam.

Abereiddy used it for up haulage, Porthgain had steam engines for haulage and mill drive. Both Trwynllwyd and Llwynpiod hauled block up to the mill from winches driven by the mill steam engine. Glogue had a steam mill, and Dolbadau and Fforest somewhat unusually used steam cranes. In the 1930s the former's crane was bought by Hendre Ddu quarry; a long and complex rail journey culminated in a precarious trip along the Hendre Ddu Tramway. Apparently when it reached its destination it fell off the wagon and was wrecked!

Ephemeral uses of steam included trepanning machines, which were tried out for the cutting of tunnels. There was some success at Maenofferen, (where the partly machine-cut Cooke's level remained in use as an escape route right up to closure), but at Abercwmeiddaw, it was a failure and their machine remained on site, unused for many years.

Finally it must be said that although the Welsh quarry industry has been criticised for its lack of efficiency and its reluctance to modernise, there can be few industries, certainly none so remotely sited, which have so consistently displayed so much engineering ingenuity and innovation, in the face of extreme financial constraints.

Mechanisation spawned a number of local engineering works and foundries. The best know of these was Thomas & De Winton (later De Winton) at Caernarfon, who in addition to their pioneering 'Coffee Pot' locomotives and marine engines, made a wide range of quarry machinery. Also at Caernarfon was H. Owen & Son, makers of saws etc. At Bangor was John Owen, at Tanygrisiau, William Lewis and at Aberystwyth, Greens. Porthmadog had the Glaslyn and Britannia foundries, and machinery makers such as Griffith Owen, (later Owen, Isaac & Owen), J. H. Williams and Richard Jones. Even in towns outside of mainstream slate such as Aberystwyth and Machynlleth, foundries made quarry machinery and components.

Eventually much of this expertise migrated to Newtown (Powys), where Turner Bros who, when their local woollen customers folded, made the transition to saws, planers etc. for the slate industry. They dominated this trade not only in Wales but throughout Britain and overseas.

The intensification of working through mechanisation increased the demand for other consumables, leading to their local manufacture. A prominent example being Cooke's gunpowder works at Penrhyndeudraeth. Mechanical working also demanded the availability of engineering sundries such as saw-blades, belting and lubricants, firms such as Celtic of Caernarfon setting up to meet this need.

SLATE SLAB. Usually defined as slate $\frac{1}{2}'$ thick or more, Standard thicknesses were up to 2' in $\frac{1}{2}'$ steps, the thinner costing more. Normally sold by weight in 'promiscuous' sizes and priced in three classes.

Lot 1 *2' 6' to 5' long x 1' 6' to 3' wide*

Lot 2 *5' to 7' long x 5' wide and upwards*

Lot 3 *7' long and upwards x 3' wide and upwards (more than 24 sq' area)*

Sawing to size and exceptionally large items carried a surcharge.

'Common Flagging' for rough flooring generally cost about half that of the cheapest 'Lotted' items (Lot 1 2').

Semi-finished products were also sold by weight, fully finished items by count other than vessels such as cisterns that were priced according to cubic foot capacity.

Special sizes could be very large, the biggest known being the 20' x 10' slab produced in 1862 at Clogau. Slab weighs about 1 ton for 150 sq./ft per inch of thickness so if this slab was of 2' thickness it would have weighed over $2\frac{1}{2}$ tons.

6. EMBELLISHMENT & EDUCATION
Enamelling

As has been said, one outcome of mechanical sawing, planing and so on, was the development of non-roofing products. Gravestones moved from being a plain rectangle with maybe a rounded top, to a riot of finials and flounces, often comprising complex assemblies dowelled together, tombs became scalloped and fretted. Other slab products abounded, apart from its wear-resistance making it the heavy-duty floor covering of choice, it found many architectural uses such as cills and copings, and above all thresholds and steps. Its imperviousness made it ideal for cisterns (sold as flat-packs), pigsties, urinals and cladding generally. Slate's high specific heat made it perfect for dairy slabs and domestic larder shelves.

Whilst some quarries did this sort of thing in-house much of the manufacture of such downstream products, was done in off-site, independent factories, were often set up alongside a quarry rail route. The Clwt y Bont works was on the original Dinorwig tramway, Humphrey & Owen's Crawia Slate Works was a complex of manufactories sited between the Padarn Railway (to bring in block from Dinorwig) and the Llanberis branch railway (to send product out). Inigo Jones works at Groeslon was set up on the Nantlle tramway, with an associated works being sited at Bryngwyn station on the North Wales Narrow Gauge Railway. Although curiously the ephemeral Llifon works nearby at Hafod Boeth lacked connection to anything. Later Pant Rhyd, Peblig Mill and Glanmorfa slate works would all be sited on the Llanberis Branch of the London and North Western Railway.

Some works began with a merchant at a port installing a saw to cut to customers' requirements slab bought in random sizes. Richard Williams and Davies Brothers, both of

Porthmadog, being notable examples. Thomas Jones had a place at Port Dinorwig and Fletcher's were for a time at Port Penrhyn.

There were others at Bethesda and Machynlleth, and at Pwllheli. John Williams, now incorporated into Cerrig, proved one of the most enduring of all. At Bangor at various times were Dixon's, William Jones John Thomas, W E Thomas and five or six Williams'. There were at least half a dozen at Caernarfon, that included at various times, R Evans, Fletcher's, (Later amalgamated with Dixons), Robert Griffiths, Owen Jones, Nichols & Owen, John Owen, Owen Roberts and. Williams & Morris. John Owen had a works at Blaenau with J.J.Riley who also had a place at Deganwy.

In south Wales the Cardigan Mercantile Company has long passed its bicentennial. More distantly there were the Minera Slate Works Wrexham, Corfield and Morgan at Cardiff and Sessions at Cardiff and Gloucester. Many of these merchant/manufacturers had a great influence on trade and price levels, buying stocks ahead of production, bankrolling quarries, or even taking them over to safeguard supplies. As happened with J.J.Riley who took on Hafodlas and Rhos quarries, and indeed his intervention in the Moel Tryfan quarries safeguarded their survival. Davies Brothers of Porthmadog bought into Wrysgan and Diphwys, Carters of Liverpool put money into Cwmmachno. One of the most important products were chimney-pieces that had once been just a pair of uprights with a cross-piece, but had become elaborate entablatures, and with the houses being erected in their tens of thousands, in the new industrial towns having at least four fireplaces; chimney-pieces was the business to be in.

The only problem was that people did not want to sit at a fireside reminiscent of a gentlemen's convenience or a pigsty, hence many were daubing paint on their chimneypieces to disguise their prosaic associations. Slate needed to avoid looking like slate if it was to find domestic acceptance, which was where the Enamelling process came in. This was quite simply the painting of slate artefacts and stoving them to give a permanent and durable finish - but easier said than done.

There were several processes, but the great pioneer was George Eugene Magnus a writing slate manufacturer of Pimlico and owner of the Valentia quarry in the west of Ireland, who first developed the process to imitate marble. He already had a well-established trade in both his Valentia product and in Welsh slab with customers as diverse as Buckingham Palace and Pentonville prison. His slate had gone into many public buildings including the new Houses of Parliament and besides more mundane warehousing use, 26 miles of it provided safe and stable shelving for the Public Record Office.

Thus when he devised his enamelling process, he had an established client base, so despite being unashamedly called 'Mock Marble', panels, pilasters, wall linings and even staircases of Magnus Ware found its way into the grandest castles and mansions here and overseas. Napoleon III and Indian potentates and other crowned heads were supplied. The Duke of Wellington is recorded as ordering *Two Dressing Table tops in Lumachelle inlaid with black @ 38/- (£1/90) each.* Chimneypieces, stove fronts, pedestals, console tables, knick-knacks and whatnots graced more modest homes and pot-stands supported aspidistras in countless best-room windows.

Branching out into a variety of finishes, Magnus's success was spurred by winning the Society of Arts medal at the Great Exhibition of 1851. (The Duc Honore de Luynes, President of the Awarding Jury, was one of his customers).

The product was claimed to be more durable than marble and soon advertisers were proclaiming as Owen Morris of Porthmadog was in 1856 –

Cistern tanks, wine coolers, pig feeding troughs, urinals, head & footstones for graves, tombs & monuments, clock faces &

sundials. Enamelled, thus various kinds of Marbles. Porphyries and other costly materials are faithfully & beautifully imitated at a fraction of the cost of the articles represented.

Likewise in 1857 Magnus himself was listing in the *Illustrated London News*, one of the media heavyweights of the time, a somewhat esoteric assortment of articles sacred and utilitarian – *Enamelled slate chimney pieces, Cabinet formed stoves, Stove fronts, Baths, Washstand tops, Pedestals, Slabs for console and ornamental table tops, Marbled wall linings, pilasters for halls and vestibules, Plain ditto for dairies baths and wash houses, Urinals, Vases, Fonts, Altars, Mural tablets, Monuments Tombs etc.*

There were many other uses. Tables and even chairs had an obvious appeal in termite-infested climes. It is said that in the Seraglio at Constantinople Magnus' seating cooled the Caliph's concubines. The extent to which Magnus Ware was a 'must have', among the fashion-conscious gentry, is shown by the proprietors of both the Penrhyn and Dinorwig quarries embellishing their respective residences with it, despite it being made from competitors slate (Their own slate was unsuitable for enamelling).

Magnus and others seem to have shrewdly appreciated that there were at that time an expanding body of *Noveau riche* who were not so *riche* as they would like people to believe.

Prior to painting with tar varnish or commonplace pigments, pieces to be enamelled had to be dried at 60°-70°F, possibly for up to 6 weeks in the case of thicker slabs, to eliminate all entrapped moisture.

Even when completely dry, the slate was still sensitive to any rapid heating or cooling, so when put in the oven heating to the 220°F stoving temperature had to be very gentle indeed. After some 18 hours, the oven was gradually let down to around 120o F before the pieces could be removed. Any premature opening of the oven could result in disastrous cracking.

Then came the tricky bit - putting in the marbling, wood-effect or whatever. This was done by dipping in water in which were stirred immiscible oily pigments, which by various secret sleights-of-hand with bits of stick, rags and sponges, produced the desired result. That in turn was followed by re-stoving.

Not all slate could withstand the thermal shock of the process, Magnus mainly used Aberllefenni slate where the Narrow Vein Ordovician rock was ideal, and established a dedicated manufactory (Later known as Matthews' Mill), in the village. The area became quite a centre for enamelling, Braich Goch quarry at Corris, Rhiw'r Gwreiddyn quarry nearby at Ceinws and, Gartheiniog quarry in the adjacent Angell valley all having ovens on site.

Eventually most enamelling was in the hands of independent specialists such as the Towyn (later Maglona Quarries) Company operating at the Bodtalog Mill, Tywyn before taking over Rhiw'r Gwreiddyn quarry. They also for a time used the Ratgoed quarry's oven, which was sited at Machynlleth, partly to save on coal carriage and partly for labour availability, and indeed to enable them to employ women, whose presence on a quarry site was a big no-no. From 1899 to 1904 the Cambrian Slate Works associated with Decorated Fireplace & Materials of London, was enamelling chimneypieces of Llwyngwern slate at their Machynlleth works. (Revived as the New Cambrian Slate Works in 1909).

Enamelling was also being done in various parts of country, for instance Sessions had ovens in Cardiff and Gloucester, and the Newport Enamelled Slate Co that had 10 saws and 2 planers. There wee a number in London including Langer, Powell & Magnus and also with a somewhat esoteric niche market in enamelled slate plaques for brewers to put in the wall of tied houses, was Aston &

Green Co Ironworks, Stratford.

Enamelled slate well suited the municipalities of northern England enabling them to fit out Xanadu-like public buildings with minimum impact on the public purse. It was extensively used in public baths, Newcastle upon Tyne Gallowgate Baths being an outstanding example. Opened in the 1854, the partitions between the cubicles (These were bathing baths not swimming baths) of the 1st Class section were separated by slate panels tastefully enamelled in pale green. Patrons of the 2nd Class were apparently assumed to be less aesthetically appreciative so had to make do with unadorned slate. To serve this market Hull became quite a centre for enamelling, having both the Kingston Enamelled Slate Company and the Hull Enamelled Slate and Marble Company.

All these enamellers favoured south Meirionnydd slate. In fact the big north of England enamelled chimneypiece firm, Hall, Harber & Thorne bought both Llwyngwen and Ratgoed, and the 1950s Bow Slate Company of East London involvement with Aberllefenni and Braich Goch arose from a safeguarding of supplies.

This preference for south Meirionnydd slate helped Aberystwyth to become an important enamelling centre in the later 19th century, using material from Llwyngwern, Hendre Ddu and several small quarries on either side of the Dyfi estuary.

Ellis and Owen were probably established there shortly after the Cambrian Railways (Neé Aberystwyth and Welch Coast Railway) arrived in 1864, leasing Glandyfi quarry to ensure a source of suitable slate, after about 15 years they were taken over by Hosking & Miller who planned a new works at the bottom of Penglais Hill, but in the end seem to have remained faithful to their Cambrian Street premises. Peter Jones ran the Briton slate works in Cambrian Place, and was associated with John Jenkins who ran Cwm Ebol quarry at Pennal in the 1880s & 90s afterwards taking on

Glandyfi. William Griffiths' owned the New Enamelled Slate Works on Llanbadarn Road.

An Aberystwyth speciality was the production of pictorial paintings on slate by artists such as Alfred Worthington, in place of the transfers often used elsewhere.

There was some enamelling of Caernarfonshire slate, although the Aberglaslyn Slate Quarries Enamel Co at Cwm Caeth quarry near Beddgelert almost certainly never got going, Hafodlas near Betws y Coed did operate ovens on site. Manufacturing merchants Nicholas & Owen, the Seiont Slate and Marble Works, Humphries & Co and Fletchers all had ovens at Caernarfon, as did John Thomas, H.Williams and W G Owen at Bangor.

Latterly some enamelling was done at Pentrefelin mill near Llangollen using material brought down the Oernant Tramway from quarries on the horseshoe pass. Allegedly this was done by an 'Australian' process.

Rosebush quarry in Pembrokeshire advertised enamelled slate but if they did sell any it would have been made by Langer, Powell & Magnus. On the other hand Dolbadau also in Pembrokeshire did have their own oven, which it is claimed, used a unique method, possibly of Continental origin.

The most notable of these enamelling specialists was Inigo Jones at Groeslon. Original set up to make writing slates they diversified into potentially more lucrative enamelling. They found that their Nantlle slate would not stand thermal shock so had to use Meirionnydd Ordovician material, Blaenau was suitable but they eventually settled on slate from the south of the county, buying up quarries such as Cae Defaid near Dolgellau and Cymerau near Corris, to secure supplies. In addition they had supply arrangements with Gartheiniog and Talymerin quarries in the upper Dyfi area.

With the rejection of Victorian knick-knackery in the early

20th century, the enamelled market narrowed, domestic uses concentrating on chimneypieces, usually coated black and often decorated with gold lining and pictures of a very high standard. These black chimney pieces that may well have originally been imitating Derbyshire black 'marble'. were extremely popular. Although as early as 1895 architect M.H.Bailie-Scott was railing against slate enamelled fireplaces, suggesting that they be thrown out or at least *'concealed by drapery'*. (One wonders what he would have thought of today's £2000 plus prices for salvaged items?)

Certainly by the early 1900s prices for such fireplaces were being trimmed, but fortunately as the demand for domestic pieces ebbed, the need for switchboards and so on, for electrical purposes developed. As a stable, non-conducting material, enamelled slate was ideal and a big trade for black enamelled slabs developed for power stations, substations, factories, electric railways and tramways. It was widely used aboard ships and the 'Queens' and other ocean liners had control panels of Braich Goch material. For a time enamelled slate was also used to mount domestic fuse-boxes.

For electrical work, the face and four sides were coated and stoved. After cooling the treated surfaces were buffed to a high polish whilst the back was painted but not stoved. This market continued into the 1970s, by which time spraying had replaced the traditional dip, splash and dab.

WRITING SLATES

Mechanisation has been referred to in connection with slab products, but writing slates or ciphering slates as they were more correctly called, were the first products to be fully mechanised.

Over three-quarters of a century before the Education Act of 1870 put an obligation on local authorities to provide free schooling for all, London Quaker Joseph Lancaster had set up the 'British' 'Penny-per-week-per-child' schools movement, to counter the almost universal illiteracy and innumeracy of his time. His British and Foreign Schools Society rapidly grew, particularly in Wales, readily appealing to the chapel-going workers since unlike the 'National' schools it had no connection with the Church of England and its English/Boss/Landowner connotations.

These schools were based on a single room with just one adult teacher supervising juvenile monitors each in charge of a different age group. Both 'sums' and handwriting were taught very much by repeatedly copying out exercises, hence were highly 'inscription intensive'.

One has only to think of the present cost of individually hand-made paper, which was the only paper there then was, to realize that no charitable school could have afforded it. Lancaster calculated that to provide a class of 60 with paper, quills and ink for a year would cost £99.

On the other hand 5-dozen writing slates could be had for £1 and even this figure, he advocated, could be further reduced by salvaging slates from demolished buildings. Allowing each scholar 100 slate pencils per year would cost £2. There was an additional bonus that re-shaping a quill was a skilled job, whereas sharpening a slate pencil was not, plus mixing ink with infants can have unfortunate results.

Writing slates were fundamental to affordable education, but were not of course a new invention. Chaucer in his 13th century *Treatise on the Astrolabe* mentioned writing on slate and there were many references to slate and soft slate pencils over the years. Also the term 'On the Slate' originating from a publican keeping tally of drinks by chalking on a piece of slate, but now referring to any form of credit; is very ancient indeed.

The educational initiatives of the late 18th century created a vast market that despite hygienic fears due to pupils cleaning them with spit, did not cease until well into the 20th century. Indeed their use was prolonged by the belief that the use of pencil and paper gave rise to eyestrain in the young.

Besides founding the schools, Lancaster also for a time (1797-1811) manufactured and exported slates and pencils until commercial factories caught up with demand He charged 2/-(10p) per dozen for slates and 1/- (5p) per 100 for the pencils, the former price being achieved by making the items a tiny 6' x 3', as opposed to what became the standard size (11 5/8' x 7 5/6' x 5/32')

The first mass production factory was established at Port Penrhyn in 1798, but Penrhyn was producing writing slates by hand long before that. Thomas Pennant observing in 1778 that they had 25-30 men making framed writing slates and had sold 133,000 in the past year consuming 3000 cubic feet of timber. One does suspect that while the Slate Tax was in force the writing slate trade was somewhat inflated by describing consignments of roofing slate as 'unframed writing slates' and so escape the impost.

In the course of the 19th century demand steadily grew, culminating in a torrent in the 1870s to meet the needs of the new municipal schools, thus over the years, the Port Penrhyn factory was followed by many others.

At the little port of Pwll Fanog was the grandly named Britannia Imperial Writing Slate Works, where timber was landed and slate brought across the Menai straits from Port Dinorwig and Port Penrhyn.

Although writing slate manufacture called for the best raw material and even when fully mechanized, was still comparatively labour-costly, it sold into a very price-sensitive market. Thus margins were fine but with volume and close attention to efficiency; it could be big business.

Bowydd quarry had a small slate works on site but this was exceptional, where a quarry did have its own factory, it was more likely to be situated in the neighbouring settlement, so that women and older and less fit men, could be employed. When Bowydd built their second (Newborough) Mill it was sited in Blaenau Ffestiniog itself, likewise Bryneglwys quarry's small works was in nearby Abergynolwyn village. As well as being unusual in making writing slates from Ordovician rock, both were also unusual in being quarry owned, since although Penrhyn quarry was the first big producer, writing slates were invariably made by independent manufacturers, mostly at places such as Caernarfon or Bangor where the vast quantities of imported softwood for the frames could be landed.

There were notable exception to this port location, such as Glandinorwig, which eventually comprised three factories at Deiniolen. When they closed early in the 20th century their inventory included a reciprocating gang-saw (such as can be seen at the Slate Museum) to reduce logs to planks, which were cut into frame components by 3 circular saws. Further machines planed, sawed the ends to form the corner bridle joints, the slot on the long sides, the pin on the short, (Bridle joints were stronger than the earlier halving and could be produced by sawing alone). A further machine cut the grooves, and another drilled in the middle of one of the shorter sides, the $\frac{1}{4}''$ hole for the string that would enable it to be hung from the nail on the side of each desk.

To work the slate itself there were 4 saws and 4 polishers, there was also a machine to scribe the squared pattern that was usually specified for the reverse of a standard school slate. Sometimes instead of the scribed grid (picked out in red paint) lines and other patterns including maps might be asked for.

A machine wired together the four components of the frame (since gluing had been found unsatisfactory in damp schoolrooms!) and finally another machine rounded off the corners.

It is curious that although the tram road that passed through Deiniolen was closed in the early 1840s, the works survived, the first substantial slate works of any kind to operate without rail connection.

The other notable non-quarry, non-port writing slate factory was Inigo Jones. Established in 1861 it was well placed to meet the demands of the Education Acts, but they switched from this cut-throatedly competitive trade to the more profitable enamelling. They did continue in the writing slate business at least until 1939 when they were quoting a Somerset dealer 12/9 (64p) per dozen plus carriage They prosper today as specialist slate workers, long surviving the Nantlle Tramway that was the reason for their siting.

Writing slates, probably Welsh, were being sent to New England by a Dutch exporter in the 17th century and the overseas market ultimately took quite large numbers. In fact parts of the world still use writing slates from Europe, still supplied by Dutch merchants, but sadly no longer sourced from Wales.

7. SHIPS & TRAINS
By sea and rail

There is in Wales, particularly in the northwest, a long maritime tradition. With the expansion of the slate trade, shipbuilding, seafaring and their attendant occupations became a substantial industry whose fortunes were intertwined with those of the quarries. Slate brought prosperity to ports such as Caernarfon, Pwllheli, Aberdyfi, Barmouth, Aberystwyth, and to a lesser extent, Conwy, Cardigan and even Solva. It raised Bangor from an Episcopal village, it created Port Dinorwig, Port Penrhyn and greatest of all, Porthmadog.

One today speaks of 'Green field' development; Porthmadog was a 'Green water' development since until W. A. Maddox built the Cob to reclaim the Glaslyn estuary, no dry land existed where it now stands. It became one of the greatest sailing-ship ports of Wales its cargoes going worldwide. Unlike cosmopolitan ports such as Caernarfon, almost every vessel using Porthmadog was locally manned, this, rather than the Calvinistic influence, accounting for the paucity of pubs and absence of brothels in its gridiron streets.

Brigs, brigantines, barques, barquentines, snows and schooners of all kinds were built by the hundred at the ports and creeks of Gwynedd. Between 1826 and 1913, the 8 yards at Porthmadog and Borth y Gest alone built over 260 ships of from 30 to 400 tons These little ships, some manned by as few as 4 local men and boys, were willing and able to sail to any part of the world.

Oak for framing was selected by the shipwrights from the standing trees of nearby estates, but planking called for imported pitch pine bringing prosperity to local timber merchants. In all the ports block and rope makers, blacksmiths, carpenters, sail makers, chandlers and so on also flourished. Foundries in addition to supplying the quarries made ships' fittings. Retired Captains or in some cases their wives, taught navigation.

A number of ships belonged to quarries, the Cefn Ddu Company had one early in the 19th century, not long afterwards Samuel Holland had his own ship, and in the 1850s Aberllefenni had a steam ship. Llechwedd, Penrhyn and Dinorwig had fleets, as did several large merchants. Many were independently owned, title being divided into sixty-fourth shares, typically a number being held by the master with the rest split between local tradesmen, shopkeepers, farmers, possibly ministers and even quarrymen. The sums involved were not necessarily great, as in spite of their sturdy, close-framed construction, builders charged little more than £10 per ton, and old but sound vessels were available for a fraction of this. With luck, returns could be good, but like any maritime venture, risks were great and to share them, owners clubbed together to form Insurance Societies.

These Insurance Societies did not charge premiums, but made calls on their members if and when a loss took place. Latterly they provided cover for sailing vessels when the steam-mindset maritime insurance market shunned them. These Societies survived up to WW1, when the rate of sinkings finally overwhelmed them.

The seamen certainly suffered as much discomfort and danger as the quarrymen. Dangerous though quarry work was, (Penrhyn, by no means the most perilous quarry, recorded 258 fatalities between 1826 and 1875); the risk to life in a small sailing ship was even greater. Apart from deaths from falls and accidents or being lost overboard, most vessels eventually sank usually with all hands. Plus there were diseases caught in foreign ports and illness from living in wet clothes for weeks on end. Both crews and owners also shared the economic hazards of the industry, for when demand dropped, freight rates fell and vessels and seamen were idle.

Cargoes were not confined to slate. The agriculture of northwest Wales, poor though it was, produced some surpluses. Livestock could be driven to market but things like dairy products could not. By around 1820 growth of regular sailings enabled such items as butter from south Caernarfonshire to be sold in London. The inbound traffic was just as beneficial as hitherto scarce commodities such as grain, could readily come in as return cargo. Holland and other owners regularly brought in provision shipments, Assheton-Smith of Dinorwig brought in a cargo of grain to be sold at cost to necessitous quarrymen. Local agriculture also gained since lime and phosphates could be readily brought in. With mechanisation and increasing prosperity coal became a commonplace in-cargo, often with lighter goods such as baskets of crockery stowed on top of the coal.

The great railway boom of the mid 1840s brought no trains to Wales, but it did create a new market for slate to roof the stations, the sheds and the new railway towns, reversing the slackness, which had set in at the start of the decade. This initial railway boom was checked by financial uncertainties in 1848, but in the 1850s, took off again with renewed vigour, fuelling slate demand not only for the railways' own needs but also the demands created by the new-found national prosperity of the railway age. The quarries, slate towns and ports flourished.

This 1850s rail-building surge did bring railways to Wales, at first just along the north and south coasts, each hell-bent on reaching as close to Ireland as geography would allow. Their actual construction had little social impact. There was little local recruitment to the vast peripatetic gangs of 'navvies' few of whom showed anxiety to stay on when the line was finished. The railways indirectly brought some investment, Thomas Savin, who built much of the Cambrian Coast line was a founder director of the Diffwys Casson Slate Quarry Company of 1863, Henry Dennis invested profits from railway building in the Cambrian quarry at Glyn Ceiriog and Sir Daniel Gooch of the Great Western invested in several slate companies.

However in 1852 two short spurs irrevocably involved the main-line railways in the slate trade. A $1\frac{1}{2}$-mile branch from the Chester to Holyhead (L.& N.W.R) line ran down to Port Penrhyn. A similar 1 mile of track ran from the Bangor-Caernarfon line to Port Dinorwig. Product from the quarries still came down their respective railways to the ports, but from then on, it could be trans-shipped not onto boats but into railway wagons. Thus half the total Welsh slate output had direct access to the UK rail network; serving notice that the little ships' day was done.

Not that the effect was immediate, custom, habit and high rail charges kept the ships in business for another 50 years and more, but no longer did quarries or their customers have to be within reach of a seaport or a canal. By the mid 1860s, small quarries to the south of the Mawddach estuary, such as Henddol, Golwern and Bryngwyn could develop, carting their few hundred tons of product to what is now called the Cambrian Coast line that ran (and still runs) from Aberystwyth to Pwllheli, with an inland connection via Machynlleth. Several other small quarries could take advantage of it and Llanfair could abandon their loadings onto little boats on the Atro and Tyddyn Shieffre could divert its tramway to the railway. Paradoxically, when in 1868, Arthog quarry replaced their tramway to the river with an incline to the railway, and built a nice new mill to handle the expected extra throughput, they closed within a year. Oddly Fron Goch with the railway passing its door never used it and when their jetty was wrecked in a storm in 1884 they closed.

From 1867 the Cambrian Railways, also provided an outlet for Minllyn quarry, via the private standard gauge Mawddwy Railway, which in turn, enabled the Hendre Ddu tramway to serve Hendre Ddu, Maes y Gamfa, Gartheiniog and Talymeiryn slab workings, as well as providing transport to farms in the road-less Angell Valley.

By 1860 the GWR. Ruabon-Dolgellau line enabled such workings as Deeside, Moelfferna, Penarth and Cletwr (Pale), to really get into business, and gave slate brought down by tramway from the Llangollen Horseshoe pass workings an alternative to the canal. Deeside and Moelfferna loaded onto the G,W,R at Glyndyfrdwy via the Deeside Tramway, built in 1871 to the unique gauge of 2' 6", it astonishingly, had wooden rails (sheathed with iron plates). Such strapways had been an anachronism for half a century and apart from a short section in the Melynllyn hone quarry, and possibly also at Hafod Las, it is unlikely that any such rails had been installed since Chwarel Ddu and Manod had laid them before Waterloo. Originally it had only served the Deeside quarry, running via their Nant y Pandy mill, to the head of an incline at Glyndyfrdwy. Sensibly, when it was extended to Moelfferna only 5 years later, the extension was in conventional steel track. The whole was gravity worked, horses pulling back the empty wagons in the original Ffestiniog Railway manner (although their horses walked, not rode, downwards).

Penarth quarry had an incline to the railway, but Cletwr closed before its planned incline could be built.

The 1869 standard gauge Caernarfon-Llanberis branch dramatically transformed the fortunes of the numerous quarries to the south of the village, most loading onto it via the mighty Ffridd incline. This reduced their carriage to Caernarfon quay from at least 5/- (25p) per ton to well under 2/- (10p), and enabled Glynrhonwy Lower to abandon its traction engine, that on one occasion ran away, attacking Caernarfon Castle like some fearsome siege machine. For the first time, these quarries could enter into serious competition with the mighty Dinorwig on the other side of Llyn Padarn. From the traffic point of view it was such a success that the proposed sub-branch to Cwm Gwyrfai was not built, but whether the cost of its 9 river crossings in 9 miles was ever recovered is doubtful.

Unfortunately the railways did not benefit all inland slate undertakings. The 1868 L.& N.W.R. Betws y Coed branch ran on the eastern bank of the river, where there were no worthwhile quarries, thus further marginalizing Dyffryn Conwy slate. In the Llangynog area, quarries such as Craig Rhiwarth, still had to cart to Llanymynech, just as long a trip as for the canal. (The Tanat Valley had a railway in 1904 - at least 30 years too late). Being within reach of a standard gauge railway was becoming increasingly important hence from around 1870 no quarry Sale Particulars were complete without an allusion to its 'proximity' to at least a 'proposed' railway.

There was a further downside. There were many tiny isolated workings at places such as the Elan valley in mid Wales, where small quarries had for centuries provided slate adequate for local requirements. With the best north Wales slate freely available at the nearest railway station, their crude product could only be shifted at giveaway prices. In fact when the Maenclochog Railway was built to serve the Pembrokeshire Rosebush quarry, one of its first slate cargoes was not Rosebush slate out but north Wales slate in! Their 'Plan B' of using the line to bring holidaymakers to this bleak and cheerless might have had more success had the hotel not been a tin shack.

Successive reductions in railway rates increased rail's share of home trade. Exports increasingly were railed to ports such as Liverpool that could handle larger vessels.

Blaenau, had only a limited option to load onto the Cambrian Railways 'Beddgelert' siding, reached by Ffestiniog tracks being back-run on the Croesor track. Thus ships held sway at Porthmadog until the huge Minffordd Ffestiniog–Cambrian interchange opened in 1872. Although for many years only a minority of tonnage went by rail, Porthmadog's almost exponential expansion was checked. The plans for a vast harbour inland of the Cob were abandoned, leaving the great steam flour mill built in anticipation of it, hundreds of yards from where a ship might berth.

Since 1864, the Corris Railway had no longer run to the port at Derwenlas, but terminated at Machynlleth station where output could be transferred on to the Cambrian main line. Theoretically it would be shipped at Aberdyfi, but increasingly ' what went on rail stayed on rail'. The 1873 the L & N.W.R backed Glyn Valley Tramway serving the Cambrian and the Wynne quarries, ignored the GWR main line, actually crossing it to reach the L & N.W.R owned Montgomeryshire canal. It was soon realised that no matter who owned it, the canal was passé so when the Glyn was steamed in 1888, it was diverted to Chirk station.

Not all these rail-borne tonnages represented a loss to the ports. Tiles still cost more to make than slates, only transport costs enabled local tiles to remain competitive at inland locations. By the early 1870s there was scarcely any part of the U.K. where rail borne Welsh slate could not undercut the price of tiles. Thus much of what the railways carried was new business.

In 1874 well over 20,000 tons of Blaenau slate was loaded onto at Cambrian Railways at Minffordd, but still four times that tonnage was put on ship at. Porthmadog. These Porthmadog shipments ceased to grow after 1878, but held up well for another 20 years and it would not be until 1905 that rail captured the majority of Blaenau output.

At Port Penrhyn and Port Dinorwig their earlier rail connection and their quarries being by now less buoyant than those at Blaenau, meant that their sea borne trade dwindled earlier than Porthmadog's, being overtaken by rail in the 1880s, with the L&NWR establishing a depot in Cheshire to handle the output. Even so substantial shipments, much in quarry owned vessels, continued up to WW1, and some slate trade was retained at Port Dinorwig and Port Penrhyn until the 1960s.

In 1868 the Caernarfonshire Railway (Later part of L.& N.W.R.) built their Caernarfon to Afon Wen branch, subsuming much of the Nantlle Tramway, whose roadbed it approximately followed from Caernarfon to Penygroes. Four years later a sub-branch to Talysarn further truncated the Nantlle line. This cut the Nantlle quarries' carriage cost to Caernarfon quays from about 3/ (15p) to 2/3 (11p) per ton. Obviously much was not unloaded and stayed on rail, but it would be 1900 before the tonnage sent by rail exceeded that shipped at the port, and even then, in several subsequent years, less went by rail than by sea.

This slowness of rail to win business is shown by the Caernarfon - London rates for 1880 - 17/- (85p) per ton by rail, 10/- (50p) by sea. This also applied in reverse, general cargos carried coastwise into Wales from say Liverpool, did not entirely disappear until the 1960s, when they were displaced not by trains but by lorries.

However the effect of the railway on the port of Conwy was terminal, from 1863 product from Rhos, Hafodlas, the Lledr valley quarries and Cwmmachno (the latter rapidly building up its workforce to 200) no longer had to be lightered down river from Trefriw but could be loaded at Betws y Coed station. From 1879 as the L&NWR pressed on to Bleanau the Lledr valley product could use Dolwyddelan station, with Tyn y Bryn having a siding right into its yard. Again most stayed on rail, little being shipped out at the rail-connected 'slate' dock at Deganwy.

However it was not the steam locomotive but the steam ship that had the most dramatic effect on activity at the slate ports. Its arrival presaged the end of shipbuilding, already threatened by competition from low-cost Canadian yards. Steam engines were at first installed in wooden ships such as the 50 hp De Winton unit in Aberllefenni's Aberdyfi built 'Quarry Maid' of the 1850s, but progress soon demanded hulls of iron. The adzes of Wales had to yield to the riveting-hammers of England. Due to the limited bunker capacity of early steamers, sailing vessels were able to hold their own for long-range shipments, but by 1872 a DeWinton powered steamer was trading with the River Plate.

Although Porthmadog did lay down a few vessels in the 1890s and some building continued until 1913, by 1880 shipbuilding had all but ceased in north Wales. Iron and steam also increased the size of ocean-going ships and although the likes of Penrhyn and Dinorwig operated fleets of iron steamers from their own ports, more and more deep-sea cargoes sailed from major ports such as Liverpool, increasingly reaching the dockside by rail. Thus even ahead of the decline and depression in the quarries the great partnership of shipping with slate, commenced its ebb into oblivion.

The last great slate railway was the North Wales Narrow Gauge Railway of 1877, part of a grand concept, of having a network of narrow gauge railways throughout northwest Wales. In a sense, it ran from nowhere to anywhere. It started at bare wind-swept Rhyd Ddu, where apart from Snowdon climbers the only traffic was a few tons from Llyn y Gadair, Bwlch Cwm Llan and possibly Ffridd slate quarries. Having failed to get access to Caernarfon, it started from Dinas, on the L&NWR. Afon Wen branch, from where it was intended that slate would be carried to the port. Again once slate was in a railway wagon it tended to stay there, further contributing to Caernarfon's decline. A number of quarries in the Gwyrfai valley were served, but apart from Glanrafon, which it helped grow to a 250-man operation, and the much smaller Hafod y Wern, few were of any consequence. Its main slate traffic came via its Bryngwyn branch, fed by a long incline coming down from the head of the Nantlle valley, which gave direct access to several quarries that hitherto had been dependent on a ramshackle, multi incline connection to the Nantlle Railway. The largest was Alexandra, which was reached by a most spectacular mile and a half looping, 'Alpine' rail line, down which for a time they sent over 4000

142

tons per year, others such as Braich and Moel Tryfan were able to get into the 2000 ton class, thanks to the N.W.N.G.R. Had it its opening not coincided with a severe recession in the slate trade. After an almost terminal decline into the first years of the 20th century, it was revived by connection to Cilgwyn in 1923, but the tonnage, which that quarry was by then turning out was a poor fraction of the 7-8000 tons they had once produced. There was a further revival in 1934 when it was extended to Porthmadog as the Welsh Highland Railway, using part of the Croesor tramway, but by that time there was virtually no slate traffic to be carried.

The reincarnated WHR does now reach Caernarfon, using the very track bed of the L&NWR whose obduracy prevented its progenitor from doing so.

In 1879, the overworked and long outmoded Penrhyn tramway was replaced by the steam-powered Penrhyn Railway. Its terminations were the same as the horse-gravity tramway, but a more circuitous route obviated the need for inclines. The same year the Corris Railway was also converted to steam.

It is obvious that not all railways achieved their hoped-for tonnages. The expensive (2 mile tunnel through solid granite!) 1879 L.& N.W.R. Blaenau extension up the Lledr valley attracted little traffic. Of the Blaenau quarries; only Llechwedd was able to conveniently reach it. Though they could either load onto railway wagons or have their quarry wagons carried pic-a-back to the Deganwy slate quays, they used the facility mainly as a weapon to obtain reduced rates from the FR. Other quarries made some use of the L.& N.W.R, particularly W.S.C.'s successor Oakeley, but they did not have a direct link to it until 1934. The 1882 GWR. Blaenau branch from Bala, offered spectacular views for passengers, but never succeeded in capturing much slate traffic. Apart from a trifle picked up from the quarries around Llan Ffestiniog, it mainly served as a feeder for the FR., carrying Graig Ddu quarry trucks, again pic-a-back, the couple of miles to Blaenau. Thus virtually only continuing the function of the Ffestiniog and Blaenau railway, whose alignment it approximately followed. Similarly the tunnels and bridges of the L.& N.W.R. Bethesda branch of 1884 brought some benefit to a handful of small independent quarries but none were directly connected.

South Wales had the quaint 2 mile Abereiddi tram road built in the 1850s to link that quarry with Porthgain harbour, but also surprisingly, in view of the small outputs, two standard gauge lines were built chiefly to carry slate traffic. The 1873 Cardigan Railway failed to re-enliven the Pencelli and Penlan quarries but it served Glogue well enabling it to employ more than 80 men and survive until 1926. The line did not reach Cardigan itself until 1885, too late to save the Fforest quarries, but enabled some Cilgerran diggings to abandon their Teifi boatings and survive to the 1930s. The Maenclochog Railway of 1876 did enable Rosebush quarry to reach the GWR but its 'boy-with-a-handcart' tonnages brought as little success to the line as did the attempts to popularise Maenclochog as a tourist destination.

Although lines like this brought scant reward to their builders, they brought general benefit to local communities, many of which without the siren lure of slate traffic would not have had the advantages of rail transport. Indeed some of the little tramways such as the Ratgoed, Croesor and Hendre Ddu, proved vital links to isolated communities.

Railways also changed employment patterns. Labour catchment was no longer limited by the distance a man could walk, and in some cases gave a quarryman for the first time, a choice of employer, thus if he was laid off it eased the problem of obtaining alternative work. (Provided he was not blacklisted!) On the other hand, it meant, as would become manifest towards the end of the century, that during a strike an employer could more readily bring in outside labour. The railways altered barracking and lodging practices, many more men could now live at home and barrackers and lodgers could now come from much further afield. As for instance the occupants of the Anglesey barracks at Dinorwig, who left their Llanidan homes at 3.00 am on a Monday morning to walk to the ferry to Port Dinorwig.

The main line railways offered cheap workmen's tickets, the FR. and Talyllyn provided workmen's trains. Quarrymen were carried on the Penrhyn steam railway almost from its start. Later the Padarn had workmen's trains, (used by the Llanidan men) but prior to this, men were permitted to use their own man-powered vehicles. These 'Velocipedes' usually had 4 seats, each equipped with pedals. In the late 1880s Pantmawr quarrymen paid 2/- (10p) per month to use 'Velocipede' on the Croesor tramway .

(The only other known instance of a line being officially used for 'commuting' with private 'vehicles' was at Craig Ddu. There men descended the inclines on *Ceirgwyllt* (Wild cars). These resembled a modern skateboard, which ran on one rail of one track, with an outrigger to a wheel running on one rail of the other track. At one time the voluminously skirted Rhiwbach schoolmistress used one to return home to Blaenau in the evening. There are apocryphal reports of two or even three men riding on one, but certainly a friend of the author's when a child rode on his father's lap 'as a treat'.

The railways also had an effect on education. Before motor buses a child in an isolated village would have difficulty in continuing their education beyond the village school stage, without costly boarding out.

The steam locomotive also had a great impact on internal quarry transport. The first quarry to have a loco was probably Glynrhonwy Lower in about 1866 almost certainly a De Winton. Although Dorothea still had a horse or two in the 1950s, it had steam locos by 1869, which called for the laying of 2' track for them to run on, as their existing rails were to the 3'6' Nantlle gauge. Dinorwig had locos by 1870, shortly followed by the Welsh Slate Company, and in 1874 by both Llechwedd and the newly amalgamated Votty &

Bowydd. Penrhyn had them by 1876, eventually building up to a fleet of more than 30. Like Dinorwig they eventually had a loco on almost every one of their many galleries, as well as using them in the mills areas and at their ports. Glynrhonwy Upper put in their first by 1877, which ran both in tunnels and on a frighteningly flimsy platform cantilevered out from a rock face. The same year Pen yr Orsedd began to build up their fleet to an astonishing 12.

With the coming of the N.W.N.G.R. several of the larger quarries it served put in locos. Alexandra, Glanrafon and Moel Tryfan each had 3. At about the same time, Cilgwyn, Pen y Bryn and Tal y Sarn, also went in for them and by 1880 even little Coed Madoc had 3 De Wintons. Eventually quite small quarries, such as Fron, Pant Dreiniog, Rhos, Abercwmeiddaw and Manod used steam traction. One of the most interesting uses was in Cambrian quarry at Glyn Ceiriog where steam locos hauled through their almost 900 yards long tunnel.

Little steam locos, grumbling and teetering along undulating tracks became almost as characteristic of slate quarrying as the drum house and incline. They were still being acquired, second-hand, well into the 1930s. Some remained in use until the 1960s, gallantly defying the onslaught of internal combustion, that had started to appear in small numbers at the beginning of the 20th century, supplanting steam in a big way during the inter-war years. Some of these Diesel and petrol units were new but most were second-hand, including many ex WW1 army items, with a number being lash-ups built in the quarries own workshops.

Outside the quarries, apart from limited use of Diesel by the FR., in the inter-war years, and the primitive concoctions of the Hendre Ddu tramway, the slate railways, as opposed to the internal quarry lines, remained faithful to steam. Though most of these are long gone, thanks to enthusiasts, such as those of the FR. the Talyllyn and other groups, the sound of puffing and whistling, still echoes in the Gwynedd mountains.

8. THE GOLDEN YEARS
1860-1870

By 1860 Welsh slate could look back on thirty years of growth, but it had been an unsteady climb along a giddy switchback of peaks and troughs. The build up of the 1830s, was followed by the booms and setbacks of the 1840s. The 1850s started well with the Great Exhibition and the abolition of the tax on brick; then the Crimean war dampened demand, but its end brought new peaks.

Prices generally had mirrored demand, but, whereas the trend of output was inexorably upward, that of prices was not. No matter how brisk the times, prices never rose more than about 10-15% above the bumper era of 1814/15 and always within 4 or 5 years had fallen again.

Then, in 1860 the switchback stopped. All through the '60s, it was no longer boom and bust but boom and boom, until by 1869; prices were 25% up on those of ten years before. Nor were there any setbacks in output, total Welsh production reached 350,000 tons. The Bethesda area remained dominant producing over 100,000 tons, but by now almost 10% of that was coming from independent quarries such as Pantdreiniog, Tan y Bwlch, Bryn Hafod y Wern and Moelfaban.

Blaenau's tonnage almost equalled Bethesda's, largely due to the Welsh Slate Company's output almost doubling in less than five years. Both Holland's, and Mathew's had five figure tonnages, with Cwmorthin and Llechwedd not far behind. Diffwys and the amalgamated Votty & Bowydd were not much smaller, and half a dozen others had four figure outputs. It is a measure of the optimism of the times that although Diffwys had failed to match the expansion of its neighbours, when sold in 1863 it fetched £120,000, 120 times its 1801 cost.

At Llanberis the 80,000 tons produced by Dinorwig's

2400 or so men, dominated the area, but with the now amalgamated Glynrhonwys and their half dozen neighbours employing over 250 men, their contribution was not negligible, and would shortly expand further with rail connection. Nantlle's near 2000 men accounted for 40,000 tons, about a quarter produced by Dorothea's 500 men, and with Pen yr Orsedd temporarily faltering, Cilgwyn, Pen y Bryn and Tal y Sarn's, 800 men accounted for much of the remainder. The rest of the Welsh industry amounted to about 20,000 tons.

Right through the 60s, the trade press complained of delivery times of up to 47 weeks. Quarries were able to pick and choose to whom they sold. Large minimum order quantities were demanded, Penrhyn and Dinorwig for instance, exacting surcharges on orders of less than 30 tons. Quarries competed for manpower pushing wages up in some cases to exceed 5/- (25p) per day. Blaenau average daily wages were cited by G.J.Williams as –

	Quarryman	Miner	Labourer
1860	4/3 (21p)	3/3 (16p)	2/6 (12.5p) 3/- (15p)
1865	5/- (25p)	4/2 (21p)	3/- (15p) 3/6 (17.5p)
1870	5/6 (27.5p)	4/6 (22.5p)	3/6 (17.5p) 3/9 (17.6p)

There was a spate of re-openings of previously unsuccessful quarries, (such as Alltgoch at Aberdyfi), these being invariably accompanied by press accounts of ambitious plans. The 1862 Companies Act facilitated investment causing unprecedented speculation, and in the four years that that followed it, 58 companies were formed to run slate quarries in north Wales. Some such as Hafodlas and Rhiwgoch were genuine and successful floatations to put workings on a sounder financial footing by attracting new capital for expansion, but many were attempts to off-load fundamentally unprofitable quarries,

All this prosperity was too good to last and in 1870 the

Franco-Prussian war halted the climb. Back to the old ups and downs? Far from it, in 1872, the market recovered and prices resumed their seemingly unstoppable rise. By 1875 Blaenau prices for Princesses were £13.50 per mille, against the £8.25 of 1850. Ladies were £5.50 against £2.75 and unlike earlier boom times, the smaller sizes showed even greater gains, Doubles fetching £2.25, up from £0.75. In the same period wages had risen but other costs had not, so there was now real money to be made. Penrhyn was said to be netting over £100,000 per year, and Welsh Slate were reported as making well over £1 per ton clear profit on their 60,000 ton output, even after paying a royalty of 4/6 (22.5p) per ton to the Oakeleys, (who were thus collecting almost £14,000 p.a. from this one quarry alone). This was not a boom, it was a bonanza.

Demand exploded, some quarries' attitude to customers bordered on the cavalier. Increasingly onerous minimum order quantities and all sorts of surcharges were imposed. Some insisted that orders be executed in sizes and grades to their, not the buyer's, choice. There even developed something of a 'Black Market', with desperate users paying over the odds to get supplies. Unfortunately buyers' anxiety to secure slate was not always matched by alacrity in paying for it. This was nothing new, but increased tonnages at higher prices meant larger debts being carried, straining many a quarry's finances. In fact in 1877 at the height of the boom, Maenofferen was being threatened by its creditors, and the Cwmorthin Company was close to failure.

It is a measure of the optimism of the times that in 1873 only a few miles from where the Gorseddau mill at Ynyspandy remained as a most prominent reminder of the follies of a generation before, Prince of Wales quarry was expensively developed. A layout similar to and only slightly less ambitious than Gorseddau was constructed. To obviate the extravagant 12/6 (62.5p) cost of carrying to Caernarfon over the mountain to Cwm Gwfrai, the Gorseddau tramway was extended and re-gauged to 2', and a De Winton loco bought. With 200 men at work it briefly reached a respectable 5000 tons, but in spite of venturing underground and making a further opening at the nearby but almost inaccessible Princess quarry, good rock eluded them. With mounting losses on a falling market, it closed in 1886.

With huge price increases even for the poorest product, the humblest of diggings had profit potential. The cautious entrepreneur had to be wary when seeking even a short-term take note much less a formal lease. With landlords anxious to maximise royalties now imposing minimum employment clauses, he might find himself forced to pay men to dig uselessly. Even so, the trade press was reporting 'New Openings' almost every month, most of which came to nothing, as virtually every worth-while site was already taken. Every likely looking bit of rock was dug or tunnelled, in increasingly improbable locations, usually backed by highly suspect promotions. At the village of Fron there were reports of diggings in back gardens!

The trade press habitually carried warnings against unwise speculation, which were just as habitually ignored. Little more than a rumour of slate, was enough to get a company floated. Searches were made further and further away from proven areas, sometimes with luck, more often without. Men beavered away in such places as Cwm Brechiau, in south Meirionnydd. Having brought to the surface perhaps a thousand tons of almost useless rock, they repeated the same futile exercise at Gyllellog. At Fronheulog and other places in the Tywyn hinterland, there were other frantic, and usually vain, diggings. Having failed to lay rails from a tiny scratching at Gwastadfryn in the furthest recesses of the Dysynni valley, to the Talyllyn Railway at Abergynolwyn, some optimists planned a railway the 11 miles to Aberdyfi. In south Wales at Ystrad Ffin, $1\frac{1}{2}$ miles of highly engineered road was actually built to reach an insignificant outcrop.

In 1875, at Cambergi, near Corris, a group of industrialists, laid out terraces, built an incline, mill etc., leaving them with no money to work the quarry. They abandoned within 2 years, having scarcely made any product at all, and most of that was from rock illicitly dug on neighbouring land!

At Escairgeiliog, near Machynlleth, the Cambria Wynne Slate Quarry Company beggared themselves, opening Cwm Gloddfa and building a grand mill. Local men took it on, but they too ultimately failed, with the proverbial third owner eventually making something of a go of it.

In the Porthmadog hinterland there had been, in the mid 1860s, a couple of moderate (30 men) developments, Berthlwyd, and Gerynt, but neither survived more than 10 years, and the modest Dolfriog had an even shorter life. By the mid 70s there was renewed interest in the area with openings at Hafoty and Hafod Uchaf, both employed about 12 men, and had water-powered mills (although machinery was never installed at Hafod Uchaf), neither lasted long. Shortly afterwards Cwm Caeth was opened also with a small mill. Nearer Porthmadog there was a revival at Porthreuddyn, where a very tough slab, which made excellent doorsteps was produced. But the more than a dozen other attempts in that area to revive old workings, or make new ones, met with scant success.

If absolutely useless rock was encountered, it was confidently stated, *'Excellent material will be found when a greater depth is reached'*. It rarely was, although there was some truth in this as rock near the surface could well be degraded by weathering. Enthusiasm was expressed for improbable developments as being *'On a new north facing opening'*. Again with some truth, as slate taken from a working face in direct sunlight could prove too dry to give a good split.

Some developments bordered on the bizarre, at

Cyfanned where lead had been worked from around the 1840s, the crushing of ore was abandoned, and attention turned to the slate vein that their workings had fortuitously encountered. Something similar may also have occurred at Hafod Boeth. Conversely metals were allegedly found in the course of slate working, as happened at Dolgarth, Braich Goch and elsewhere, such reports may have been exaggerations to encourage investors, but it is possible that the moderately successful copper mine at Cwm Dwyfor arose out of unsuccessful slate trials.

Not all developments were unsuccessful, unscrupulous or crazy. In 1874, fairly good rock was found at the head of Cwm Orthin and opened up as Conglog, building a mill and an extension of the Cwmorthin tramway. This modest quarry was worked part time by two brothers towards the end of its 30-year life. They presumably made money, as it is alleged that the postmaster at Tanygrisiau, who acted as their banker, absconded with their accumulated takings! Such working of tiny quarries part-time by just one or two men, who also held down 'Day jobs' in a larger quarry, was an ongoing feature of the industry.

Some new workings in the Llangollen area such as Craig y Glem and Craig Wynnstay, were modestly viable, as was the 3 or 4 man underground working at Cwmmaengwynedd a little to the south and at nearby Llangynog there were several new diggings.

In southwest Wales the slate famine overcame any misgivings about quality and there were new developments, most notably at Rosebush.

In 1873 the Mining Journal carried extracts from a series of articles in the Caernarfon and Denbigh Herald. They give a valuable insight into the state of quarrying at the time as seen by a layman (Reproduced in full in *The Slate quarries of North Wales* Edited by Dr. M. J. T.Lewis)

Of Dolwyddelan the correspondent reported, *'Prince Llywelyn and Penllyn are being worked by companies, a few men are at Rhiw Goch but Fedw is idle'.*

In the south of Meirionnydd he said that *'Bryneglwys has 260 men working on 5 Levels and in the hills, barracks, houses and a Writing Slate factory. At Gaewern, the Talyllyn Slate Company have some chambers open, there is a spacious machine room, all rubbish is sent down an incline the loaded wagon rolling downwards enabling a weighted ballast wagon to return.* (I.e. a single acting incline) *Braich Goch has 200 men and 2 machine rooms, one being at Gaewern. The new Cambria Wynne has 50 men on slab work only. Aberllefenni has workings on 3 sites and there are a further 3 quarries, Cymerau, Ratgoed and Hendre Ddu to the north. Mr Buckley has workings at Dinas Mawddwy'.*

Of Nantlle, he said, *'7 Veins are worked, the principal quarries being Alexandra, Moel Tryfan, Braich, Fron, Pen yr Orsedd, Cilgwyn, Gallt y Fedw, Pen y Bryn, Dorothea, Talysarn, Cloddfa'r Coed, Coed Madoc, Gwernor, Tŷ Mawr* (Tŷ Mawr West?), *Nantlle* (Nantlle Vale?), *Ty'n y Weirglodd, Nant yr Allt* (Tan yr Allt?) *and Fronheulog. Of these Dorothea is the largest with 450-500 men, owned by John Williams & Company. Cilgwyn employs 260 men and has abandoned 2 of its 4 pits, whilst Pen y Bryn employs 300 men in 4 pits. John Robinson is said to be the owner of several quarries through the Talysarn Slate Quarry Company including Gallt y Fedw, where only 12 men are working, and Gloddfa'r Coed which is flooded. Braich is a large pit on 3 floors, with 140 men and where the Dixon Manual Drill is used, with one man turning the drill, whilst another pumps water into the hole'.*

A particularly picturesque description was given of Dorothea – *'Rockmen are working upon different ledges of rock, some with levers forcing open splits in the rock, others regularly plying the long chisel. Rubblemen were noisily throwing waste rubble into small iron wagons, which as soon as loaded, ascend the inclined chains'.*

Of Dinorwig, he said, *'Mr G. W. D. Assheton-Smith's quarry includes the old Garret section and the new, comprising*

153

Wellington, near the old quarry, Victoria further south, Braich above Victoria and Matilda and Sophia above Wellington. There are inclines to Garret, Wellington and Victoria. Allt Ddu one of the oldest is worked as a pit. The hours are 6 a.m. to 5.30 with meals from 10-11 and 3-3 30, taken in cabins of 30 or 40 men. New houses are replacing barracks'.

Of Cwm Pennant he said, 'There is Prince Llywelyn, previously known as Hendre Ddu [Not to be confused with Hendre Ddu in southern Meirionnydd] and the recently re-opened Moelfre has 20-30 men and a fine water-wheel for sawing and planing. Prince of Wales now on 7 galleries is still carrying slate over to Rhyd Ddu, but has purchased an old tramway'.

At Bethesda, 'Penrhyn has 2800 men at work, there is a hospital among trees and there are 6 water balances in use. Pantdreiniog is being worked by the Bangor and Pantdreiniog Slate Company and Tan y Bwlch by the Port Bangor Slate Company. Bryn Hafod y Wern, run by the Royal Bangor Slate company has a pit 74 yards deep'.

In the Blaenau area, after mentioning the 278 men at Diffwys and the 310 at Votty & Bowydd, at the Welsh Slate Company's quarry he became almost poetic 'Imagine such a chamber – the daylight streaming through the upper opening, the bottom only to be recognised by the small lights of the workmen, and yourself perched midway between dawn and midnight on a small wooden bridge, while the horrible rumbling of the explosion comes rolling through the passages till the bridge beneath your feet vibrates in conscious fear. At Drum he rather fell into condescension 'I reached the quarry at noon, and was allowed the privilege of steaming my clothes before a peat fire in the weight-taker's hut. The men soon came filing in, each man taking a can from the fireplace. That can contained neither tea nor coffee but buttermilk. I entered into off hand conversation with the men and soon found that in politics they were eminently radical in sympathies, generally warm hearted and as impulsive as Celts in general'.

All the time, expansion was continuing, much of it

attributable to exports. From 1861 to 1881 Nantlle output, very much export driven, increased from 30,000 to 74,000 tons, but Blaenau went from under 70,000 to approaching 150,000 tons.

Some Blaenau tonnages

	1840	1859	1879
Wrysgan	?	1235	2078
Diffwys	?	?	5567
Maenofferen	?	700	8366
Cwmorthin	?	?	10736
Votty & Bowydd	?	8964	12092
Holland's	10580	10676	13739
Mathew's	2390	9287	15161
Llechwedd	-	7900	18269
Welsh Slate	9337	26236	43296

Since the beginning of the century the output of Bethesda and Nantlle had expanded fourfold, that of Llanberis sevenfold, whereas Blaenau expansion was more than a hundredfold. This was reflected in the population growth of Ffestiniog parish from 732 in 1801 and to 11,274 in 1881. Penrhyn and Dinorwig continued to be by far the largest units, but their 1882 outputs of 111,000 and 87,000 tons respectively, would prove to be their zeniths.

Inland quarries, thanks to the railways, were doing well, the Corwen area raised over 4000 tons in 1882, and in the same year, the Oernant quarries produced over 3000 tons. The quarries on Cefn Ddu benefiting from the 1869 Llanberis branch of the L&NWR were boosted further by the 1878 extension of the Ffridd incline and the amalgamation of Cambrian, Cefn Ddu and Goodman's. This pushed their output to some 5000 tons per year, but they were entering a mature market where buyers had become used to the famous names, making them vulnerable when a downturn enabled buyers to be choosier. The same thing applied at Corris where the steaming of the Corris railway came too late for them to be a force in the market-place, at least as far as roofing-slate was concerned. In Dyffryn Conwy even at the height of the boom scarcely 6000 tons was produced, a far cry from the over 25,000 of a couple of decades before.

Not that Wales was the only source of slate. The rest of the U.K. (which then included Ireland), was by the late 1870s, producing over 50,000 tons, but this was still dwarfed by the Welsh total of 450,000 tons. The Welsh quarries were also more profitable, their sales averaging 53/- (£2.65) per ton, whereas the rest of the U.K. could barely manage 37/- (£1.85). Added to which, the 14259 men in the Welsh quarries each averaged over 31 tons per year, but in the rest of the U.K. the average was only some 28 tons. Imports did not yet pose an overwhelming threat but ominously their value in 1878 was £20,000, three times the total of barely twenty years before.

To some extent the men shared the good times. Over a period of 30 years wages had increased considerably, in the 1840s, as little as 1/- (5p) per day, for an adult labourer was not unknown, with a top bargainer making 3/- (15p). By the mid 70s almost double these figures were commonplace with some Blaenau men making 7/- (35p). Besides which, in the same period, the cost of living had fallen. Flour at 3/- (15p) the half-peck, had not gone down, and in fact went up after the bad harvests of 1875-78. But the vital tea and sugar had more than halved to 3/-lb. (15p) and 3½d lb. (1.4p) respectively. Soap and starch, essential to the proud wives, had also dropped by similar amounts. Quarrymen were able to indulge their craving for books, paying off peddlers weekly for weighty tomes. In Blaenau, at least, it was not unknown for quarrymen to have a live-in maid. These girls, some as young as 10, would often be relatives working for next to nothing to gain experience before seeking positions 'In service' in Liverpool. Even so theirs was another mouth to feed so their presence indicates a degree of disposable income.

Though quarrymen might now feel almost affluent, compared with their fathers, their rewards were in sharp contrast with the profits made by some of the large proprietors. Also in contrast too, with the revenues of some of the quarries' landlords, particularly if they were on an ad-valorem royalty. A small quarry, ill-sited on poor rock with uneconomic transport and onerous lease-terms, no matter how hungry the market or how high the prices, could rarely make money. But a quarry close to a rail line, able to usefully employ, say 100 plus men on good rock and with little or no royalty, could, in the mid 1870s, be very profitable indeed.

Undoubtedly some of the reports of enormous profits made at that time do not fully reflect the amortisation of development and plant, or of the wasting asset nature of any extractive undertaking. Unfortunately, many proprietors took an equally simplistic view. It is rare to find financial accounts that include adequate write-downs of equipment, and sums spent on development work were often accumulated in balance sheets as 'assets'. Unsaleable stock was, optimistically valued and funds were certainly not set aside for plant renewal. It was quite usual for any monies in hand at the end of the year to be declared a 'profit'. Folly of course but understandable where there were shareholders to be satisfied, particularly if they were family members unversed in business, whose expectations often bordered on the ludicrous.

Looking at figures in retrospect, there was another cause for concern. Any commodity price rise is an incentive to find a substitute. Except for a brief period during the Napoleonic wars when the Slate Duty had inflated prices and shipping war-risks, it had always been cheaper, to roof with slate rather than tile in places close to ports. The coming of the railways had extended this advantage to very many inland destinations. However the big price increases of the 1860s & 70's eroded slate's price advantage, until by the mid 1870s, when for instance WSC was getting for best duchesses £11.50, over 50% more than in 1865, both materials were virtually on a par in important markets such as the southeast of England. Tile makers would need to only slightly improve their methods to undercut slate.

9. TROUBLE & STRIFE
The 1880's

The good times did not last. In 1875 after almost 20 years of vigorous growth the British economy took a downturn. The building industry was badly hit, but with outstanding orders to fill and merchants' stocks to replenish, the full effects were not felt by the quarries until well into 1876 – but felt it was.

A trickle of cancelled orders became a deluge. List prices for 1877 were cut, and cut again in each succeeding year, but such buyers as there were regarded list prices purely as the starting point for a Dutch auction.

Towards the end of 1880 there were signs of recovery, some quarries that had been on 4 day working went back to a full week, and several which had closed were talking of re-opening. At the end of the year a 6000-ton order from Hamburg brought Christmas cheer to Blaenau. Nevertheless, the owners, who were now for almost the first time getting together to agree prices, shaded them further for 1881. Their reading of the prospects was correct, since demand again fell back.

With supplies freely available, buyers could be selective. Thus those quarries able to make larger sizes and higher qualities, particularly if they had a 'known name' were not dramatically affected by the downturn. However those locked into lower grades had to deeply discount their prices to move their product, seriously threatening their viability.

Figures for Caernarfonshire in 1882 based on average 'at quarry' valuation, show how much profitability varied. They are not a precise comparison as they do not reflect royalties, equipment amortisation, nor coal and other costs, but they do give useful approximations.

The two Superquarries led this League Table. Penrhyn obtained £2.43 per ton which at 39.6 tons per man-year

(Tpmy) gave a gross return per employee of £96.28. Dinorwig on £2.20 and 38.7 tpmy obtained a return of £85.14 per man, which their large workforces multiplied into very large sums, uneroded by royalties.

Some Nantlle quarries known for their thin slates in large sizes, obtained good prices. Dorothea material was averaging £3.10 and although the productivity of their 533 men, in their difficult pit-working conditions was only 31, it still gave them a revenue of £96.10 per man. A useful figure, making them, Dinorwig and Penrhyn apart, the county's most profitable unit, and the only Nantlle quarry to ever show consistent profits. By contrast, neighbouring South Dorothea although grossing a handsome £3.60 per ton, their 70 men each raised a mere 14 tons, dropping their per-man take to little more than £50.00. Pen yr Orsedd's 261 men making 7999 tons, equalled Dorothea's productivity, but since they could only get £2.60 per ton, this dropped their take to about £79.60 per man. Cilgwyn averaged the same price as Pen yr Orsedd, but again with their 300 men only raising 24.6 tons each; their figure was under £70.00.

Tal y Sarn's prices were on a par with Dorothea, but needing 400 men to raise 8210 tons they only grossed £63.60 per man. Alexandra's 195 men only averaged 23 tons but a useful £3.17 per ton pushed their revenue to almost £73.00 on each. Adjacent Moeltryfan's productivity was identical but since their prices averaged a mere £2.19, they grossed barely £50.00 on each of their 81 men. Braich was able to average £2.40 per ton but with their 124 men only turning out 21 tons each, their figure was £54.60. Coed Madoc obtained the same prices as Braich but getting less than 19 tons per man from their workforce of 100, the return was less than £45.00, probably scarcely covering their labour costs.

Over at Llanberis, Glynrhonwy was obtaining £2.20 and with their 53 men each turning out 28.6 tons, they grossed almost £63.00 per man, and at Cefn Ddu on the same price and with productivity only slightly less, each of their 197 men brought in just under £62.00. Cook & Ddol's product could only command £2.07 and with their 26 men making just 23 tons, their revenue on each was a worrying £47.61.

At Bethesda, Bryn Hafod y Wern's 65 men raised a creditable 33.8 tons each, but only realising a derisory £1.27 per ton, gave a return of about £43.00 per man. Any worries this quarry may have had about poor revenues became academic in 1889. The new Lord Penrhyn may have felt that they were taking business he considered rightfully his, or he may have been mindful of the rebuff received by his father when he had tried to annex the site. For whatever reason, he cut off the quarry's water supply that was sourced on his land. Since this 'upside down' quarry had to haul all its rock out of a pit and then send its rubbish up to a higher level again, lack of waterpower brought immediate closure.

At Cwm Machno 100 men raised over 44 tons each which even at a measly £1.75 gave the quarry £77.00 per man. This low selling price and high productivity suggesting that as at Bryn Hafod y Wern, there was a big proportion of slab. At Hafodlas, nearly 700 tons (including building block) was being raised by only 10 men, which even selling at only £1.29 per ton, gave a revenue of £86.30 from each.

Other quarries were clearly running at a loss, Glanrafon averaged over £3.00 for its product, but with its 97 men each raising scarcely 10 tons, it grossed only £31.00 per man. Even the much larger Pen y Bryn with its 234 men had a productivity figure of less than 12 tons, so even getting £2.50 per ton grossed them under £30.00 per man. The productivity of Fron's 62 strong workforce was much the same, but selling at only £2.20, pushed their per-man take down to £26.00. Nearby, Fronheulog could only obtain £2.23 but with productivity of their 98 men at 16 tons, they were realising a somewhat less unhealthy £35.68. At little Garreg Fawr 6 men could only manage 80 tons that at £2.00 per ton gave them a gross per man of under £27.00. Prince Llywelyn's 74 men raised only 25 tons each, which realised

161

under £1.00 per ton, a disastrous revenue situation. This was an example of a quarry only able to turn out small and lower grade roofing slates, being stuck with prices on a par with slab, but without slab's productivity advantage.

In all, in 1882, the 36 quarries of Caernarfonshire employed 8960 men, sold just under 281,000 tons averaging 31 tons per man, with a per man revenue of £76.00. But ignoring the 3 top performers, Penrhyn, Dinorwig and Dorothea, the 2859 men in the rest of the county produced 65.500 tons, less than 23 tons per man. Although most got around £2.45 per ton, many must have struggled to meet even their wage bills.

At Nantlle, Pen y Bryn, only recently employing over 250 men, would with its appalling productivity, shortly close. Coed Madoc facing pumping costs of £100 per month closed their Gloddfa Glai pit. The small Cloddfa'r Coed closed completely. Closures at Nantlle were liable to be permanent as idle workings were quickly snapped up by neighbours as dumps for rubbish. There had been a proposal for a co-operatively funded railway to dump into the sea near Pontlyfni but like a similar scheme to collectively drain and pump, the slump killed off such ideas. Many of the family workings, on tiny sites with no rail connection, had closed. Once there had been well over 40 undertakings at Nantlle, by the 1880s amalgamation and closure had reduced this to about 15. According to a contemporary report, only 3 of these were breaking even. In 1884 even Dorothea's profits would be seriously dented when water broke in, drowning 7 men, (believed to be the most serious single accident in a Welsh slate quarry), eventually involving £30,000 on remedial work.

In the Llangollen & Glynceiriog area in 1876 there had been 8 quarries with about 600 men producing nearly 20,000 tons. In 1882 only 3 quarries were open, their 160 men raising less than 4000 tons. Everywhere quarries were closing, some never to reopen. In this rigid economic climate, only the most efficient could survive.

During the next few years many more undertakings, particularly those with poor transport, would close. Some small and marginal, such as the 7 man Bwlch y Ddwy Elor, but also larger ones like Cedryn and its associated Cwmeigiau, who in spite of (or rather because of) the big sums expended, gave up trying to triumph over their difficulties. Similarly Hafod y Llan failing to reap a return on their epic inclines, closed. A host of openings or re-openings of the heady 60s and 70s failed. Not that good transport necessarily brought success, for Corris with its newly steamed railway suffered as badly as anywhere and while quarries on the rich Narrow vein would survive those such as Abercwmeiddaw on the poorer Broad vein would succumb. Unhappily too, the great prosperity brought to the quarries to the south of Llanberis by the railway, proved short-lived. Some closed, others operated on a reduced scale, and Gallt y Llan at Nant Peris was finally defeated by poor rock and lack of rail connection.

At Blaenau in 1882 about 4000 men in 20 or so quarries raised something over 130,000 tons, with revenues per man averaging around £100. However with the Welsh Slate Company achieving perhaps £150, and Llechwedd over £130, returns at some others must have been nudging down towards the £60, which with heavy coal bills, would not have been rosy. The statement made at the time that of the 15 quarries in Blaenau, only 4 were profitable, may well have been correct.

Little wonder the WSC so boastfully and smugly received visitors

'While at Blaenau Ffestiniog we made our way to the Palmerston Slate Quarry, which we were told was the largest and most productive in Wales. The landlady of the Baltic Hotel found us a highly respectable guide, who conducted us up the great heaps of shale, and past the finishing sheds to a narrow-gauge line, along which the huge blocks of slate are brought

from the pit's mouth on trucks. On one of these we were bidden to take our seats, the guide sitting just behind us and holding us on carefully, whilst two lads pushed us along through a tunnel about 50 yards long, dark and rather moist. On reaching our destination, where we came to more sheds filled with machinery, we alighted and walked down some steps into the first chamber of the black smoky mine; there are nine beneath it, right into the bowels of the earth. The miners, who number between seven and eight hundred, were then enjoying the open air during their dinner hour, and were sitting or lying about near the pit's mouth. Considering the fearful atmosphere so many of them have to work in from six in the morning till 5.30 in the evening, they, most of them, looked very robust and healthy; they were all very civil and well behaved to us as we passed in and out amongst them, and there seemed a good deal of kindly feeling and good fellowship between themselves. The miners earn from 23s. to 25s. a week, and the slate finishers 45s. This mine made £83,000 clear profits last year, but this was unusually good. It yields an average profit of £50,000 or £60,000. The shaft we went down was pitch dark, and the air was most disagreeable to breath. A miner lad went before us with a lantern; our guide held me by the arm and my sister followed us closely, carrying a bit of lighted candle, set in a lump of clay, in her hand. We came upon bridges across shafts letting air down to the chambers beneath, where we saw, dimly burning, ever so far down, the lights of the poor miners. The quality of the slate in this quarry is very good, and the mine has already been worked 80 years. Our guide showed us the water-works which pump the water out of the mine, and the slate just as it is after it has been blasted, huge blocks worth about £4 each, which are conveyed to the pit's mouth on trucks, part of the way drawn by horses and then by machinery with wire ropes up the steep incline to where the narrow-gauge line takes it to the finishing sheds where it is split, cut in squares, and then taken off to the railroad, to be forwarded to all parts of the world. We took a look at the great engine which sets all the *different machinery in motion in the finishing shed, where nothing is done by hand now-a-days except the actual splitting of the blocks of slate, which is an easy task when once the two wedges are driven in. The guide has a fixed charge of 5s. for taking people over the mine, and we were glad to give it to him – he was so civil and so careful over us.'*

From *Thorough Guides, North Wales*,
Part 1 1892 pp 178/9

However the WSC's equanimity was about to receive something of a setback. Pressing to increase productivity to compensate for lower sales and lower prices, they took a reckless approach to working practices. Their sales had peaked at near 50,000 tons in 1875, by 1882 they were down to under 35,000 tons, but by cutting corners, they achieved this with a workforce almost halved to little more than 700, an astonishing near 50 tons per man, way ahead of Llechwedd whose consistent 40 plus tons of large, top-quality roofing slates was regarded as an industry benchmark. W.S.C probably reduced the pillar width to less than the proper 30', always a temptation, as the pillars represented good, easily worked rock. They certainly failed to take proper care to precisely align their chambers with those of Mathew's and Holland's that were above them. It was alleged that they did their measuring with a '*Three-foot walking stick*'. They had been prosecuted in 1874 for failing to keep proper plans of their workings. Since they were only fined 2/6 (12.5p or half what their guide's tip!), risking further penalties must have seemed a better bet than employing a surveyor. In December 1882 the inevitable happened and there was a serious fall. Two months later, whilst management was still figuring out how to get the affected district re-started, another, much bigger fall occurred. Reputedly over six million tons of rock came down, all but destroying much of the quarry, (fortunately without causing any injury) and seriously damaging both

Mathew's and Holland's quarries.

Both the Mathew and Holland quarries were now in W.E.Oakeley's hands. Having managed the estate for some years on behalf of his aunt, the widow of W.G.Oakeley, W.E. had finally inherited in 1878. Not content with his handsome royalty income, he wanted the quarry profits as well; so one of his first actions was to decline to renew the expiring leases on these two quarries. Buying the plant with loans from the Rock Insurance Company and from bankers C.Hoare & Co, he set about running them himself. This proved to be not one of his best-judged moves. Anticipating having to give up possession the quarries were in a mess, Mathew's in particular having been irresponsibly worked with no regard for the future. More seriously, the late 1870s was no time to entering the slate industry. Now with his two quarries all but wrecked and facing the prospect of a serious diminution of the royalties from W.S.C. that were urgently needed to service his loans and pay for his ongoing extensions to Plas Tan y Bwlch, Mr Oakeley was not a happy man.

He eventually won a protracted legal action against Welsh Slate but since there was no chance of his £110,000 compensation award being paid, he seized their quarry and set about merging it with his existing two. At the end of the century a steam shovel was still clearing the debris.

Cwmorthin had furiously pushed their annual output into five figures, also partly by pillar robbing. In 1884 the inevitable happened and there was a major collapse, not on the W.S.C. scale but enough to render almost half the workings unusable. A subsequent examination by Thomas Jones, Oakley's engineer, found *'pillars less than 10 feet thick instead of the proper 30 feet'*. In fairness it must be said that 'pillar robbing' and 'cupboarding' (cutting recesses in pillars) was regrettably widespread. Nor was this 'Slice off a cut loaf' philosophy confined to the 19th century. West Llangynog closed in 1937 due to a collapse caused by pillar robbing to meet an urgent order.

The fall broke the Cwmorthin Company. The quarry was reopened in 1889 by the New Welsh Slate Company, a re-incarnation of the old W.S.C. They never prospered and in 1900 Oakeley, by then operating as a limited company, took them over. In all, the great Oakeley quarry, an amalgamation of Holland's, Mathew's, Welsh Slate, Nyth y Gigfran and Cwmorthin, would ultimately have 12 mills containing 500 saw tables, almost 50 miles of rail track, and 11 miles of compressed airline. But for all its size, Oakeley, like other Blaenau quarries, would never again replicate the profits of the 60s and 70s.

In 1883 the market remained weak. Caernarfonshire quarries held up fairly well but the brunt fell on Meirionnydd, where competition in the export market forced substantial cutbacks in output.

Examples of cutbacks 1882-1883

	1882		1883	
	Output	Men	Output	Men
Caernarfon				
Alexandra	4550	195	3721	182
Cefn Ddu	5640	197	4040	172
Cilgwyn	7430	300	4956	215
Dinorwig	87429	2757	85000	2710
Dorothea	16598	533	15841	481
Fronheulog	1642	98	1364	69
Moel Tryfan	1880	81	1781	70
Penrhyn	111166	2889	110382	2838
Prince Llywelyn	1685	74	315	42
Rhos	1285	45	1005	40
	239305	7169	228405	6819
	-		4.5%	-4.9%
Meirionnydd				
Abercwmeiddaw	4173	188	2875	80
Cwt y Bugail	2459	73	1662	40
Deeside	105	42	600	34
Graig Ddu	3140	110	807	36

Minllyn	2830	108	1468	71
Penrhyngwyn	250	47	54	20
Ratgoed	434	15	382	8
Wrysgan	2078	96	1396	51
	16459	679	9244	340
			-43%	-49%

By 1884 prices of even the best slates were 30% or more below the 1876 peak and by 1886 the total Welsh tonnage had fallen to less than 400,000. Imports that had been encouraged by the recent high prices took an increasing market share. Besides the traditional European sources, slate was now also coming from the United States, where many quarries were worked by Welshmen who had emigrated during previous depressions, forming nostalgically named communities such as Bangor

A report in the Mining Journal of 1869 mentions difficulties in several Pennsylvania quarries due to the widespread use of the Welsh language among the 4-man gangs who introduced Welsh methods of working. Wages of 40p-60p per day made possible by productivities of roofing slate close to 50 tons per man-year must have been a big incentive to emigration. The same report mentions, 1000 Writing Slates per day being made by one man cutting and two men 'smoothing'.

The fall in trade was accompanied by an entirely new factor. No longer could the employers arbitrarily cut wages and lay off 'hands', since in 1874, following the frustration by some owners of earlier attempts, the North Wales Quarrymen's Union had been formed.

Unionism came late to the slate quarries, as revolutionary theories that had found ready support in English mills and manufactories, did not readily take root in a culture more versed in the Mabonigion than in Marx. The various uprisings, both agricultural and industrial that had occurred in south and mid Wales earlier in the century, had no counterparts in the north. The chapel rather than a union or a political movement was the instinctive focus of solidarity, and a strong focus it was, chapel loyalties were fervent and remained so in rural areas up to the mid 20th century. Their influence was formidable, forming an alternative society, with a rigid hierarchy of the minister, (who might well be an ex-quarryman), deacons and other officers, who carried great moral authority among their congregations. Though sharing a common dissension from the Established Church, rivalry between differing chapels, even those of the same denomination was fierce. It was possibly only the realisation that chapel loyalties were too disparate (There were well over 30 chapels in Blaenau Ffestiniog alone), to effectively further their interests, that caused the men to turn to unionism.

Unsurprisingly, the NWQMU was largely a Penrhyn and Dinorwig initiative. The proprietors of both had shown commendable concern for the welfare of their workers by the building of hospitals, schools etc. and in the provision of (small) pensions and so on. Unfortunately they had always run their quarries in an authoritarian style, with scant regard for *Chwarae Teg* (fair play) so innate in the Welsh psyche. They are said for instance, to have paid higher wages to churchgoing men, condoned the favouritism and corruption rife amongst their letting stewards and middle managers. In fact it was probably dissatisfaction with such unfairness rather than pay and conditions that was foremost in the minds of the union founders.

Most of the other big quarries were run by owners, who whilst not always totally benevolent towards their employees, understood them better, many sharing their Liberal and Chapel views. Also Penrhyn and Dinorwig were both virtually monopolistic employers in their respective areas, whereas in such places as Blaenau and Nantlle there were opportunities for dissatisfied men to find work in other quarries, particularly in the buoyant middle 70s.

A contemporary report in the Carnarvon and Denbigh Herald remarked on -

'The better feeling in Blaenau quarries as opposed to Carnarvonshire due to the Liberal and Non-conformist sympathies of the owners and the speaking of Welsh by the superintendents, as well as to better wages'.

The benevolence of management was alliteratively instanced by citing *'The provision of a Pudding Room by Mr Percival'* They went on to attribute -*'The men of Blaenau being less given to drinking and debauchery, than those elsewhere'* to the (Rice) puddings provided by Mr.Percival, proprietor of Votty and Bowydd quarry. This initiative was, course, like Lady Newborough's Cocoa Rooms, an attempt to encourage milk consumption as an aid to health.

In some quarries such as many in Nantlle, the 'them and us' comprised not so much masters versus men, as both, collectively, versus the likes of Penrhyn and Dinorwig. The Darbishires, owners of Pen yr Orsedd, actively welcomed the formation of a union, and there were even some Nantlle owners who held office in the NWQMU. These factors were reflected in the figures for union membership that by 1878 totalled 8000. At Penrhyn over 90% joined and at Dinorwig about 83%. Yet in Nantlle only 25% were unionists and at Blaenau scarcely 10%.

There were other ingredients to complicate industrial relations. Most men being Bargainers considered themselves not 'Wage slaves', but independent contractors. They felt they had common cause undivided by craft or skill, since top rockmen, tradesmen and the humblest labourers might share the same *caban*, attend the same chapel and were probably related anyway.

There was also the problem of Language and Nationality. Apart from the actual difficulty of communication, many English owners and managers tended to have a 'Colonial' outlook, seeing themselves as bringing civilisation to these natives who spoke only in an unintelligible tongue. On the other hand the 'natives' would have little esteem for persons ignorant of the 'Language of Heaven' and its accompanying culture. Although the 1901 Census would record that of the 5281 persons in Bethesda, 2091 were bi-lingual, the actual numbers that could speak English would be much lower since anyone with the slightest smattering, of the language would undoubtedly have boasted of such a cosmopolitan accomplishment.

Apart from operating in an unusual industry, the NWQMU was itself unusual. Normally when a union was formed, officials were elected from among members who often held more extreme views and possibly were less devoted to the work ethic, than the men they represented. Initially the leaders of the NWQMU were not quarrymen, mainly because acceptance of office would have meant dismissal, but partly because it was wished to have men of standing and negotiating experience. The first president J.L.Jones was the owner of several small quarries, and also prominent were a bank manager, a doctor and several schoolteachers. The general secretary, later president, W.J.Parry was the son of a quarryman but had built up a substantial business, describing himself as a *'Builder's Merchant, Oil, Powder and Dynamite Merchant and Implement and Quarry Tool Agent'*. He also had accountancy qualifications and was Agent to the Cenfaes Estate. W.J.Williams, who succeeded Parry as secretary, was a practising professional accountant. An unlikely assembly perhaps, but Parry in particular would prove an outstanding leader, his total bilingualism invaluable in dealing with management.

Immediately following the formation of the union there had been a clash at Glynrhonwy. Membership was prohibited and when the men ignored this injunction they were locked out. With demand for slate brisk and alternative work available at other quarries, this caused more problems for management than for the men. Within 3 weeks the quarry was reopened, with union membership tacitly tolerated. Shortly afterwards there was trouble at Dinorwig. Thomas Assheton-Smith II had died in 1858 leaving the estate to his ten-year old nephew, George W. Duff. When young George attained his majority in 1869 he assumed the Assheton-Smith name and set about sorting things at the quarry. By 1874 his various tinkerings including alterations to the payment structure, having generated a lot of ill will, the men walked out. When they returned five weeks later, it was substantially on their own terms.

The big test came at Penrhyn. Colonel Douglas-Pennant had been ennobled in 1866 and reviving his predecessor's Irish title, was now First Baron Penrhyn of Llandegai. Colonel or Lord, he was still the man to beat, and beat him they did.

The actual cause of the 1874 Penrhyn dispute was not about wages although there was considerable discontent over the pay structure, distortions of which meant that good workers producing much first-class material might be worse off than less able or less diligent men making little more than rubble. Nor was it directly union related, but merely a trifling tiff over a collection made in working time. Such collections were commonplace whether for distressed colleagues or for wider causes, such as those made towards the establishment of Universities at Aberystwyth and Bangor, but this one was in aid of the Dinorwig strikers, which to his lordship was a definite non-starter. The dispute grew into a full blown stand-off, which lasted over two months but resulted in a shake out of senior management and in the signing of the Pennant-Lloyd agreement (named after the Penrhyn Estate Agent). This 1874 agreement was a landmark not so much because it improved and codified the working conditions, gave the men some voice in the running of the quarry and acknowledged the need for a minimum wage, but because its very signing recognised for the first time, delegates' rights to negotiate on behalf of the men.

During the rest of the 1870s, there were few serious disputes, the only major one being at Rhos in 1877, which although it lasted two whole bitter years, was purely a local matter. But when the downturn started to bite at the end of that decade, bringing wage cuts and lay-offs, there was more general trouble, particularly at some of the less profitable but strongly unionised quarries at Llanberis and Nantlle. From 1879 on, there were strikes at Cook & Ddol, Goodman's, Cambrian, Glynrhonwy Upper, Cefn Du, Cilgwyn, Braich, Alexandra, Pen yr Orsedd and Moel Tryfan. At Bryn Hafod y Wern, there were 4 strikes in seven years.

There were wage reductions and lay-offs at larger Caernarfonshire quarries such as Dorothea, Penrhyn and Dinorwig, but these were generally less drastic and were negotiated without serious confrontation. Blaenau quarries with their greater profitability, were less affected as they could pay above Caernarfonshire rates, which by the mid 80s, in the smaller quarries, were at best 4/3 (21p) per day, with for instance Cilgwyn paying under 4/ (20p) for top men. Penrhyn was paying up to 5/ (25p) per day but even this contrasted with the 7/6 (37.5p) some men had been getting a few years before.

No union could fight harsh economic facts, there was disenchantment with this route to betterment and membership dropped away, falling to well under 3000 by 1884. The men increasingly turned back to their chapels as a focus of solidarity.

At Dinorwig, things had started to go really sour in 1880 when W.W.Vivian was appointed general manager, his success in commerce (and his being the son of a peer?), apparently overriding his lack of experience of controlling a large workforce and his ignorance of quarrying. He was charged with the task of improving the profitability of the quarry, which had always failed to match Penrhyn's performance. This was mainly because of geological problems, with bad rock having been worked around rather than boldly removed, rubbish dumped with little forethought as well as the hotchpotch development, particularly in the Allt Ddu & Chwarel Fawr districts. Besides which, Penrhyn tended to get better prices, more perhaps due to their agents' skilful marketing, than any superiority of product.

These difficulties Vivian could in the short term do little about. To try to get more out of the men was something he could and did tackle. There were five years of mounting tension and dissension, but no actual conflict.

Reference has been made to the close connection with the land felt by the quarrymen, particularly those of north Caernarfonshire. This was in fact a carry-over from the old metal mine practice of farm hands working part-time. Thus the custom of taking days off or of leaving work early, to attend to their own holdings or to help neighbours with theirs, was strongly ingrained. As Bargainers, which most of the men were, they saw nothing wrong in this. If they chose to sacrifice earnings, they felt that only they were the losers. A manager such as Vivian trying to maximise output, by running things on factory-like lines with hours governed by the hooter, viewed matters differently. Thus much dissension was attendance-related.

As is usual in such matters, a small event turned discontent into disorder. In addition to the regular quarry holidays, it had become usual for the men to take a day off at the end of the 4-week month. When in 1885 some of the Dinorwig men, observing this tacit custom, were ordered back to work, resentment built up. Shortly after this when men were seen by an under-manager, waiting for the hooter not at their workplaces, but at the edge of the quarry site, a whole gallery was suspended. Although Vivian did not fully support his under-manager, he did not completely rescind the suspension. Following further disputes about working on the last day of the month, and the holding of meetings on quarry property, there was a lockout.

Fifteen weeks of idleness followed, with some negotiation, much bitterness, a little vandalism, but no violence. There were even elements of farce. There was much glee when Assheton-Smith was prosecuted for winging a beater whilst out shooting. The Dinorwig Band, when ordered to surrender their instruments, (which as with most of the numerous quarry bands were provided by the owners), very publicly played them as they marched in to return them. Then, finding no one at the quarry that would accept them, they marched home again, much to the delight of onlookers.

Eventually, largely due to the intervention of John Robinson, the owner of Tal y Sarn quarry, the men were persuaded to return. The terms were substantially those dictated by Vivian, rules would not be relaxed, new working practices would be introduced and manning would be cut by some 500.

The shortage caused by the Dinorwig shutdown helped prices to firm a little for 1886, and with some improvement in trade during the latter part of the 80s they were by 1889 around 5% up on the low of 1884/85. Although still a full 25% less than the 1876 peak, there was now a little more scope for managements to be flexible and conflict receded. At Blaenau trade was good and confidence was returning, as demonstrated by the Greaves' in 1887 further extending their Llechwedd holding, by leasing part of Friddybach farm from the Rev. Haygarth,

Having 3 landlords, (The others being Lord Newborough and W.G.Oakeley) exacerbated the problem faced by quarries, having more than one landowner. For royalty purposes, separate accounts of tonnages would have to be accurately maintained for each, that with the best of goodwill could cause dispute. In fact when Tan yr Allt closed in 1879 this was partly because of problems of apportioning dues between 4 landowners.

Nantlle too, was busy, although some quarries such as Coed Madoc had declined and the likes of Brynfferam and Fron were on almost nominal outputs, Pen yr Orsedd had almost restored its manning to the 400 it had been in the 1860s. Cilgwyn's 318 and Tal y Sarn's 360 payrolls were almost their best and Dorothea's 550 was their highest ever. Alexandra was doing well with 230 men, South Dorothea had a remarkable 104 and Cloddfa'r Coed an incredible 150, equalling Moel Tryfan's total. Several of the intermittently worked smaller diggings were revived.

On the other hand, at Penrhyn serious and portentous events were taking place. In 1885, Lord Penrhyn, now a sick 85 year old (he died the following year), passed control to his son, George Sholto Gordon Douglas Pennant. The heir, pushing 50, having spent most of his adult life watching his inheritance grow, had lately seen decline threaten. Undoubtedly spurred by his close friend Emilius Alexander Young, one of the company's auditors, he had smouldered, impatient to remedy what he perceived as his father's senilities, and Wyatt, the manager's, weaknesses.

The new master immediately arranged for Wyatt to retire 'due to ill-health', and over the heads of better-qualified applicants, appointed Young in his place. Young was at once able to show that his predecessor had been lax in his accounting and by this means confirmed his employer's confidence in him. Young may have been a competent manager of figures but as a manager of men he was definitely less than outstanding. His deficiencies would soon become apparent and it is puzzling why, in the ensuing years, he continued to enjoy the new Lord Penrhyn's backing for his so often unwise policies.

The Penrhyn/Young team was encouraged by the decline in the strength of the Union, for the NWQMU was both in membership and its influence on affairs, a shadow of what it had been a decade before. They, with some justification, felt that the Pennant-Lloyd agreement had handed too much power to the men, but instead of seeking to re-negotiate, they unilaterally abrogated it. In addition they made it clear that they intended to run the quarry with a firm hand, cracking down hard on union 'activities'.

There followed a decade of discontent

OUTPUTS AND MANNING OF NORTH WALES SLATE QUARRIES 1883

Bethesda

Penrhyn Lord Penrhyn	111,617 tons	2838 men	39 t/man
Bryn Hafod y Wern	1263	54	23
Pantdreiniog J Williams	245	13	19

Llanberis

Dinorwig G W Assheton-Smith	85,000	2710	31
Cefn Ddu Llanberis Slate Co	4,040	172	23
Up'r Glynrhonwy			
Up'r Glynrhonwy S'te Co	2,072	80	26
Glynrhonwy			
Glynrhonwy Slate Co	1,789	70	25
Cook & Ddol	631	26	24
Caermenciau			
Caermenciau Slate Q Co	300	12	25
Brynmawr Bryn Mawr Slate co	160	?	-

Nantlle

Dorothea Dorothea Slate Quarry	15,841	481	33
Pen yr Orsedd Penyrorsedd Slate Q Co	8,257	230	36
Pen y Bryn Pen y Bryn Slate Co	5,083	240	21
Cilgwyn Cilgwyn Slate Co	4,956	215	23
Alexandra Alexandra Slate Co	3,721	182	20
Coed Madog Coed Madog Slate Co	2,879	135	21
Braich Braich Slate Co	2,200	99	22
Moel Tryfan Moel Tryfan S & S Q C	1,781	70	25
South Dorothea South Dorothea Slate Co	1,750	92	19
Fronlog New Fronheulog Slate Co	364	69	20
Fron Vron & Old Braich W S Q Co	650	?	
Caermenciau	300	12	25

Brynfferam Brynfferam Slate Co	252	18	14
Nantlle Vale Nantlle Vale Slate Quarry Co	150	20	7
Llwyd Coed W Jones	78	6	13

Conwy Valley

Prince Llywelyn Prince Llewelyn Slate Co	1,315	42	31
Rhos Capel Curig Slate Quarry Co	1,005	40	25
Hafodlas Betws-y-coed S & S Co	289	11	26

Cwm Gwyrfai

Glanrafon Glanrafon Slate Quarry Co	1,725	92	19
Plas y Nant Plas y Nant Slate Co	672	28	24
Bwlch y Ddwy Elor	160	7	23
Garreg Fawr Betws Garmon Slate Co	96	6	16

Cwm Pennant

Prince of Wales	?	9	-

Ffestiniog

Rhiwbryfdir Welsh Slate Co	26,108	655	40
Llechwedd J W Greaves & Sons	24,723	553	45
Cesail Oakeley Slate Quarries	13,372	507	26
Votty & Bowydd V & B S'te Qu's	11,923	374	32
Gloddfa Ganol Oakeley Slates Quarries	11,617	345	34
Cwmorthin Cwmorthin Slate Co	10,709	441	24
Maenofferen Maenofferen Slate Quarry	8,230	244	34
Diffwys Diffwys Casson Slate Co	5,656	228	25
Rhosydd New Rhosydd S Q Co	5,587	181	31
Rhiwbach Ffestiniog Slate Co	3,187	130	24
Cwt y Bugail Bugail Slate Co	1,662	40	41
Wrysgan Wrysgan Slate Co	1,396	51	27
Craig Ddu Craig Ddu Slate Co	80	36	22
Parc J Staveley	351	15	23
Conglog New Conglog S & S Co	313	17	18
Voelgron Jones & Owen	112	4	28
Bwlch y Slaters Bwlch y S's Q'ry Co	71	?	-

Corris

Braich Goch B G S Q Co	5,085	238	21
Aberllefenni R D Pryce	4,814	78	27
Abercwmeiddaw Aberc'm'w S Q Co	2,875	80	36
Llwyngwern	915	35	26

Cymerau H N Hughes	762	29	26
Ratgoed H N Hughe	382	8	48
South Meirionnydd			
Bryneglwys W McConnel	7,996	282	28
Minllyn Carlyle Slate & Slab Co	1,468	71	21
Hendre Ddu	878	36	24
Henddol Walker & Co	401	40	10
Cwm Ebol Cwmebol Slate Co	260	9	29
Gartheiniog Jenkins & Owen	250	9	28
Penrhyngwyn	54	20	3
Golwern Walker & Co	50	4	13
East Meirionnydd (As was then)			
Moelfferna M'lfna & D'side S & S Co	1,601	81	20
Deeside ' '	600	34	18
Penarth Jones & Phillips	498	10	50
Cletwr Llandderfel Slate & Slab Co	12	3	4
Denbs & Monts			
Moel y Faen	1625	84	19
Clogau (Berwyn)	1022	75	14
Hendre Ddu	878	?	-
Pant Glas	73	35	21
Craig Rhiwarth	329	15	22
Cwmmaengwynedd	10	2	5

The quite good productivity at WSC & the Oakeley quarries and even after the Big Fall was due to much of the fallen rock that had to cleared, being useable block The strong position of the Ffestinog area is shown by their having (Other than the two ' Superquarries') 7 out of the 8 with 300 + payrolls.

10. TRIUMPH & TRAGEDY
The 1890s

By 1890 the fragile recovery of the previous couple of years was faltering and price lists were trimmed, but list prices were one thing, invoiced prices another. An 1890 Aberllefenni Price Card exists which shows overwritten reductions of up to 5/- (25p) per ton on some slab. Also inked in are discounts of $17\frac{1}{2}$% less 10%, less $2\frac{1}{2}$%. So that for what was almost their top slab product, listed at £4 per ton, they were quoting only £2.71.

Tonnage at 410,000, was better than it had been, but was still nearly 40,000 less than late 70s peak. A year later output was below 400,000 tons and manning at less than 13,000, was almost 2000 down. Much of the drop fell on Nantlle, where by 1891 a number of the smaller workings had closed and others had slashed manning, hours and wages. Penrhyn and Dinorwig retrenched and even booming Blaenau was affected. The once mighty Diffwys failed and although it was restarted, it never recovered its former eminence.

A couple of years into the decade an upturn in the building industry brought a renewed demand for slate. By 1894, this had become almost a stampede. In spite of production being lost by the freezing weather at the end of the year, outputs were nudging previous records. Everywhere there was a turnaround, Nantlle more than regained its lost trade, and Blaenau's climb once looked unstoppable. Several quarries such as Penarth that had failed to keep open in the recent slack times restarted. Even the trifling Egryn was developed underground. Attempts at new openings were renewed although the chances of finding new, workable rock were slim. Typical of these was Ffynnon Badarn, near Corris, where optimistically, a tramway was planned to reach a trifling outcrop hundreds of feet up a cliff.

There was success south of the Dyfi estuary. For many

years some slate had been dug there, but there was now more serious activity. Glandyfi was busy supplying slab for enamelling at Aberystwyth, and there were new openings at Morben and at Tyn y Garth as well as some smaller diggings. Their combined outputs briefly reached several thousand tons, but they would become early casualties when the slab market declined.

By 1896 prices not only stood at a remarkable 25-30% above those of 1890, but also held for 3 years. Even when trade eased a little in 1899, lists were still above anything seen for more than twenty years. Small investors were also regaining confidence. The directors of Wrysgan for instance included A N Williams a draper and D Roberts a grocer.

However the 90s were most notable, not for the trade recovery, but for three portentous events –

1. The Llechwedd stoppage of 1893.

2. The publication in 1895 of the *Report of the Enquiry into the Merionethshire Mines*

3. The Penrhyn stoppage of 1896-7.

All leading up to the cataclysm of 1900.

To deal with the Mines Report first. Although the enquiry's remit was confined to the underground workings of the one county, it served to publicise the dangers and hardships in slate quarrying generally. Although the Chairman Sir Charles Foster (as he later became) was above suspicion, much of the evidence was not, being provided by understandably biased management, and by employees fearful of their jobs. More flagrant was the evidence of medical men employed by quarry owners. Whilst the standard of medical attention given by quarry doctors was invariably of the best, their impartiality when matters of compensation were involved was often questionable. The term 'Natural causes' was sometimes elastic, and 'Visitations of God' on such devout communities were surprisingly frequent. For this reason there were recurrent moves to put sick clubs outside of quarry control, or to permit opting out of membership, so that medical advice independent of quarry influence could be obtained.

Despite robust rebuttals from medical and management witnesses, the report made clear how unhealthy and hazardous slate quarrying was. It showed that although gas posed no dangers of explosion or asphyxiation, it was more dangerous to work in an underground slate quarry, than even the most notorious of coalmines. Roofs crumbling, falling rock, blocks slipping during handling, missed footings in the dark, stumbling near the many sheer drops, running down by wagons – there were a hundred dangers. It was scarcely safer in the open quarries. Wet or greasy rock, and precipitous pits reached by rickety ladders, presented additional hazards. In all workings there were winches and hand cranes whose ratchets slipped, sending winding handles spinning to kill or maim. Blasting had been made safer by the obligatory provision of blast shelters, and by firing at fixed times with bugle and flag warnings, but horrific accidents from shot firing were still commonplace.

At the smaller, remoter quarries, an injured man could be a very long way and a very long time, from medical attention of any kind. At some of the larger quarries his chances might be better. Besides the hospitals at Penrhyn, Dinorwig and Oakeley, other owners at Blaenau Ffestiniog had put the town ahead of many municipalities by sponsoring a hospital in 1848. These institutions were competently staffed and by the standards of the time well equipped, founding a tradition of care, which the hospitals of north Wales still ably continue. Indeed Penrhyn hospital was a pioneer in the use of anaesthetics, and Dinorwig in the development of X-Rays and amputation prostheses. However even with a hospital on site, it could be a lengthy and painful journey for a patient to reach it from a distant workplace. Thus fractures and other injuries not ordinarily life-threatening, could result in death, or at best, permanent disablement.

The report drew attention to the chronically bad diet of the men, although this was passed off as a *'failure by the wives to provide proper meals'*. It highlighted the great incidence of diseases, particularly pulmonary complaints, some 50% of male deaths being from respiratory causes. These, some witnesses attributed, not to dust, damp and bad housing, but to drinking *'stewed tea'*. It would be the 1920s before the canard that slate dust was 'beneficial', was finally laid to rest. Even so it was the 1930s before dust extraction and dust suppression was seriously tackled, and dust-induced lung diseases were recognised as compensatable complaints, for which employers could be held liable. Since by this time many employers had gone out of business, victims were denied any source of redress. It was not until 1979 that a Government scheme was enacted to grant such men, or such few of them who were then still surviving; appropriate compensation.

The report also drew attention to the awful conditions prevailing in barracks and the plight of men who having walked many miles in rain to work, would spend the day in wet clothes, either on exposed open rock faces, draughty sheds or in watery conditions underground. As a result, serious disability was more likely to be the result of disease than traumatic causes. Added to which, even in the large quarries with sick pay schemes, economic necessity could force an ill or injured man to return to work before recovery was complete. For all its faults the report was a damning condemnation of conditions in the industry.

The Llechwedd strike of 1893 was the first ever serious dispute at Blaenau Ffestiniog, and indeed was to be the only one of any consequence for almost a century to come. Over the years there had been occasional brief strikes, but disputes were invariably settled quickly, amicably and without rancour. The managers who were virtually all local men with a sound quarrying background, were always ready to listen to and act on, genuine grievances properly presented. Blaenau owners were also for the most part realistic over concessions.

When trade took an upturn in 1892 a wage increase was sought, although the basic 5/-(25p) per day which was granted at the end of the year, was not far short of the men's expectations, some dissatisfaction remained. This dissatisfaction was strongest at Llechwedd, where undoubtedly due to the increased wage costs, the Greaves brothers (sons of J.W. who had retired in 1870 and died in 1880), felt the need to tighten up on working practices. Also due to the constraints of water supply, some men had to work on a 'split-shift' basis that involved them in unpaid waiting time. J.E.Greaves did not help matters by dismissing the discontent as being merely due to *'Union activities'*. Actually with only about a quarter of the men belonging, and many of them being in arrears with their dues, the Union did not loom large at Blaenau.

In May of 1893, when a man allegedly finishing early was ordered back to work, 486 men, almost the entire workforce, walked out. The strike lasted 16 acrimonious weeks before the men came back, having gained few concessions.

The 1896-7 Penrhyn dispute was to prove a more serious matter, and its effects would spread far beyond that one quarry. The seeds had been sown in the previous decade or two, in 1896 they sprouted. Not that the germination was without nurture, for Young, motivated by a profit sharing contract, pursued a drive for ever greater efficiency, suspending, sacking and abrogating long-tolerated practices. Much resented was his introduction of outside contractors to clear waste and rubble. Exception was also taken to the appointment of 'Safety Inspectors' who were perceived as management spies.

There was growing disenchantment amongst many of

the men with the Union. The widening of the franchise in 1884, having ended the Tory landowner's grip on Council and Parliamentary seats, it was felt that Union officials were using their positions to further personal political ambitions. Their position vis-á-vis management was questioned, even W. J. Parry, being heavily dependent on his supply contracts with Penrhyn quarry, suffered some mistrust. (This anomaly was corrected when Young, alleging overcharging, ceased to do business with him). Increasingly, politicians were also seen as exploiting the problems of the industry in general and Penrhyn in particular for self-advertisement.

On several occasions during the 90s there had been times when management's intransigence, might have met with more robust responses but a combination of confusion and indifference averted any positive action by the Penrhyn men.

The appointment in 1896 of D.R.Daniel as full-time organiser, put Union matters on a firmer footing, and in fact a strike was planned for 1897, if the demands for wage increases and so on had not be met, (by which time Union finances were expected to be in better shape). However in September 1896 these plans were overtaken by events. A number of men were suspended for having taken a day off to attend a political rally.

A complete stoppage ensued.

The Union was too ill-funded to offer much support but many men were able to find other work. Some were taken on by other slate or granite quarries, others by the contractors building the Snowdon Mountain Railway, and the waterworks at Lake Vrynwy. A regrettable number left the area for good.

It was August 1897 before there was an agreement to return to work. The Union claimed that *'Substantial concessions'* had been won, but Young's view that he had *'Obtained complete victory on every point'*, was probably a more accurate assessment of the outcome.

With the Penrhyn dispute settled, and management's

right to manage apparently vindicated, the industry forged ahead. Blaenau's growth found a new impetus and Nantlle positively boomed, Pen yr Orsedd alone employing 450 and turning out 13,741 tons. In the northeast, Moelfferna's manning leapt to almost 200, four times their total less than a decade earlier.

Again there was a spate of new but usually hopeless diggings. At remote Cwm Du in the upper Dyfi there was an attempt to make a fresh opening and several non-hopes holes were tunnelled in the Arthog area. Maes y Gamfa emboldened by the success of its chimneypiece trade, built a connection to the Hendre Ddu tramway.

By 1898 tonnage for the Welsh industry nudged an unprecedented half million, with manning nearing 17,000, but a close look at the statistics might have given pause for thought. Penrhyn and Dinorwig did not fully share this growth and in some quarries output actually fell, Votty & Bowydd's 1898 figures being well short of their 17,000 tons of 1897. Generally however, the prospects for the New Year of 1899 looked bright, the slight difficulties at the Cape causing no anxiety in the industry. But as it became clear that Boer farmers were running rings round the British Army, business confidence was affected, Bank Rate rose, the building industry faltered and orders fell off. There was concern, but little serious worry in an industry so well accustomed to temporary setbacks.

In early 1900 continuing bad war news kept trade flat. Following the national euphoria in May at the relief of Mafeking, there came reports of British advances. These and the election defeat of the Liberals regarded by some as *'Dangerous reformers'* meant that towards the end of the year, business optimism was widespread. Those in the slate trade looked forward to an imminent return to the growth that the course of the 19th century slate had doubled the population of Meirionnydd to almost 49,000 and trebled Caernarfonshire's to almost 127,000.

Then came the second great stoppage at Penrhyn.

It is difficult to make any comment on the 1900-1903 cessation of work without immediately taking sides. It has been called a Strike, it has been called a Lockout, and even now, in parts of Bethesda, it may still be wise to be wary of which term one uses. But whichever term one does use, it was immediately apparent that 1897, serious though it was, had merely been a trailer of the main event.

To pursue the same analogy, the scenario was now somewhat different. The conciliatory W. J. Williams, the Union secretary, had resigned as had the president, the able W.J.Parry. The old team of outside men, whose interests embraced the Radical cause on a broad basis, had been replaced by quarrymen, whose interests were more narrowly focused on the industry. They were men who perceived that a quarter of a century's persuasion had achieved little, and that a more vigorous and militant approach was called for. Not all the men approved this change of emphasis, which caused some further disenchantment with the Union. This apparent decline in the support for the Union and its leadership did not escape the notice of management.

In 1899, a trivial incident had occurred, which whilst illustrating the delicacy of relations, also tells us something of the men's character. Lord Penrhyn made it known that he would refuse to allow his daughter (one of twelve!) to accept a wedding present from the men, apparently because the collection had been organised by the Union. This caused resentment out of all proportion to its importance. Even more inflammatory was Young's edict at the end of the year that Bangor Fair days would no longer be holidays.

Young was on a high, the quarry showed a profit of nearly £120,000 in 1899, of which his share was over £3,500, enabling him to live in a style to which he was rapidly becoming accustomed. (He employed 4 domestic servants, 2 nursemaids and a governess; he had a yacht and in 1899 boasted that certain of his investments had increased in value by £30,000). That year his second-in-command D. Pritchard fell ill and had to retire. Whilst never disloyal, Pritchard had been a moderating influence on some of Young's worst excesses. His successor was H.P.Meares who, having been an engineer in India was well accustomed to dealing with 'native labour', had no intention of being a moderating influence on anybody. Thus backed, Young introduced various economies such as reducing the rate of new pensions, from 7/6 (37.5p) to 5/- (25p) per week, and restricting them to *necessitous men of good character'*. It was said that he dismissed for alleged misconduct several senior men nearing retirement to avoid paying them pensions. When it became apparent early in 1900 that profits (and hence his cut) were likely to be down, his attitude became draconian. In April, knowing that the Union was short of funds, he forbade the collection of union dues on quarry property. A measure, which having regard to the wide scattering of the men's homes, should have made continued collection almost impossible. Far from harming the union, this edict had the unexpected effect of causing a flood of applications to join or re-join.

Throughout the summer of 1900 there was friction at Penrhyn not only between management and men, but also between the men seen as accepting the rigid regime and those who resisted it. In October, there was trouble in a gallery where there had previously been disputes and suspensions over lettings. Violence broke out, quarry property was damaged and a man was injured. The next month there were further disturbances, resulting in police intervention. Twenty-six men were prosecuted and although eighteen were acquitted, all were dismissed. The magistrates fearing trouble, sought military assistance, but when a large number of quarrymen abandoned work to march to Bangor in support of their victimised colleagues, there were no incidents. Management responded to this absenteeism by suspending the whole quarry for two weeks, at the end of which time, when Bargains were re-let, a number of men were not offered work. Almost the entire near 3000 workforce walked out, and the quarry gates were shut behind them. This was neither a strike nor a lockout, it was war. The issues were complex, but the men's grievances were aptly summarised at the time by Richard Greaves (Who had taken over management of Llechwedd from his brother J. E.) as – *'The contract system, the managers' lack of practical experience and a general nostalgia for the times when things were slackly run'.*

The Radical London press took an immediate interest and dispatched reporters, making the dispute a matter of countrywide debate. In fact in December, when the first real discussions took place between the Union and management, they were brought together largely by the efforts of Clement Edwards, a Daily News journalist. At these discussions management did offer some concessions, but they were so trivial that the men rejected them out of hand. (Clement Edwards' daughter related some of her father's reminiscences to the author, when he had the pleasure of accompanying her on her first visit to Penrhyn quarry, over 80 years later).

Increasingly, prominent Radical politicians such as David Lloyd George identified themselves with the dispute, but how much this was due to a real concern for the issues, or how much it was an opportunity to get personal press coverage is not clear. Certainly, attempts were made to couple support for the Penrhyn men with opposition to the South African war, likening the quarrymen to the Boer farmers, a comparison that both parties would doubtless have hotly repudiated. Matters remained relatively quiet for some months, with the quarry at a standstill. In June 1901 when Lord Penrhyn reopened the gates offering work to all those who would accept his terms, about 400 men opted to do so. Resentment was fanned by a rumour that these men received a sovereign each from his Lordship personally and allegedly, an increase in wages. Events now took a more serious turn, there were periodic disturbances, *'Y Bradwyr'* (The Traitors) and their families, were threatened; troops were again called in and arrests made.

New Year's Eve brought the first ugliness, there were violent clashes and troops were deployed in strength. Such scenes were not repeated, but throughout the whole of 1902 there was stalemate. Lord Penrhyn refused to deal with what he called 'deputations' and hardened his attitude, all attempts at arbitration failing. There were evictions from quarry-owned cottages, occupied by strikers or men who had obtained work elsewhere, the properties being re-let to 'loyal' men. Messages of approval for Lord Penrhyn came from many quarters, Assheton-Smith of Dinorwig being understandably one of his warmest supporters. This support did not however prevent him from poaching Penrhyn's customers, and taking on Penrhyn men, increasing his workforce to over 3000. By 1903 Penrhyn affairs had become a subject of Parliamentary debate, but more as a stick for Liberal members to beat Tory landowners in general, rather than quarry owners in particular, which further clouded the local issues.

In April that year Lord Penrhyn won a libel action against W. J. Parry. The previous year Parry had re-opened Pantdreiniog quarry providing work for 50 men, a costly enterprise which together with the libel costs, the loss of his Penrhyn contracts and a serious fire at his yard, almost bankrupted him. Whilst Parry no longer held office he still very much epitomized the men's cause and his setbacks were seen as a moral gain for Lord Penrhyn. Union funds, meagre from the start, and despite being augmented by other workers' movements and by public appeals, were dwindling.

On the other hand, the quarry was doing relatively well,

the workforce augmented by outside men, such as lead miners, had edged up to 1100, and with the bargain teams reduced from four to three, unprecedented productivity was claimed. (By concentrating the reduced workforce on easily worked faces, postponing maintenance and suspending all development, higher than normal tonnages per man could well have resulted). This enabled management to refuse to countenance any talk of full re-engagement, it being claimed that *'not above 2000'* would be required for full-scale working. By late 1903 the Union with outside support fading was fighting a rearguard action, with fewer than 600 men actually on strike. On 7th November with an increasing number of men applying to be taken back, a vote to end the strike was passed by a small majority.

The men were utterly defeated, the village was demoralised, even the chapels so central to the quarrymen's solidarity, lost much of their influence. The pre-eminence of Bethesda in the affairs of the industry evaporated. Within 4 years Lord Penrhyn was dead, within 5 years the NWQMU, with Penrhyn membership at an all-time low had, with the appointment of R. T. Jones as its sole full-time official, become Blaenau Ffestiniog centred.

Besides those moving to other slate districts, 200 Bethesda men had emigrated, a similar number had found work outside the industry, many going to the collieries of south Wales, (where their skill with timbering and general adaptability, was much sought after). Those that remained and all their counterparts in other quarries would find themselves in very changed circumstances in the years to come.

LIST OF MANNING AND OUTPUTS OF MEIRIONNYDD UNDERGROUND SLATE QUARRIES 1895

Men below ground. Men above ground. Tonnage

Blaenau Ffestiniog

Oakeley (Rhiwbryfdir, Cesail, Gloddfa Ganol)

	736	916	56589
Llechwedd	222	264	15615
Votty & Bowydd	251	212	14537
Maenofferen	167	161	11047
Cwmorthin	183	108	6910
Rhosydd	108	78	4962
Wrysgan	41	55	3006
Diffwys	57	29	1136
Par	14	15	409
Bwlch y Slaters	5	11	270
Moelwyn	4	-	76
Manod	2	-	-
Fronboeth	-	1	-
Conglo	-	-	-
Foelgron	-	-	-

Corris

Braich Goch (+Gaewern)	58	90	6044
Aberllefenni	73	59	4440
Abercorris	14	21	3884
Cymerau	11	10	530
Ratgoed	7	5	232

South Meirionnydd

Bryneglwys	97	88	6385
Minllyn	12	8	550
Penrhyngwyn	3	-	4
Henddol	-	1	-

East Meirionnydd (now Denbighshire)

Moelfferna	40	84	4955
Penarth	-	-	-

11. THE GREAT DECLINE
The 1900s

It is said that the industry never recovered from the Penrhyn dispute. Indeed the start of its steep and ultimately near-terminal decline coincided with that calamitous stoppage, but the decline largely arose from other causes. At most the Penrhyn events accelerated a contraction that external factors had already made inevitable.

The peak year of output was 1898, thus by the time the Penrhyn gates were shut, demand for Welsh slate was already falling. Although the late 1890s had seemed a boom era, in fact Welsh slate's share of the total potential market decreased. By 1895 imported tonnages had reached an unprecedented 20,000, and boosted by the shortages and price rises during the Penrhyn stoppage, their inexorable advance continued. Again the inroads that tiles made during the slate shortage of the early 1900s had their beginnings in the high prices of the 1870's. In addition galvanised sheeting and so on, now offered a quick and cheap alterative to the laborious laying of slate or tiles, for agricultural and industrial buildings. By the turn of the century even the roofs of some quarry buildings were sheeted.

The Penrhyn stoppage has been blamed for the almost total absence of outside investment in ensuing years but in fact capital inflow had already almost vanished. In 1866, prospectuses totalling almost a million pounds were issued, most of which were taken up. Apart from some flurries during the mid 1870s, offerings steadily tapered off until in 1899 there was just one £8000 company floated.

But there had been a more insidious factor, lack of modernisation. The slate industry entered the 20th century with a methodology established in the first half of the 19th. Obviously this was in part due to the dearth of new money coming in, but chiefly because of the 'boom or bust' nature of the industry. In good times with profits rolling in, there seemed no need to invest, and in bad times with mounting losses, there were no resources to do so.

A further factor was the endemic reluctance to accept new ideas – the slate industry was a bastion of '*We've always done it like this*'. For instance, pneumatic drills that owners such as the Darbishires of Pen yr Orsedd had proved successful in the late 1880s were still rare a decade later. It was alleged that power drilling produced cracks in the drill-holes into which powder penetrated causing a shattering of the rock. Mechanical drills did indeed produce more waste, which increased the cost of rubbish clearing, but this was a small penalty against drilling being up to fifty times faster. Even taking full account of equipment costs, power drills more than halved the price per foot of shot-hole drilling, which was a major part of extraction costs. Even the men who would be relieved of the dreadful toil of the *Jwmpah*, opposed powered drills. Penrhyn did not adopt them until 1912 and Dinorwig did not use them until 1919, even in the 1920s some managers were still expressing reservations about them.

Again, in order to make a start at the foot of a working face, where no suitable natural joints were manifest, compressed-air channelling machines (Basically air drills on a traversing frame) were available to quickly cut a 'free end' yet they were not taken up even where compressed air was available. As late as 1923, Captain (later Colonel). Martyn Williams-Ellis grandson of J. W. Greaves, who joined Llechwedd in 1919, stated '*The majority of quarries are still continuing to waste rock by blasting for footings*'.

Wire sawing is also a case in point. Cornish slate quarries that were using them by the beginning of the 20th century, demonstrated that they could almost eliminate extraction waste and produce blocks with at least one sawn end thus facilitating mill work. Early wire saws, consisted of an endless wire typically 3/16' (4.75mm) thick, cutting the rock by being fed with sand and water. These wires might be several hundred yards long, led over pulleys to a distant steam engine. Modern ones are self-contained units with integral compressed air motors, cutting by diamond-impregnated collars threaded onto the wire. Apart from some experiments at Oakeley in the 1930s, they were not used in Wales until the 1980s (at Maenofferen, Llechwedd and Aberllefenni).

Mill sawing was the outstanding example of out-datedness. Diamond saws were available in the 1900s (In fact a John Jones of Bwlch y Slaters quarry filed a patent for one in 1903) yet well into the 20th century, some quarries were still using sand saws, the rest still had Greaves pattern machines devised in the 1850s, the sole later upgrade being the occasional substitution of Tungsten Carbide tipped blades. This reduced blade-changing downtime but did nothing for rates of cut since it was impracticable to run the saws at high speeds Carbide demanded.

The case for diamond saws was overwhelming, even the earliest machines had a feed rate of up to 12' (300mm) per minute, at least 4 times that of the traditional saw (modern machines routinely work at, 30' (750mm) per minute.). This obviously dramatically speeded work, but these saws were much more versatile, they could traverse, obviating the slow and laborious task of exactly locating the block on the table, both ends of blocks could be sawn on the same set-up and the lesser feed forces eliminated the need to secure blocks to the table. A further advantage was a cut devoid of saw-marks, so that the sawn edges of slabs often do not need further finishing. Steel blades may start off at 24'(600mm), but re-sharpening soon takes them down to 20' (500mm), reducing their depth of cut and their peripheral speed and hence their efficiency. Diamond blades can be much larger, up to 80' (2000mm) and more, and maintain their diameter regardless. They also cut many thousands of feet without attention, as against the tens of feet of a steel blade. The

195

obviation of the almost daily chore of blade changing in itself can in itself mean a 10% gain in operating time. Diamond saws were such an improvement that contemporary advice on their installation warned that the output would be so much greater than the 15 Cwt or so per day of steel saws, that the entire handling arrangements of the mill would have to be revised to cope.

Such high outputs with saw speeds of 1500 rpm called for many times the approximately $\frac{1}{2}$-1 hp needed by the old tables. This could only be met by electrical power.

The first electrified quarry might have been Dorothea as in 1896 a costing exercise fully justified the £16,000 estimate for a hydro-plant. It was only legal problems over water rights that forced the scheme's abandonment, hence when ten years later they had to upgrade their pumps to de-water their 550' deep pit, they installed an archaic Cornish steam pump.

Llechwedd experimented with on-site generation in 1891, putting in a full-scale 500 kW hydro plant in 1904. This showed immediate economies over clumsy, high maintenance water wheels for mill driving and incline power. For pumping, electricity obviated the use of the curious pumping-cum-haulage water wheel remotely sited above a shaft at Owain Goch. Unusually, they also used electricity for drilling.

In the meantime the innovative Moses Kellow, having consolidated his position as manager of Parc quarry by marrying the owner's daughter, re-opened Croesor in 1895 after a 17-year closure, where also in 1904 he had installed electricity. His 350 Kw, 500V hydro installation of his own design was very much 'State of the Art' being 3 phase A.C. For mill drive and winches 10 hp motors were used, there was a 30 hp. loco and a 90 hp winder. DC. Excitation was provided by a dynamo that also lit the mill, part of the workings and Kellow's house. Moses Kellow also developed (and manufactured on site) a patent hydraulic drill that was not widely adopted due to the vast quantities of water it both consumed and discharged (mostly over the operator!). He invented a hydraulic channelling machine and developed an innovative high-pressure pump. His many creations included hydraulic motors and various dewatering equipment. He made improvements in sawing and in underground working methods. Whilst not all his devices were completely successful, he was arguably the most ingenious engineer the slate industry ever had.

At both Llechwedd and Croesor electricity enabled the mill engine to be replaced by a motor but the installation would not have been able to support the independent drives that diamond saws would have called for.

The first public electricity supply was from the Yale Company's 589 KW Dolwen hydro plant of 1899. Votty & Bowydd, as a major shareholder, took most of its output, enabling them to abandon their steam engines, but not to consider diamond saws. These had to wait almost 30 years until the 28 MW Maentwrog hydro station came on stream.

Supply on a wider scale was offered in 1905 by the North Wales Power Company's 6 MW Cwm Dyli power station. Pen yr Orsedd immediately took advantage of it, followed by Oakeley and Dinorwig and a few years later, Maenofferen. In 1930, the latter augmented this source with its own hydro plant. Its 24' Turbo-impulse wheel was rated at 345 hp. Water at 915 cu/ft per min. on a 250' head, turning it at 550 rpm producing 257 KW at 510/580v.

These first public suppliers charged 1d (.4p) per KWh, equivalent to .313p per hp per hour. This in coal terms was equal to £2.80 per ton, (2½lb /hp/hr.), over double the actual price of coal. However the far greater efficiency of electricity, the fact that it was only used as needed instead of having a boiler continuously in steam (and required no fireman and little maintenance), outweighed the apparent higher cost. When after WW1 the price of electricity halved and that of coal almost doubled, the case for electrification became overwhelming.

In the meantime quarries with electricity remained in the minority. Penrhyn did not have a supply until 1912, and was not fully electrified until 1938, (by which time it had its own 330Kw hydro plant as well as taking something like 1.5 Mw from the public supply). Gradually over the years a few others including Bryneglwys (which also supplied Abergynolwyn village), put in hydro units, and others put in Diesel generators. It was a slow process, Dorothea in spite of their early electrification plans, only finally put in a Diesel unit in the 1930s. Some such as Llwyngwern, Manod, Moelfferna and Penarth powered their generators with producer gas engines. The engines worked well enough but cooking coke to obtain this noxious and barely flammable fuel was a black art. In 1928 Capt. Matthews of Manod quarry complained of *'The hours lost each day as men struggle to start the gas engine'*. Even in 1930 at Blaenau, with two hydro stations just down the road as it were. Cwt y Bugail, Graig Ddu, Rhosydd and Wrysgan were all without electric power.

One of the first, if not the first to use a diamond saws was not one of the 'biggies' but Moelfferna who, realising their error in equipping with sand saws, installed an Anderson Grice machine and appropriate oil-engined generator in 1923. The daunting outlay on blades was overcome by renting them on the basis of the number of feet cut, a practice that afterwards became quite customary. The blade/motor unit was mounted on a travelling bridge that was advanced by hand, the block remaining stationary, Modern machines have power feed, the feed motor speed automatically controlled by the amperage demand of the blade motor.

In spite of the fact that at least ten times as much rubbish as good block had to be shifted, improvements in handling were almost entirely confined to good block. For instance, when Cambrian was efficiently sending its block to the mill via their tunnel beneath the workings, they were still laboriously up hauling most of their waste.

Such things as water-balances were clung to, even in quarries with an electric supply, in the belief that they were 'free', yet it was shown that the slowness, high maintenance and labour intensiveness of such devices made them far more costly to run than electric haulages. In 1938 Votty and Bowydd were still using a water balance which the Quarry Managers' Journal described as *'70 years old, lifting only one truck at a time and taking five minutes to do so. Men at the top and the bottom are required to operate the valves, as the automatic stops have not worked for many years.'*

Again, many Welsh quarries had been in the forefront in the adoption of steam locos, but they were retained long after electric traction had been shown to be more economical, (and could be run on lighter track). It was understandable that due to the problems of overhead wires, particularly underground, Moses Kellow's initiative in using electric locos was not widely copied. But even when suitable accumulators became available, battery-electric traction was not very widely taken up. Such units were more expensive to buy and run than wire-fed electric locos but were proven cheaper than steam and certainly more economical than the horses that were still widely employed.

A 1912 calculation showed a horse as costing 17/6 (87.5p) per week to feed, plus 2/3 (11.5p) for depreciation, and £1.00 driver's wages, while the weekly costs of a battery loco were over £4.00. But, although the loco cost twice as much it could do five times the work Conductor type locos were reckoned to run out at around £3.50, whilst to keep a loco in steam could cost almost £6.00. Llechwedd at least, would eventually use all electric traction with, by the early 1930s, battery locos underground and overhead-wire on the surface (the latter being mostly in-house conversions on old steam locos under-frames). Despite this example and even when cheap and versatile internal-combustion locos became available, many quarries clung loyally to old, and often worn-out steam locos, a further manifestation of the conservatism of the industry.

Anyway, up to date or not, in the early 1900s quarries vied to make up the shortfall caused by the Penrhyn stoppage that had abruptly cut Welsh output by almost 20%. In spite of some slackness in the building trade, it was all go, with by 1903, the best slate fetching more than the peak prices of 1876.

In Nantlle, Moeltryfan put in 7 new saws in 1904 to bring their total to 44 and had a record payroll of almost 300, (105 Bargainers, 52 Rubbishers, 34 Badrockmen, 44 Untoppers, 3 Weighers and 39 on various duties). Daily wages averaged from a little over 5/- (25p) for the Bargainers to not much more than half that for the Rubbishers. Braich Rhyd had 58 men and was putting in a new drainage tunnel and Braich itself had 80 men and 13 saw tables. Fron had 39 men, with 8 saws in the mill (they had taken on 50 men when they re-opened in 1901, but this included men on development). Of the big quarries only Cilgwyn and Alexandra, each with 200 men at work were below their best ever but still were fairly buoyant. In spite of this general briskness, some of the smaller workings fared less well. Brynfferam, for instance, after stumbling on with a handful of men, had folded in 1902.

At Llanberis, Cefn Ddu had around 125 men at work, (including 20 at Bwlch y Groes) and Cook & Ddol had 25 men and had installed 7 new saws. In Cwm Gwyrfai, Hafod y Wern employed 36. In the Bethesda area at Moel Faban, Afon Wen and Cwm Bychan, 16 men, 8 men and 2 men respectively, found employment that was denied them at Penrhyn. Elsewhere some very small diggings were revived, such as the ancient Tal y Fan near Conwy where 7 men were working.

In Caernarfonshire as a whole, times were undoubtedly

good, although not as good as a County Council publicity leaflet claimed. This leaflet issued partly to counteract the impression that the Penrhyn stoppage had paralysed the whole county, stated that 99 slate quarries in the county were working; a considerable exaggeration.

In the Blaenau area 18 quarries were going flat out, with even the smallest doing well. Llechwedd had a record payroll of well over 600, Bwlch y Slaters with 52 men were talking of expansion and considering putting in electricity, even planning to light the chambers. (They didn't!) The somewhat marginal Pantmawr had their 20 men making fresh underground developments. Blaen y Cwm had 12 men, and was making new works, as were Graig Ddu and Cwt y Bugail. Little Foelgron had 8 men, Drum 4 and Croes y Ddwy Afon had an astonishing 62.

Further south such scratchings as Rhaeadr got in on the act, and near Denbigh, Aber's 3 men and Nantglyn's 4 were busy anachronistically hand-working their slab products, taking advantage of the larger quarries preoccupation with roofing slate. Several workings with just a couple of saws and half a dozen men such as Aberdunant, Bryn Glas and Cwm Teigl that had been squeezed out by the big guns were re-activated.

This euphoria was short lived, for apart from the extra tonnage as Penrhyn's production built up, the building industry took a further downturn. Blaenau suffered an additional setback when their main export outlet, Germany, imposed a 30% import duty on slate. By 1904 with imports booming, the market went into surplus, bringing to a stop the shortage-driven price rises.

The 1905 lists came out 5-7% down, and there was an unprecedented further mid-year price cut, a step which had not been necessary even in the tough times of the late 1870s. Wages were reduced by around 5% and men were laid off or put on short time. There was a wave of strikes particularly in the Nantlle area, which were not entirely unwelcome to owners carrying heavy stocks and hard put to meet wage bills.

A continuing fall in demand drove tonnages for 1906 almost 25% below those of a couple of years before, with prices slashed by a similar percentage. In the Nantlle area Cilgwyn held up well with 217 men and Fron was up to 44, but generally things were grim, Alexandra was down to 190 and Moeltryfan to 243, many of whom were on short time. Others such as Nant y Fron only recently a 100-man operation, slid into closure. Elsewhere several smaller quarries such as Croes y Ddwy Afon, Foelgron and Henddol closed. The newly revived Aberdunant also succumbed but Cwm Teigl and the recently re-opened Arthog clung on with a mere 3 men at each. Against the trend the Pantdreinion/Tan y Bwlch/Moel Tryfan co-operative was doing well with around 100 men and Hafod y Wern increased its payroll to 54.

The tiny diggings that jobless Penrhyn men had started in all sorts of unlikely and out of the way places north of Bethesda, folded. Those that did find rock, often had to carry their make many miles at the end of the day to be sold for a few pennies to help feed a family. Some had found nothing; scarcely any repaid the labour of tunnelling and the erection of crude shelters.

It was becoming clear that the 1901-1904 mini-boom had been just a respite from an inexorable shrinkage, Hafod y Wern recruiting heavily in 1905, was virtually at a standstill a year later. Bwlch Cwmllan, never able to afford the rail link to the NWNGR that would have obviated the expensive cartage to Rhyd Ddu, stumbled into nothingness.

The industry was in trouble, deep trouble and no part of it more so than the slab trade. Some folk might still want slate on their roofs but not on their floors. The fashion was for mantelpieces of timber not slate, concrete lintels, windowsills and doorsteps were coming into widespread use. Galvanised tanks and cement rendering were displacing slate on the farms. Gentlemen now relieved themselves against Messrs. Shanks' wares, and the gruesome slate privy seat was now just a chilly memory. Even in the graveyards, the more pretentious tended to be memorialised in alien stone.

A lucrative market was wiped out when it was realised that the most discerning cueist could not distinguish billiards tables with the 1' thick Italian beds from those with the traditional 2' thick Welsh ones. Penrhyn did retain some billiards table trade with Germany, but it is said that in fact the slabs were required for fabricating vats for the production of explosives! The newfangled electric installations did call for slate switchboards, but their requirements were as yet modest. The problems of the slab-dependant quarries were compounded by some mixed-product units using their market muscle to poach their customers. Braich Goch fell victim in 1906, gutting the village of Corris, partly from these competitive pressures, partly due to having dispersed boom-time profits, leaving management unable to fund urgent development work.

Export prospects were far from good. More overseas countries, nurturing indigenous slate industries, imposed tariffs, which even where these did not actually close a market, forced prices down. Vainly men showed their protest, particularly again in Nantlle by a number of strikes. From 1907 to 1909 sales sagged further, listed prices did edge up, but whether many buyers actually paid increased prices is questionable, particularly as import prices were tumbling. A London merchant who had paid £7 5 0 (£7.25) for a mille of French slate in 1906, claimed he could by 1909 obtain the same grade and size for £5 2 6 (£5.125). Oakeley laid off 350 men, but as always, there were little diggings that somehow bucked the trend. The abandoned and isolated Powys quarry revived and nearby Cwmmaengwynedd found work for 20 men, about five times their usual number, but these were ephemeral exceptions.

1910 and 1911 were better years, with some slight recovery in sales and some firming of prices. But the Pantdreiniog/Tan y Bwlch/Moel Tryfan co-operative once a 270 man operation, failed, leaving just Pantdreiniog to continue under new ownership until 1926. All the several attempts at worker ownership proved fragile. Co-operative working at Cook and Ddol was no more successful than had been the Union working of Llyn y Gader in 1881.

In 1912 tonnages dropped again. Bad debt increased, with even some reputable merchants failing, owing substantial sums to quarrying firms. In 1912 Pen yr Orsedd lost £582 and Tal y Sarn £82 when Smith of Nottingham went through, and that summer several other Nantlle quarries reported bad trade and credit problems. In fact most in the Nantlle area were finding times hard, Gloddfa'r Coed which had once employed 150 men were now down to 7. Those on Crown leases were seeking abatement of dues. It being pointed out that a quarry lease was typically at 30/- (£1.50) per acre, whereas similar land was let for agriculture at only £1. Plus Crown royalties ran at 2/ – 2/6 (10p – 12.5p) against the 1/6 – 1/10 (7.5p – 9p) charged by many private landowners. It was claimed that anything up to 40 tons or more of debris had to be shifted for every ton of slate made. At 9d (3.75p) per ton this could add up to almost half the average selling price of £3 10 0 (£3.50) per ton. In addition, several Nantlle quarries were spending 2/- (10p) on pumping for each ton of slate made, and one was said to be spending 5/- (25p) per ton. Even the ever-buoyant Llechwedd laid off 90 men.

For 1913, prices were boldly jacked up to levels close to 1903-04 figures, which did help margins a little, but helped imports a lot, making Britain for the first time ever a net importer of slate. An untimely strike in the building trade pushed Welsh production down to 300,000 tons, and manning to 9000, a drop of nearly 40% in little more than a decade. Tan yr Allt closed making some 70 men idle, nearby Fron was fading fast. Rhiwbach failed, as did the following year, the very efficient Parc & Croesor Company, and in Meirionnydd generally many found trade difficult.

One tiny section of the industry that did seem to hold its own were the little quarries producing whetstones. These hones besides being used by woodworkers for their edge tools, also replaced the traditional wooden rips which, coated with grease and sand, were used to sharpen scythes and sickles. Handfuls of men managed to survive at tiny sites at Pen y Pass, in Nant Gwynant, in the Ogwen Valley, on the Glyders and at Llyn Crafnant, each making 2 or 3 tons per year. All that was required was a source of close-grained rock. With such a small weight of product no elaborate transport was needed. Thus with a tonnage value of perhaps £30, these little ventures could be relatively profitable. Melynllyn had a water-driven sand-saw, as did Penrhiw that survived until almost 1920; when it was squeezed out by the same pressures of factory-made product and foreign competition as beset the slate industry proper.

With the 1913 price increases seen as counter productive, prices for 1914 were cut by 5%, with inevitably, a reduction in wages; exacerbating the problems caused by layoffs and giving rise to disputes such as the 4 month strike by the 220 men at Alexandra. This Alexandra strike heralded a new direction in industrial relations, as it was an official Union call-out. The strikes around 1905-06, with the NWQMU in disarray, had been backed by the chapels rather than the Union. The more serious confrontations of earlier years, although union supported, had not been actually initiated by the union. This change was due to the energetic leadership of R. T. Jones who, having greatly increased the Union's membership, had taken matters out of the hands of the quarry lodges and placed them firmly in the central committee's control. Within a few years Jones would achieve almost 100% membership, enabling the NWQMU to speak with one voice on behalf of all the workers in the industry.

The old order was also changing on the management side. Besides there being a new Lord Penrhyn, E.A.Young had died in 1910. Two years later W.E.Oakeley, little more than an onlooker since his quarries had been in the hands of a limited company dominated by Hoare's bank, also passed on. New men were emerging, owing their position to ability and energy rather than descent or privilege. They would bring new ideas and a new ethos, not only to the industry but also to society in general. Like their predecessors they would hold office as Councillors, Magistrates, High Sheriffs and Lords Lieutenant, but unlike them, as servants of their communities rather than as masters.

But of course, far greater changes were at hand. In early 1914 trade remained slack, but by mid year there seemed grounds for sober optimism. The long dry summer did pose problems of water shortage, but the shooting of a foreign princeling in an obscure Balkan town, cannot have caused great anxiety in the cabans, the taverns or even the boardrooms of Bethesda and Blaenau.

12. DOGGED STRUGGLES
1914-1939

The outbreak of war in August 1914 put the slate trade into confusion. Commercial confidence ebbed, the building industry wound down, orders were cancelled and exports (and imports) vanished. All shipping movements were strictly controlled, quarry steamers were commandeered for war service, some such as the Penrhyn vessel Linda Blanche soon to be torpedoed. Rail carriage was uncertain, civilian consignments often being left in sidings to clear the tracks for troop trains and 'Jellicoe Specials' carrying coal for the fleet. Several quarries closed and most others went to short time working. A number had their financial problems exacerbated by large sums outstanding from German customers.

However by 1916 in spite of the ban on building, it was not the shortage of orders or the problems of transport that was constricting output, but the shortage of men. A great many had volunteered for the forces, others had taken jobs in war factories, a number of which had been set up in or near the quarries, taking advantage of the industry's equipment and technical expertise. One such factory making shells at the FR.'s Boston Lodge works requisitioned. Llechwedd's steam haulage engine. (An electric motor was installed as a replacement).

In 1917 the slate industry was classed as non-essential and many of its remaining men were conscripted into the forces or directed into work of 'National Importance'. The standard pay for the latter being £2 12 6 (£2.62) per week, plus 17/6 (87.2p) lodging allowance. This was widely considered derisory, but to slate workers it must have seemed handsome. A few quarries broke with tradition by employing women in their offices. Women such as Miss Kane who owned Pen yr Orsedd in the 1850s had been involved in management, women had helped their menfolk by carrying slates from tiny early diggings and girls at one time tended strings of pannier-ponies. This apart, female employment was unknown. Some quarries barred women underground even as visitors, in the belief that a death would ensue.

Additionally, the non-essential classification put the quarries at the back of the queue for coal and other vital supplies. Blaenau output with fewer than 900 men at work dropped to 20,000 tons, less than a quarter of the immediate pre-war total, Llechwedd had 110 men compared with a peak of over 600. Other areas were slightly less badly hit, but the 1917 Welsh total of less than 100,000 tons and 3000 men was little more than Penrhyn or Dinorwig could have turned out a few years previously.

Quarries increasingly were having to turn business away, and merchants' yards and quarry banks were bare of even the most unsaleable varieties. Wartime paper shortages meant that even writing slates were in demand. With only 10 quarries of any size still open, demand greatly exceeded supply.

In January 1918 The Slate Trade Gazette reported '*We are informed that for some time the demand for slate has been double the output and that, as a consequence, there is likely to be a slate famine within a few months. The difficulty is, and will continue to be, the provision of adequate labour*'. Prices that had only risen by 5% since 1914, were sharply increased, followed by unprecedented quarterly revisions, which by October brought them to almost 50% above the record levels of 1903/04.

The war's end in November 1918 failed to bring any immediate surge of orders so the 1919 price list showed only modest advances, but as soon the building industry found its feet, buyers almost stormed the quarries gates. By July 1920, six-monthly jumps had taken prices to almost double those of late 1918. The Slate Trade Gazette reported in May

1920, (just prior to a further price hike), *'Best Portmadoc Blues which sold for £11 13 0 (£11.65) in 1914, fetched £27 10 0 (£27.50) last July, are now fetching £35'*.

With foreign suppliers busy with their own problems, the UK quarries had a clear run, most of the quarries such as Bryneglwys and Diffwys that had closed during the war, re-opened. A new company took on Rhiwbach, one of their first actions being to raise the charges on their tram road, to the dismay of the user quarries. Maenofferen solved the problem by arranging to run out through Votty & Bowydd (until 1928 when they bought out Rhiwbach Quarries Ltd). Bwlch y Slaters went over to road haulage (via the Cwm Teigl road), one of the first producer to forsake rail completely. With Blaen y Cwm failing to survive the war, that left just Cwt y Bugail lumbered with the increased charges.

Amalgamated Slate was formed to re-open Cilgwyn, Alexandra and Moeltryfan quarries, and soon employed over 400 men. Several of the small Nantlle workings were revived, and elsewhere even doubtful sites such as Nantyr in Glyn Ceiriog, had a new lease of life.

As regards capital, some new money was coming in, sometimes from unexpected sources, such as the 1920 purchase of Croes y Ddwy Afon and the following year of Rhosydd, by Colmans (of mustard fame). Several companies were formed, such as a £20,000 flotation to re-open Fronlog and the £35,000 company at Cwm Machno. In south Wales there was a £40,000 scheme at Glogue, to erect a 100' x 38' mill with 4 saws and 2 planers all water-turbine powered, as well as a plant to make bricks from waste. Despite the failure of the £300,000, Welsh Slate Combine offering, the two quarries involved, Cwt y Bugail and Braich Goch were successfully floated separately. But overall, capitalists generally stayed away.

Also staying away were the men. Many quarrymen had found in the forces, better food and better clothing than they had previously known. They had discovered that what the Army called a barracks was very different from say, the Rhosydd connotation of the term. After the wages paid in munitions factories, even the enhanced rewards now being offered in slate quarrying seemed paltry. Plus, there were those who could never come back, as memorials in every quarrying village testify, these were sadly numerous.

Although the skills of quarrymen were welcomed in the Royal Engineers, most proudly joined the Royal Welch Fusiliers whose distinguished traditions can be traced back to Agincourt. Their losses in France were heavy even by WW1 standards, one quarter off all skilled slate makers died. Nor were losses confined to the employees, several owners and their relatives died, among the most poignant was the death of Sir Robin Duff in November 1914, just 3 weeks after inheriting Dinorwig from his father, Sir Charles Assheton-Smith. (Before he had had the opportunity to follow the family tradition of adopting the Assheton-Smith name). It is believed that no industry suffered proportionately as many casualties in WW1 as did Welsh slate.

Apart from the shortage of men, particularly skilled men, there was a shortage of plant. New equipment was expensive and on extended delivery, and high prices were asked for such second hand items that had escaped being melted down for armaments. There were however plenty of War Department locos coming onto the market. Many of these engines, that had supplied the army's trenches and depots, were American-built using technology proved on the Ffestiniog Railway half a century before. Thus there were opportunities to modernise rail motive power, if nothing else. Some of these locos were Diesel or petrol engine units, giving some quarries their first introduction to this more economical form of traction. (Capt. T.P. Crossland's decision to replace his steam loco by a Simplex petrol unit in the long tunnel at Cambrian quarry was based on his seeing them at work in France during the war, so successful was this that a similar Planet loco was bought in 1929).

More significant in the longer term, was the great number of motor lorries the Government was releasing. Moel y Faen and Clogau had already abandoned the Oernant tramway, product being taken to Llangollen station by steam lorry. The availability of motor lorries encouraged other quarries to consider road haulage and in fact Llwyngwern bought a motor lorry to reach Machynlleth station, rather than pay for repairs to their Corris Railway bridge over the Dulas. Indeed slate could now be economically worked entirely independent of rail connection. Cwm Bach near Tremadog, one of the very few entirely new openings in the 1920s, was totally road haulage dependent.

Some slate shipments resumed, but not only were exports little more than token, but also the post-war shortage of vessels made coast-wise shipping expensive. Even after sea-freight rates collapsed, a reduction in railway rates would ensure that most U.K. distribution would be by rail. Caernarfon even handled an unprecedented slate import! (Italian slab for a manufacturing merchant in the town), and within a few years the port would be described as *'Deserted and grass-grown, with even harbour buildings being re-roofed in asbestos sheet'*.

With a fierce U.K. demand, the industry did the best it could and in 1920 neared 200,000 tons, a creditable recovery, but still only two-thirds of the worst of the immediate pre-war years. Coal continued to be scarce and expensive, serious shortages arising during the 1921 coal strike. Thus waterpower regained some of its old importance, but for several weeks in the dry summer of 1921, water shortage made up to 2000 men idle. Conversely, Dorothea would soon have too much water, for in 1922 there was a recurrence of the flooding problem, which had been disastrous in 1884 and had caused a stoppage in 1910. There were no casualties but almost 200,000 tons of ground collapsed into the pit carrying away a Blondin and two public roads. (12 years later the mess was still not fully cleared).

There were also industrial relations problems looming. In 1918 when even agricultural labourers were doing better than quarrymen, a minimum wage had been established and at least the outline of a sliding scale, tying wages to slate prices. By 1921 comparatively generous concessions on wages and hours had been recommended by both the employers' bodies, the North Wales Quarry Owners Association, who now included; Amalgamated Slate, Dinorwig, Dorothea, Penrhyn, Pen y Bryn, Pen yr Orsedd, South Dorothea, and Tal y Sarn, and the Ffestiniog & District Quarry Proprietors Association comprising Graig Ddu, Llechwedd, Maenofferen, Manod, Oakeley, Parc & Croesor and Rhiwbach. Oddly, Rhosydd and Diffwys belonged to the substantially Caernarfonshire N.W.Q.O.A, while Votty & Bowydd hedged their bets by belonging to both. These two associations (who merged in 1930) were a sort of gentlemen's club of the more affluent quarries, who could afford a more liberal attitude towards pay than their smaller competitors. Understandably those working in some of the more marginal quarries were aggrieved, as were their employers who suspected the Associations of trying to squeeze them out. Much robust correspondence was exchanged

In 1921, in spite of the problems, production was up again, tonnages well exceeding 200,000, with pundits predicting *'Ten to fifteen years of prosperity'*. But users faced with shortages and high prices, were already turning to other sources and other products. Reports began to appear that certain sizes were in poor demand, then towards the end of the year, amongst a flood of order cancellations, the queue for deliveries vanished.

It was clear that prices for 1922 would have to be slashed with wage rates reduced in accordance with the sliding scale. But, when the 1922 lists were published they had not gone down by the announced 18%, on which the wage reduction had been based, but only by 10%. Though this cut was less than the dramatic fall in living costs that occurred during late 1921, the men, understandably, felt they had been cheated out of almost 1/ (5p) per day. Furthermore, the owners thought the minimum wage was too high and they pressed to reduce it by a third. Whilst few employers would oppose the concept of a 'living wage', there was the fear that if a minimum was too close to what a poor bargain would pay, the team might be tempted to produce little or nothing.

In March there was trouble and by June almost the whole of the industry was on strike. Though a few quarries stayed idle for up to four months, most men were back in two weeks, substantially on management's terms. Throughout the industry the settlement gave little satisfaction to either side, as managements were committed to wage rates tied to list prices which were often much above levels at which sales could actually be made. The men, certainly those on short time, were still taking home poor wages. At the end of the year, with heavy stocks particularly in the smaller sizes, the 1923 lists came out a further 10% down, triggering a corresponding fall in wages. Over a couple of years average earnings fell by a third and the minimum wage was down from 12/6 (62.5p) per day to 6/6 (32.5p).

Many of the industry's problems were beginning to look fundamental. For instance, increasingly house building was by big national firms and by direct-labour municipal authorities. These big buyers demanded vast numbers of identical items, to a close specification, with tight delivery dates and possibly non-performance penalties. Few slate quarries could meet such terms, but almost any tile maker could. The continental quarries were fast recovering from the war, and although imports were well below the immediate pre-war totals, they were growing apace and in 1921 exceeded 6500 tons, with France again the main source but with Portugal sending an increasing share. Exports were a mere 3-4000 tons. The 120,000 tons that Germany had once taken had vanished and Australia once an 8000-ton market was now a trickle. A press report of the time pointed out that in *'recent years the slate industry had shown no growth, but the tile industry is now three times what it had been'*.

During 1923, difficulties continued, whilst few men were wholly unemployed, many were on short time, with Saturday working the exception. Total output fell to 160,000 tons, with the Caernarfonshire quarries being particularly badly hit, some such as Pen yr Orsedd temporarily closing. In the northeast, Deeside, tied to the declining slab market and with ageing machinery, closed.

Blaenau's position remained relatively strong. Wrysgan, which had re-opened in 1922 under new ownership, was putting in new plant. Oakeley re-opened Nyth y Gigfran by tunnelling in from its own upper workings, so eliminating the earlier vertiginous operations on narrow ledges. Bwlch y Slaters expanded, taking in the adjacent Old Manod site, Cwt y Bugail would shortly flourish under new ownership and, Glogue, south Wales' one remaining quarry of any consequence, installed 4 additional saws.

Also against the general trend that favoured the larger units, Hendre Ddu was successfully revived, but at Glyn Ceiriog the curiously named 'Square Slate Quarries Ltd' had less luck taking over tiny Nantyr from the proudly named but nonetheless defunct, National Welsh Company. In Cwm Gwyrfai, there was a flurry of activity. Hafod y Wern re-opened albeit briefly, after a decade of near idleness as the Victoria quarry. Rhos Clogwyn, re-started on a modest scale, abandoned their incline, reaching the NWNGR by a ropeway. A buyer was found for Treflan and Llyn y Gadair was revived. Several quarries, such as Bryn Hafod y Wern, were now being worked on a small scale by men unable to find other employment, sharing profits, if any, between them. This 'Free enterprise', incidentally, did not appeal to the Union (now amalgamated with the T. & G.W.U.), who stipulated in 1923 with a nice ignorance of economics that they must pay each other at least £2 per week.

There was some improvement in trade in 1924 but financial returns remained poor. Government help was sought, particularly in the matter of the use of slate for official buildings. Representations were again made to help quarries on Crown land by the abatement of royalties, and assistance was sought to combat imports.

There was talk of strengthening 'Brand Images' but an attempt by Votty & Bowydd to do this, failed partly due to the problems of marking the product. An industry-wide publicity campaign to promote the use of slate was mooted but it was thought that the merchanting system made this too difficult. Merchants were coming in for a lot of stick at this time, it was alleged that they were increasing their mark-ups to compensate for lower prices, it being said that instead of the traditional 10-15% they were now getting 15-20%. Some were said to be regarding the extra 60 they got in every Mille, not as an allowance for breakages, but as part of the count and making claims for any mille that was not of 1260 saleable pieces. It was also said that they were lax in emphasising to buyers that the Welsh mille meant 1200, whereas import prices were based on the bare 1000. In fact the whole question of count was confused. Most quarries sold by the mille, although a few such as Croesor sold by the actual 1000, as did most London Merchants. Elsewhere the mille still ruled and at least one court case arose through a dispute over how many was a 'thousand'.

There was also disquiet at the varying names given by various quarries to differing qualities, buyers were confused by such terms as 'Best', 'First', 'Strong Deep' and so on. The number of varieties offered was criticised. (Penrhyn was listing nearly 250 different items).

Credit, always the bane of the industry, stretched to 3 or 4 months, and there were bad debt problems. The traditional method of solving 'cash flow' difficulties by holding back wages (which were by now generally weekly) was of course no longer an option. With money tight, big stocks of unpopular sizes both at the quarries and in merchants' yards on consignment terms (i.e. paid for when sold), were an embarrassment. There was still a tendency to always seek to make the biggest and best slates that could be made out of a particular block, even when perhaps smaller and cheaper slates were in better demand. Critics pointed out that it was better to make a product that could be sold rather than a nominally more profitable one that could not.

By 1925 trade was picking up and short time working became the exception and there were reopenings at Henddol, Llanfair, Westminster, Foelgron, Moelfre (after a 40 year closure), and a brief re-opening of Tal y Sarn. New companies were formed at Llangynog and Graig Ddu, the latter putting in a new oil-engine compressor to work drills, a winch and a pump. Both Croes y Ddwy Afon, and Rhiwbach put in new saws and compressors, but when Chwarel Ddu, revived as Castle quarry, ordered a solitary 10hp pump such expenditure was considered sufficiently newsworthy to be reported in the trade press.

Outputs improved further in 1926, in spite of the coal strike causing some hold ups, and in 1927 the quarter million tons was exceeded for the first time since the war. But the growing pressure of imports which had leapt to almost 50,000 tons, kept prices weak at about $17\frac{1}{2}\%$ below the 1921 peak.

In 1928 trade was slack, by 1929 it was stagnating. Some optimism remained in what was left of the slab trade, with tiny Craig y Cribin re-opening after many years idleness, but Hafodlas' closure was more typical of its continuing decline. This was reflected in contractions in the independent manufacturing trade. Williams Eureka at Port Dinorwig had been taken over by Dixons of Bangor and in 1924 they amalgamated with Fletchers of Victoria Dock, Caernarfon. As Fletcher-Dixon they maintained their ability to make large fabrications, such as a tank produced in 1930 reputedly 24' long, 9' wide, 11'6' high made of 38 slabs of Penrhyn slate 2½' thick, weighing 28 tons, but their billiards tables and enamelled products had dwindled to almost nothing. (The firm was eventually taken over by Wincilate and absorbed by Inigo Jones of Tudor works Groeslon).

A more than 10% reduction in the 1930 price lists failed to stem a steepening dive into recession. At first Dinorwig managed to keep their 2000 men on full time, partly because they had captured much of Nantlle's Irish trade. Thus Nantlle which had already lost nine quarries since 1914 (Blaen y Cae, Braich, Cloddfa'r Coed, Cloddfa'r Lon, Gloddfa Glai, Gwernor, Tal y Sarn, Tan yr Allt & Tŷ Mawr) was further hit, with Fronheulog, Pen yr Orsedd, Dorothea and Pen y Bryn all laying men off in the New Year. Nantlle was also choking on its own debris. There being limits to how high it could be piled and how many disused pits could be filled. There was a revival of the old idea of a collective rubbish railway to the sea, but finding finance for such a project was out of the question.

By March 1930, depression was spreading. Many more quarries announced short-time working, even Dinorwig having to go onto a 3 day week. Some such as Glynrhonwy and the hitherto buoyant Bryneglwys suspended work completely. In June, 600 Welsh slatemen were reported as unemployed and 2000 as being on short time. By the end of the year, little more than 200,000 tons had been sold and many of the men who had been on short time were now totally without work. There were shock failures such as that of the Llanberis Slate Company, operators of Cefn Ddu and Chwarel Fawr. Happily import tonnages were also down, partly due to a new requirement to mark them 'Foreign', but they still topped 40,000 tons.

In 1931, in spite of prices being trimmed by a further 5% there was no respite. At the start of the year the totals of slate quarry workers reported at various Labour Exchanges as unemployed or on short time were; Bethesda 1456, Llanberis 1322, Penygroes (Nantlle valley), 532, Bangor 58, Blaenau Ffestiniog 86, Porthmadog 83, Pwllheli 2. By June 1931, the Union reported that for the industry as a whole, only 700 men were working a full $5\frac{1}{2}$ day week, 1000 were on 5 days, 2750 were on 4 days, 2100 were averaging $2\frac{1}{2}$ days and 130 were unemployed. Such figures suggest that employers were trying to avoid total lay-offs, though hard economics might have favoured total temporary closure. In Nantlle there were further body blows. Both Pen y Bryn and Old Pen y Bryn failed, likewise Amalgamated Slate, making 500 men jobless at Cilgwyn, Moel Tryfan, and Alexandra, the latter still suffering the effects of the 1927 gale which blew down the Blondin masts. In 1922 there had been 11 firms operating in the Nantlle area, employing nearly 1700 men. By the end of 1931 there were just 4 employing 865. Invariably when a company went through, the men were left not only idle but with wage arrears unpaid. Such closures also had a 'knock on' effect on the quarries' suppliers, they having to cut staffing and suffer bad debts.

The hard times again fell most heavily on north Caernarfonshire, as was emphasised by house prices. In Bethesda, £30 was an average price for small properties; some two-bedroom cottages sold for £15 and quite substantial 3-bedroom dwellings only fetched £60. The Blaenau area fared better, Oakeley and others had periods of short time working, but these were mostly brief. Of the only 8 quarries in Wales having more than 100 men in full-time employment, 4 were in Blaenau. (Oakeley, Llechwedd, Maenofferen, Votty & Bowydd). Blaenau's fortunes were also helped by the few vital pence more that their products could command over the likes of Penrhyn and Dinorwig. Some Nantlle prices also held up well, with Dorothea commanding a slight premium over even Blaenau.

Imports were still making heavy inroads into the market. French prices had increased but were still way under Welsh prices. In 1931 10 ton lots of 'Best Quality' Fumay French slates were being offered at Harwich quay for £23 18 6 (£23.925). At that time Best Blaenau slate would cost about £33.60 at Porthmadog and even Seconds would have been £28.30. (As part of their marketing exercise, the importers declared that French slate was *'Guaranteed not to turn white'*. It was roundly retorted that Welsh slate *'required no such guarantee'!)* Besides the price advantage, imports benefited from the configuration of the rail network that made it easier and cheaper, to reach main markets from the Channel or east coast ports than from the Welsh slate districts. As regards home-produced competitive materials, one report priced 100 sq. ft of roofing in cement tiles at £1.50 against over £3.00 for Welsh slate.

In late 1931 the hope that the abandonment of the Gold Standard would help exports, boosted confidence. Dinorwig, which had been on a 2-week month, went to full time, and despairing of getting orderliness into the huge hotchpotch the workings had become, made a tentative new opening high up on Mynydd Elidir at Marchlyn. This project, exemplifying how the motor lorry now enabled a really major new opening to be made without any need for rail access. Dorothea, also on a 2-week month went to a 3-week month and then to full time, and even took men on. Penrhyn also resumed full week working. At the end of 1931 although the numbers totally unemployed had not fallen, there were fewer on short time. In 1932 Alexandra, Braich, Cilgwyn and Moeltryfan closed and would have stayed closed had not the energetic partners at Rhos, Owen Owen, J.J. Riley and Lord Ancaster, joined with Major Goronwy Owen DSO MP to strong-arm the new National government to make a grant enabling them to form the Caernarvonshire Crown Quarry Co. to take them over. They could not do much with Braich, but amalgamating Alexandra with Moeltryfan and electrifying, they took on 20 men and repaired the Alexandra mill that had been damaged by fire during the closure. They attempted to make a new opening (New Crown) between it and Braich, but its success was limited. Dorothea absorbed Gallt y Fedw and South Dorothea, Pen y Bryn was restarted, but within months it was again closed. The small Fronlog took over Gwernor and Tŷ Mawr East to re-commence small-scale working.

In Denbighshire, Moelfferna installed a third diamond saw to cope with the extra business they inherited when neighbour and rival Penarth closed. By this time diamond saws had an additional attraction in that they cut heavily doused in an oil-water emulsion, often avoiding the extractors that regulations now demanded for steel saws. Besides the expense of ducting, extractor fans could well absorb almost as much power as the saws they served.

In 1932 the Welsh output managed to stay above 200,000 tons, but with exports weak Blaenau's share decreased. Also, although some quarries were moving more product, returns for all but the largest and most efficient were below break-even levels. In fact in spite of the increase in the use of power of all kinds, the whole industry had become seriously less efficient. At this time Penrhyn quarry calculated that for all purposes, they utilised 3760 hp of electric power, 1740 hp of steam, 1090 hp of hydropower and 200 hp from oil-engines. This total of 3 hp per man employed was exceptional, but the average for all quarries at the time was still 2 hp. In the 1880s when power averaged well below 1 hp per man outputs in open quarries in north Wales had averaged 31 tons with underground workings slightly more, by the 1930s open workings were only averaging 24 tons/man year, with underground workings even less. The reduction in hours and a lower proportion of slab product was partly responsible and there could have been some truth in the assertion that the men *'Regard modern machinery as being to their benefit not that of the quarry'*. But worryingly the fact was that the fall in productivity was primarily due to good rock becoming more difficult to win. Average make to waste ratios had been around 1 – 15, now 1 – 20 was usual, with Penrhyn reported as getting a mere 1 – 100 in the upper galleries. Added to which journeys to the tip were getting longer and frequently involved up-haulage, Cilgwyn had almost a mile of sinuous uphill track and an engine in steam just to deal with the rubbish. Quarries were said to be spending 15% of gross revenue on waste removal.

The struggles of 1932 and 1933 brought further wage reductions as hard-pressed firms tried to balance their books. Economically, the quarries were trying to climb a down going escalator. Price reductions that should have made their product more competitive were being more than matched by the fall in the price of tiles. Tile production and imports though below their 1927 peaks, still aggregated to the equivalent of almost half a million tons of slate.

There were pontifications in the trade press alleging owners' shortsightedness. It was said with some truth, that quarries fought each other for business, rather than presenting a united front against the tile industry. Their bad state of repair was often criticised. An instance was made of the condition of quarry rail lines that required the continued use of old and inefficient double-flanged wheeled trucks, laboriously dragged over collapsing track. It was suggested that *'management would rather spend £10 per week keeping track repaired than pay £25 to replace it'*. Sound advice – to any who had actually got £25. Wrysgan was an instance of the marginal state of some quarries. Their spectacular self-acting incline, failing to 'self act', had been converted to single acting, hauling empties up by a steam engine. Unfortunately the boiler was too small so journeys stalled through lack of steam. When mains electricity was put in to drive the mill and the workshop, it was decided to electrically haul the incline. Since a third motor could not be afforded, when empty trucks needed to be raised, the workshop motor was unbolted, and dragged to the incline-head where it was temporarily installed to power the incline. Eventually an old lorry engine was used. Another incline was powered by the engine of the manager's Lea-Francis car, (Hopefully with his agreement!). At this time stringencies were not confined to the quarries. On one occasion when a man was injured at Croesor in 1930, an ambulance was called. The vehicle's brakes proved so defective that on the road down from the quarry, men with ropes had to hold it back!

In 1933 fortunes were mixed. Tonnages overall held up, with Blaenau recovering well. Hoare's bank put extra capital into Oakeley, enabling them to buy Votty & Bowydd (and 2 years later Diffwys), and to seek new rock by re-developing Cwmorthin. The dewatering of Cwmorthin Old Vein section was not a problem, but to drain 45 million gallons from 70 flooded chambers on the Back Vein, called for specialist contractors who made a 5' borehole through from the existing workings. As a result their 800 men who had been working a 10-day month, went onto full time. Hoare's Bank sought an amalgamation with Llechwedd but their £440,000 valuation of Oakeley and £90,000 for Llechwedd met with understandable derision from the Llechwedd board. Also Mrs Inge, daughter of W.E.Oakeley who had inherited part of her father's share in the Oakeley Quarries, was firmly advised to have nothing to do with it. Thus the bid fell though.

Llechwedd, although its 400 or so payroll was half that of Oakeley, was a much more valuable property partly due to the innovative enterprise of Martyn Williams-Ellis. He had extended the electrification, with a Diesel set to back up the hydro plant and had introduced electric traction. Always stressing the great economies that could be made, by improving waste handling, he put in an overhead conveyor to carry waste from his pioneering untopping scheme. Such ropeways were usual in Lake District for carrying product but apart from Cefn quarry at Cilgerran, unknown in Welsh quarries. Williams-Ellis' innovative use arose from his realisation that the new more powerful Diesel versions of the steam excavators used in Pen yr Orsedd, Penrhyn and elsewhere for rubbish removal, could be used to strip off the overburden from old underground workings. This would expose the pillars, which represented a considerable amount of good slate rock.

Oakeley had considered untopping in the 1890s but it was not actually done there until the 1980s. Several other quarries such as Blaen y Cwm untopped to a limited degree, but Llechwedd was the first to fully adopt this method, although the necessary buying out of grazing rights cost them dear. Untopping is now the basis of almost all Blaenau work. Williams-Ellis also introduced an unusual monorail system to assist with movement of finished slate from mill to stockyard, possibly copying a system that may have been used at Hafodlas. He also developed slate powder manufacture.

At Penrhyn trade was now better and they put in extra pumps, as the lowest workings were now 200' below the drainage adit. The immense task of de-watering a big pit working is shown by figures published by Major Griffith, the Penrhyn manager. These showed that each 1' of rain meant something like 22,500 tons of water entering his quarry. This deepening also meant that about a third of the 800 tons of water the water-balances used each day had to be pumped, calling for 150 hp from waterpower and 567 hp from electricity.

Elsewhere trade was thin, Dinorwig for a time laid off 400 men, Aberllefenni operated a 3-day week and many others also cut back. Dorothea added Old Pen y Bryn to their collection, continuing the trend towards fewer but larger business units. Since 1900 the number of slate firms in north Wales had shrunk from 100 to 36, their average output increasing from 4000 tons to well over 5000 tons per year.

In Denbighshire things were steady, during the 20s and into the 30s, 4000 tons or so being produced each year, mostly from Cambrian and Moel y Faen, each employing about 100 men. Most of the rest being raised by Clogau and West Llangynog with 20 or so men each. (Moelfferna at that time being in Meirionnydd). This was only half of the county's turn of the century total, but well up to what had come from there in much of the 19th century. Pembrokeshire's traditional few thousand tons, was down to a few hundreds, Montgomeryshire contributed a similar amount, but Cardiganshire, with the Aberystwyth enamelling trade gone, produced scarcely anything at all.

Northwest Wales' tonnages did improve in 1934 with all the larger quarries restoring full-time working. In March, Dinorwig worked their first Saturday for 4 years. There was further improvement in 1935; Welsh tonnage reaching almost 230,000 but only Caernarfonshire was actually up on the 1925 output, (167,000 against 164,000). Of the rest of was Meirionnydd was down by 17,000 from 72,000 in the ten years, The Denbighshire workings were down by 1100 to 3700 and West Llangynog, soon to be felled by their pillar robbing exploits almost halved to 800 tons Pembrokeshire was virtually a wipe out down to 400 tons from almost 2000. Despite being down from 900 to 700 Gilfach made Carmarthenshire's output more than Pembrokeshire's for the first time ever.

Some very slight price increases were obtained, that were partly passed on in wage rises These increases brought the minimum wage up from 7/3 (agreed at Arbitration in 1932) to 7/6 (36.25p to 37.5p). This gave a guaranteed weekly wage packet of about £2.00. Where the Letting Standard was at the 9/9 (48.75p) maximum, the top rockmen averaged just under £3.00 for a full week. By contrast white-collar pay was around double this, as emerged when a court case involving falsification by two wages clerks at Penrhyn showed their salaries to be £300 and £260 p.a. respectively. This was an anachronistic and resented echo of the time when literacy and bilingualism commanded a premium. Alexandra/Moeltryfan having closed for some months, re-

224

opened with new machinery, Garreg Fawr was revived, and an attempt was made to resuscitate nearby Plas y Nant after 40 years of idleness. There was even activity at such little slab workings as Gartheiniog.

However, the overall outlook was not good. In 1922 annual house completions had numbered 103,000, in 1935 they were 332,000, a rise of over 200%. Over the same period slate consumption had increased by only 25%. Whereas in 1922 almost half of new houses had slate roofs, by 1935 the proportion had fallen to well under 20%. For besides the cost of roofing with tiles being less, slate was unfashionably redolent of the old industrial terraces, and out of keeping with the smart new suburbias. Also apartment blocks and 'modernistic' houses with flat roofs were being built in increasing numbers. Even local loyalties were stretched, as when Pembrokeshire County Council opted for tiles. It being calculated that the heavy local slate, though no dearer would have called for an extra £7-8 per house in additional timbering.

Although a 15% duty had cut imports, they still totalled 32,000 tons in 1935, over 500% up on 1922. Exports, which now included Ireland, were a derisory 3000 tons and falling. Possibly more worrying was the fact that quarries elsewhere in the U.K. were gaining ground. In 1922 when the Welsh output was about 200,000 tons, the rest of the U.K. produced little more than 30,000 tons, a 13% market share. By 1935 a demand for the 'fancy' colours from Westmoreland and recent vigorous activity by other English and Scottish producers, had pushed their tonnages to 70,000, a 23% market share.

To fight 'fire with fire' a £365.000 'Colloidal Slate Company' was set up jointly by the big Caernarfon and Blaenau quarries to coat slates in 'Westmoreland' colours. This was not an enamelling process, but involved an allegedly weatherproof paint. The factory was strategically sited at Llandudno Junction, where the Holyhead line bringing slate from Penrhyn and Dinorwig, was joined by the Blaenau Ffestiniog branch, and was of course well placed to reach any part of the UK. Big sales were claimed, and although their products cost only about 15% extra, comfortably below Westmoreland prices, it was not a success. Latterly wholly owned by Oakeley quarry, it stumbled on until 1939. The Coleg Harlech warden's house is an example of its use,

By 1935 the decline of the granite trade having forced the Glyn Valley Tramway to close, Cambrian, with a tonnage nearing 3000 were now dispatching it all by road. The motor-lorry had become cheap and reliable and the 1930 Road Traffic Act having increased speed limits, its challenge to rail and to what remained of the coastwise shipping, was firmly established and growing.

Total U.K. tonnages edged downwards in 1936, to less than 300,000 but a strong showing in Blaenau helped Wales' share. In 1937 U.K. tonnages eased again with Scottish and Isle of Man quarries being badly hit, but again thanks to a good showing in Blaenau. despite some industrial problems, Welsh tonnage at 226,000 held up well.

The industry was becoming even more concentrated, with Dinorwig, Blaenau and Penrhyn accounting for about 80% of the output. Nantlle, where employment was little more than half its early 1931 total, produced about 10%. The other 10% came from the rest of north and mid Wales. In southwest Wales Gilfach was now the sole serious producer, Twrch quarry's last substantial order before closure being the roofing of Carmarthen County Hall.

In 1937 employment in north Wales quarries was 8223 –

LLANBERIS	2371 39% Dinorwig 2369, Upper Glynrhonwy 2
BETHESDA	1916 23% all at Penrhyn
BLAENAU FFESTINIOG	2174 26% Oakeley/ Diffwys 765, Llechwedd 438 Maenofferen 429, Votty & Bowydd 314 Craig Ddu 95, Bwlch y Slaters 65 Cwt y Bugail 41, Wrysgan 27
NANTLLE	1000 12% Dorothea/Gallt y Fedw/ Pen y Bryn/South Dorothea 359, Pen yr Orsedd 351 Caernarvonshire Crown (Alexandra /Clgwyn/ New Crown/Moel Tryfan) 185 Tyn y Weirglodd 39. Fronlog 36, Tan yr Allt 11, Gloddfa Coed 9, Fron 7, Gallt y Llan 3
DENBIGH	219 4% Cambrian 121, Moelferna 98
MONTGOMERY	22 -% West Llangynog
CORRIS	247 3% Braich Goch/Abercorris 101, Aberllefenny 131 Ratgoed 15.
DYFFRYN CONWY	175 2% Cwmmachno 123, Rhos 52.
SOUTH MEIRIONNYDD	99 1% Bryneglwys 58, Gartheiniog 26, Hendre Ddu 15.

The highlight of 1937 was the Coronation, royal occasions having always been celebrated with some enthusiasm in the slate areas. It was a public holiday; quarries such as Penrhyn paying an extra 10/ (50p) to the men and 5/ (25p) to the boys and almost for the last time, Rock Cannon were fired. These Rock Cannon were used to celebrate notable events, both local and national. They comprised a number of holes drilled in a flat rock, with incised channels connecting them. Properly charged with powder these would provide a succession of explosions. It is said that some were capable of 'playing' God Save the Queen. (Recent investigations of surviving examples have failed to produce any evidence of such cadence).

But after the high jinks it was back to the grind, in a shrunken and ailing industry, clinging to a minority share of a market it had dominated little more than a quarter of a century before. The still primitive state of affairs was exemplified, when in the dry summer of 1938, Bryneglwys had to conserve water by suspending the supply of electricity to the village of Abergynolwyn. Then with the reservoir dry and totally dependent on waterpower, all work had to stop to await the autumn rains.

Thus when war came in 1939, the industry was smaller, weaker and in worse shape to meet its difficulties, than it had been in 1914.

13. NADIR AND A NEW HOPE
1939 On

The outbreak of war in September 1939, brought an even more abrupt drop in trade than had 1914. Within weeks, Dinorwig closed their Allt Ddu and Vivian outliers. Others such as Penrhyn also closed departments, some like Dorothea closed completely. The rest ticked over, most working short time, hoping for the best. Bryneglwys kept going but suffered from a big collapse and flooding. In January 1940 Penrhyn shut down for 5 weeks, announcing that they would not be able to re-employ single men aged between 20 and 35. By this time the industry was described as *'In severe depression, with large stocks of unsold product'*. The many buildings furiously being erected for military purposes might have provided an outlet, but these were invariably roofed in other materials, some of which it was claimed, were imported.

Many quarries were to play a direct part in the war effort; the two Glynrhonwys became respectively an ordnance factory and a bomb depot, Dinorwig's extensive workshops turned out munitions components. Underground chambers in idle quarries such as Croesor, Wynne, Llanfair and Hendre Ddu (Dinas Mawddwy), were ideal for explosives storage, the latter's tramway being replaced by a road to facilitate this. Bwlch y Slaters held works of art and even abandoned chambers at still-working quarries such as Braich Goch hid munitions. Defence factories were again established at Bethesda, Llanberis and elsewhere, and the various works and foundries produced military components and the ports built landing craft. When the Daimler aero-engine factory at Coventry was bombed, a complete replica sprang up at Peblig Mill, near Caernarfon, within weeks. At Blaenau, a boot-repair factory for the U.S. Army was established in the Market Hall with beyond-repair items incinerated on the Crimea Pass. A curious of relic of this is the mock monument to the 'Dead Boots' surrounded by the resting vestiges of countless thousands of hobnails and heel-irons.

As men left to work in these and other war industries or to join the forces, more quarries closed. Others struggled on with scratch crews of the old, the unfit and the very young, Government restrictions confining their markets to emergency bomb damage repairs. By 1945 tonnage was scarcely 70,000, and of the pre-war total of 40 quarries, less than half remained even notionally open.

The end of the war brought a demand for slates to re-roof blitzed buildings but their use, except in very small sizes, was banned for new construction. This meant that there was no repeat of the unbridled scramble of 1918-1920, but the run-down quarries could scarcely cope with even this constrained market. Continuing price controls meant that they could neither afford to re-equip, nor pay realistic wages.

There were also controls on virtually everything the quarries needed to buy, timber, steel, motor fuel, coal and so on, were all in 'short supply', obtainable, if at all, only on permit. More serious was the manpower shortage. Quarry workers were granted early release from the forces, and mercifully there were many more survivors than there had been from WW1, but now as then, the returning men often opted for better-paid and less arduous employment. Several increases had brought wages well above pre-war levels, the day rate being up from 9/4 (46p) to 14/10 (74p) with piecework rates perhaps 25% more, but in the meantime living costs had risen even further.

By mid 1946 Dinorwig had only managed to build up to about 1300 men, scarcely half their pre-war numbers, and not much more than their war-time low of 1000. Increasingly difficult working conditions with obsolete plant and an ageing workforce reduced their productivity to well less than 30 tons per man. At Penrhyn things were worse, where 1000 men could scarcely raise 20,000 tons. At Nantlle, Hafod Las, Tynyweirglodd and Vron soldiered on but almost all production was from Dorothea, Pen yr Orsedd and the Crown Group (Alexandra/Moeltryfan, Cilgwyn), their payrolls around a third of their pre-war total. Outside of Dinorwig, Llanberis had ceased to be a slate-producing area. At Blaenau, Diffwys, Votty & Bowydd, Rhiw Bach and Cwt y Bugail were all turning out only a fraction of their former tonnages. Oakeley, Llechwedd and Maenofferen remaining the only substantial producers. The whole of the Welsh industry barely topped 100,000 tons, less than half the pre-war figure and not dramatically above their wartime output. In 1939 manning had been – 1261 rock men, 1346 shed men. 484 apprentices and boys and 1400 other occupations, now the headcount was scarcely half this.

Controlled prices were raised in 1946 by a derisory $2\frac{1}{2}\%$ and the next year by 5%. This made scant contribution to parlous finances, and was almost entirely absorbed by a wage award of 5/6 (27.5p) per week, and a reduction in working hours to 44. With even top men still averaging little over £5, there certainly was no stampede for quarry jobs. When in early 1947, the Cambrian quarry at Glyn Ceiriog, laid off their 70 men due to severe weather, many were taken on by the Council to clear snow from the roads. Having sampled such seemingly light and highly paid work, so few chose to return that the quarry could not re-open. Similarly, when there were strikes elsewhere later that year, a number of men obtained other employment. It has been said that the duration of one at Aberllefenni, was determined by the time it took to erect a Bailey bridge for the Forestry Commission!

It was becoming clear that little Government help could be expected. For example, agricultural workers and miners, received priority in housing, but underground slatemen were not officially classed as 'miners' for this purpose, in spite of their workplaces being legally defined as mines. Similarly, food being still rationed, coal miners got special allocations of such things as cheese, slate 'miners' did not.

In 1947 controls were relaxed to permit slate roofing on new buildings within Wales and in England if not more than 75 miles from the source quarry. This brought talk of re-activating some old sites such as Pantmawr and Parc, there was even a proposal to re-open Gorseddau! With manning so difficult, plant expensive and scarce, and with no one coming forward to invest in slate, none of these enterprises came about. There was some cheer in Porthmadog that year when a cargo of slate was loaded at the quays, but that proved to be the last ever.

All restrictions on slate supplies were lifted in 1949, but the quarries were unable to make much impact on the tile-dominated market. Many quarries could not match even wartime manpower levels, and some, such as Bryneglwys that had survived the vicissitudes of a century or more, not to speak of two wars, stumbled into closure. Several quarries were advertising surplus equipment, among them Moelfferna, hawking their incline gear, rollers, and tramway track, which the use of lorries had made redundant.

The 1951 election was largely won on promises of an unprecedented house-building programme and unlike many election promises, these were substantially fulfilled, but overwhelmingly the roofs were tiled. In 1952, even in Caernarfon, municipal housing was being tiled, since this showed a saving of £100 per house the local authority had little option to do otherwise. Not only costs were involved, skilled slaters were not to be had. Anyway such slate demand as there was, was being increasingly met by imports, mainly from Spain whose war having finished 6 years earlier than the rest of Europe had developed a substantial slate industry. The Press fulminated about the poor quality of imported slate, but although there was some truth in this, buyers were not deterred.

Trifling incidents were hailed as harbingers of resurgence, such as the 1953 loading of 100 tons of Moeltryfan slate at Caernarfon, the first slate dispatched by sea since before the war. But the slide in sales continued with stocks starting to accumulate, particularly of the smaller sizes and damp course slates, the latter being displaced by cheaper, more efficient and more easily laid plastic. This was bad news for the 'tip-pickers', who had long been an integral part of the industry particularly in Dyffryn Nantlle. Sometimes working quarries contracted them to make small slates from dumped rock on their tips, acting in effect as 'extra mural' bargainers. More often they would work the tips of abandoned diggings, (With or without permission!). The remains of their crude shelters and sometimes their jury-rig pulleys can still be seen. Their shelters were invariably sunken into the tips, not so much to avoid the weather it is unkindly said, but to avoid the Benefit inspectors!

From the early 1950s demand slipped year by year, the slab trade being all but non-existent, other than for plaques and decorative features, with gravestones suffering doubly from cremations and reconstituted stone, but in spite of severe unemployment problems in the slate districts, most quarries were still constrained by lack of men, rather than lack of orders. In 1955 the once great Diffwys finally closed, just failing to reach its bicentennial. By 1956 several pay rises had brought the labourers' day rate to £6 19 6 (£6.98) per week but the skilled men's day rate was only about 4/6 (23p) more. The effect of this was apparent the next year when Cwm Machno who in the late 1940's had been employing a good three-quarters of pre-war numbers, laid off 20 labourers, as they could not get enough rockmen and slatemakers to support them; closing completely shortly afterwards. Neighbouring Rhiwbach besides having manning problems were still tied to the use of the now rickety tramway. Having failed in their rather cheeky bid to get the Local Authority to repair the 'road' from Penmachno, they too closed. Even with the 1960 increase of 5/ (25p) per week, wages were little more than young girls were being offered in the factories now coming to the area. Plus of course factories provided dry, heated workplaces, good washing and lavatory facilities, and canteens. Certainly much better money was to be had on construction work such as the Trawsfynydd and Tanygrisiau power stations, the Tryweryn dam and in plants such as Llanwern steel works in south Wales.

Moelfferna where Thomas Firbank writing in 1952 quoted the manager T.J. Davies as saying '*I could employ 200 men but can only get 27*'; rumbled on quite profitably but by 1960 the impossibility of finding skilled replacements for their ageing workforce made closure inevitable.

Annual sales already down to 50,000 tons drifted down further, with employment well under 2000, half of what it had been 10 years earlier. Prices at over 3 times pre-war figures were approaching levels at which efficient units could profitably operate, but put slate prices even further above tiles. Also, slum-clearance and urban renewal schemes provided an abundant source of second-hand slates, their much-vaunted durability thus now proving counterproductive.

Decades of hand to mouth working had left most quarries in a disorganised mess, overwhelmed with ill-sited rubbish tips, they struggled with out-of-date methods and worn out plant. None more so than the once mighty Dinorwig. Still using traditional saws, (although most of their 500 tables were idle). Still using some steam locos, gulping prohibitively priced coal, having only pensioned off the last of their horses in the early 1950s. With only 700 men remaining and an almost negligible output, they energetically revived their 1930s Marchlyn ideas. At the new Marchlyn Mawr site, almost at the top of the mountain, reputedly a million and a half tons of overburden was cleared by the most modern machinery. New saws were put in to cope with the optimistically predicted 12,000 ton output, but it all proved a costly failure, (ultimately obliterated by the top reservoir of the pumped storage scheme). Encouraged by some firming of demand in the mid 60s they hung on. The almost total cessation of dispatches by sea, (their last steamship having been sold in 1955, the same year that Penrhyn disposed of their sole surviving vessel) and lorries replacing rail freight, made the Padarn railway redundant and in 1961 it was closed. A year later the Penrhyn line was also closed, and a year after that, the rump of their still horse-drawn Nantlle tramway took its last load from Pen yr Orsedd.

Things were no better in Meirionnydd. In Blaenau despite there being nominally 8 quarries working they employed less than 1000 men a far cry from the 1935 13 quarries with 2222 men and a further cry from the distant days of 1901 when 19 quarries employed 3516. For Corris the figures were respectively 2 & 91, 4 & 154, 8 & 329 and the rest of the county there was just Moelfferna with its 54 men as against in 1935 3 quarries with 190 men and in the halcyon days of 1901 4 with almost 400 men.

In 1967 prices were reduced, but Best Duchesses still cost about £170 per 1000, which worked out at £1.75 per sq/yd, way over any other roofing material. By 1969 the total Welsh output was only 25% of that of 20 years earlier, little more than half the UK requirement for building repairs alone. With no let up in sight, Dinorwig bowed to the inevitable and sacked their remaining 350 men.

In the meantime, Dorothea had been boldly modernising. In 1955 having by now grid supply, a 60 hp electric pump, (plus another for stand-by), had replaced the Holman beam engine. These pumps, operating at night on off-peak rates, dewatered only down to 440'. The sinc below this level being used solely for waste, thus eliminating some up haulage. A road was built down into the workings, enabling agricultural tractors and trailers loaded by mechanical shovel to handle both block and waste. Rail movements, along with their solitary horse, were phased out. One of their 20 Greaves type saws was converted into a diamond saw of their own devising by Williams of Porthmadog. Its 10 hp motor and 20' blade travelled above and across the existing table enabling the table-motion to be used to position the block for cutting. A small pulverising plant was also commissioned. Yet in spite of having invested some £25,000, by 1969 with annual tonnage less than 1000 and falling, they too were forced to close.

The next year Oakeley, now the second largest quarry after Penrhyn, dogged by the ever-increasing costs of pumping their extensive tunnels and chambers, followed Rhos and Votty & Bowydd into closure. Cwt y Bugail and Moeltryfan staggered on for a time before they too closed. In 1969 Pen-yr-Orsedd, down to 30 men with an output of only 700 tons, perceived that with so many competitors having failed, there was a prospect of survival, provided that methods were radically updated. They put in 3 Anderson Grice diamond saws, 2 with 600 mm blades, hand fed (The operator moved the table in accordance with the ammeter read-out from the 20 hp motor), and one with a 450 mm blade, hydraulically fed. They also had a locally made 600 mm saw, for the department producing 12'x12' x 3/8 floor tiles and 4'x4' x 1/2 wall tiles, with all mill waste being dealt with by conveyor. They built a road down to the workings, making the last surviving Blondins in the industry redundant, but by the late 1970s with only 15 men still employed, they too closed. By now, less than 20,000 tons of Welsh slate could find a market, mostly produced by one quarry, Penrhyn. Even the tip-pickers found their gleanings unprofitable.

At Blaenau, its population less than 50% its 1890s peak of almost 11,500, only the Greaves company carried on, probably cross-subsidised by their Quarry Tours venture. This successful enterprise, based around the old Llechwedd No 2 mill, capitalised on a long tradition of quarries as 'tourist attractions'. According to A.T. Story, writing in the 1890's *A courteous application to managers will generally result in permission being given to go over the quarries'*. So popular were these visits that at one time Penrhyn retained a retired slateman as a guide. Unfortunately regulations now restrict visits to working quarries.

At Corris, Llwyngwern faded away (becoming the site for the Centre for Alternative Technology) and Braich Goch, a shadow of its former glory, just quietly died, to be re-incarnated as a café, craft-centre, and theme cavern. Aberllefenni soldiered on solely as a slab producer. Apart from some very small scale working in the Nantlle valley, at Berwyn and at Cwmorthin, that was it. (Cwmorthin was worked underground, transport being provided by an old Landrover whose dents testified to the narrowness of the passages through which it was driven. It is a sad reflection on our times that due to vandalism their saw had to be re-sited in an underground chamber).

The industry was locked into a downward spiral, with outputs, manpower and stocks at such ebb that producers could not respond to orders when they came. Users could not rely on being able to get Welsh slate in the sizes and quantities, and at the time they needed it. Even the most sympathetic Planning Authorities had to waive their insistence on local product. By the early 1970s total employment had fallen to little more than 500. Towns such as Blaenau Ffestiniog, their populations halved, their shops shuttered, their hopes shattered were, like the industry that had created them, gripped in an abomination of decay.

Those quarries not vanishing under the bland grasses of 'landscaping' schemes, or the conifers of afforestation, seemed destined to be just sources of landfill hardcore. Their only likely product being the slates stripped from their abandoned buildings, or of slates cut from the blocks of the buildings themselves. The best hope seeming to be to become part of the tourist scene with Visitor Centres such as, Llechwedd, Llanfair, Wynne, and later, Gloddfa Ganol.

It had been said of Penrhyn 1880 *'The peculiar metallic sound emitted as the slates shoot down the steep inclines, the oft-recurring reverberations from the blasting, the enormous sombre heaps of rubbish, the materials of which are ever restless, ever working, the Babel of Welsh tongues shouting and vociferating as only a Welshman can shout, the ceaseless bustle'*. Now it seemed that such sounds would only be heard as electronic simulations.

Then, in the early 1980s there came a turnaround. The grants to restore old houses stimulated demand for slate. At the same time there was a growing appreciation of its properties that caused architects to increasingly specify it for both roofing and detail of commercial and public buildings as well as prestigious houses. Also and vitally, the soaring fuel prices of the mid 1970s had forced up the cost of kiln fired tiles, thus enabling slate prices to be advanced to levels that could make quarrying economically viable. And at last, and almost too late, Government grants became more readily available to help quarries re-equip to meet this new demand.

There had already been two bold initiatives that augured well for the future, both in sense backward integrations. In 1956 the Lloyd brothers, seeking sources for their London slate enamelling interests, bought Braich Goch and Aberllefenni, and although they had to eventually abandon the former, they vigorously modernised the latter. The acquisition of both Fletcher-Dixon and Inigo Jones give them a benevolent monopoly of slab and fine-product production.

Meanwhile at Penrhyn, the fourth Baron Penrhyn having died in 1949, the estate passed to his niece Lady Janet Douglas Pennant who made over the Castle and part of the estate to the National Trust. In 1964 the McAlpine construction group took over management of the quarry assuming full ownership in 1973.

Although these ventures differed greatly in scale, they were both unencumbered by any great experience of Welsh slate quarrying. To both proprietors the fact something had 'always been done this or that way', was, in view of the industry's decline, seen as good grounds for considering alternatives.

At Aberllefenni, the product to waste ratio that had been running at a profligate 1 to 67 was cut back to 1-3, largely thanks to the pioneering use of a Korfmann chain saw. This saw that was virtually unknown outside Germany until it came to prominence when it was used in the re-siting of the Abu Simbel temple in Upper Egypt. Later the chainsaw was supplemented by a wire saw. Handling was updated and the mill equipped with diamond circular saws and their unique reciprocating diamond gang saw. Efficiency of production of their premium slab was further improved in the 1980s, when their finishing processes were moved from Caernarfon to Aberllefenni.

At Penrhyn, one of the first actions by the new management was to rid themselves of the constraints of the internal rail system. Euclids loaded by diggers carried rubble and fork trucks handled block. Later a system of tractors and semi-trailers was put in to maintain a constant supply of block to the mills. Abandoning rails, apart from the obvious advantages of being able to move material more quickly, also greatly simplified development work and enabled larger blocks to be carried to the mill, fully exploiting the capacity of modern saws. The mills were rebuilt and re-equipped, eventually having conveyor-fed, paired diamond saws with laser measurement to optimise block out-turn.

Penrhyn were one of the first quarries to palletise all finished slate, which together with restriction of the product range enabled high productivities to be achieved. Make to waste ratio has remained something of a problem, partly because of energetic extraction methods and partly because the best rock is overlaid by inferior material. Efforts to improve this by sawing rock from the face proved disappointing.

At Llechwedd too, well ahead of any sign of recovery, manager B.Hefin Davies, (later becoming the first non-family member to head up the Greaves company), staunchly maintained his belief that slate quarrying had a future. Under his leadership Llechwedd was extensively modernised. Instead of 4 mills with 100 saw tables, reduction was concentrated at No.5 mill, with diamond saws being installed in the 1960s. Afterwards reduction was transferred to No 7 mill, re-built and re-equipped to the most modern standards. They took in Votty & Bowydd and Diffwys where, as at Llechwedd itself, the untopping methods they pioneered in the 1930s were energetically pursued. Excavators, Euclids and forklifts replaced manhandling and all use of rails, (the main incline being last used in 1964). Shot firing was supplemented by crawler-mounted jackhammers and wire saws.

Maenofferen, briefly owned by J.W.Greaves in the 1850s, was bought back in 1952 and worked underground, with wire saws, rubbish in the chambers being handled by excavator. The mill was modernised and in 1976 a new road made redundant the Rhiwbach No.2 incline, the last self-acting incline in Wales. (A road had replaced No.1 incline many years previously). The two underground inclines remained in use, controlled by the original brine bath resistors. (The sole modernisation was the replacement of the wooden barrels by plastic dustbins!)

At Blaenau there were also other happenings. T. Glyn Williams with his sons, members of a long and distinguished slate dynasty, boldly bought the Oakeley quarry site in 1970, not only as a base for their plant hire business, but also to restart slate working. Lower Quarry, (the old Welsh Slate Co.

site) became a self-contained production unit; the old Holland/Mathew quarries became Gloddfa Ganol as both a visitor centre and a production unit. The Cwt y Bugail Company was acquired and used as a springboard for the notable lawsuit that resulted in the Government yielding its hold on the Bwlch y Slaters quarry, which then became available for them to fully develop along with the Graig Ddu site. They tool an interest in Cwmorthin also reopened Pen y Orsedd, re-equipping it and the four Blaenau units with the most modern machinery. Up to date mechanical handling was devised with the Blaenau quarries working by untopping the old underground workings.

Regrettably, in 1985 the vigour with which the Williams quarries were modernised, gave rise to dispute. There followed a seven-month strike, the first of any consequence in Blaenau for over 90 years and the longest dispute in the industry since the turn of the century events at Penrhyn.

Fortunately the divisions at Blaenau healed more quickly than at Bethesda, where more than a century after 1900-1903, the descendants of 'Y Bradwyr' (the traitors) who worked during the strike, are still pariahs. But it was a setback for the town and the industry.

A spin off from the strike was the re-opening of Croes y Ddwy Afon after 60 years of idleness, by a group of dismissed workers. To augment their locally based financing they obtained apparently strong outside supporters, who also took an interest in Cwmorthin. Their untopping and mill modernisation enabled them to prosper, Unfortunately the 1990 recession that all but halved 1989s 85,000 ton UK demand, caused their backers to fail and with them both Croes y Ddwy Afon and Cwmorthin, a failure that presaged further contractions during the final decade of the century.

A fall at Pen yr Orsedd caused a suspension of work; Llechwedd facing geological problems closed Maenofferen. The Williams sold out the Blaenau operations to McAlpine, who eventually closed all three mills, transferring the

241

reduction of block to Penrhyn.

Despite the optimism of the millennium, in 2004 economic conditions succeeded in doing what two World Wars the Civil War and for that matter the Wars of the Roses, failed to do – end extraction at Aberllefenni.

Penrhyn with radical new methods and extensive mechanisation now dominates the industry in a way that exceeds the wildest dreams of the Lords in their castle. At Nantlle the Humphreys carry on their two centuries of family tradition at the little Twll Llwyd quarry. Berwyn, which survived for years as a tiny working, was taken over by a south Wales businessman in the early 1990s, to develop its potential for slab production. Braich Ddu operates on a small scale, there is some work at Alexandra and some production of building block has re-commenced at Cefn in Cilgerran near Cardigan.

Fortunately those that remain in the slate industry now, at last, have rewards comparable with other occupations. Clothing protects them from the wet and from minor injury, and machinery has eliminated the worst of the toil. Dust control has abated dust diseases. No longer are men required to hang from ropes or chains, or to work by candlelight under doubtful roofs, so accidents are now rare. No longer do we have scenes such as used to occur at Dinorwig. Where, when the locomotive whistles signalled an accident, people in Llanberis would rush into the streets to stare across the lake as the stretcher made its long and laborious journey down gallery after gallery to the quarry hospital. And then watch to see if it would be taken in through the front doors or continue on to the side door into the slate-slabbed mortuary.

All this has had to be paid for. Although productivities are, thanks to modern machinery, double the traditional 30 or so tons per man-year, capital amortisation even spread by round the clock working, imposes heavy overheads. Slate prices in 1900 were approximately four times those of 1800. In 1960 they were 11 times that of 1900. By 2000 they were more than 25 times the 1960 levels (plus VAT!)

These price levels leave the way clear for countries such as Spain with massive opencast operations unobstructed by ancient waste and structures, to offer substantially lower prices. Even in the slate areas of Wales where planners rightly insist on slate roofs, EEC regulations prevent them specifying 'Welsh' or even 'UK'. The can only specify European. Fortunately buyers in the rest of the world equate 'Welsh' with 'Best' and are allowed to say so.

In the meantime less regulated, lower wage-rate countries are already encroaching on the European market and will increasingly do so in the future, particularly as 'Country of Origin' regulations permit, say Brazilian slate, that has been finished in UK to be described as British.

Slicing up rock is bound to be dearer than a process-generated product. Despite the reputation for durability of slate, particularly Welsh slate, few specifiers are likely to be swayed by a life prediction measured in centuries and anyway slate's advantages of durability may be eroded as improvements in substitute materials are made. Despite slates now being offered pre-holed, slate will always call for more skilful laying than interlocking tiles.

There is also the problem that qualities and sizes made tend to be decided by the rock not the market. This and the ability to meet large orders, even when output is slowed by bad rock or re-development, calls for very large quantities being put down as stock. Modern 'Just in Time, Not Just in Case' business economics discourage this.

A tile manufacturer does not have these problems, he can rapidly, change moulds or mixes, needing few special skills he can afford to hire and fire to meet market demands.

Roofing slate must remain, a premium prestige product, other than perhaps the reconstituted slate made from resin and slate dust and so finding an answer to the age-old problem of what to do with the waste. For literally centuries, uses for the millions of tons of slate waste have been sought. Powdered slate has traditionally been a significant part of Penrhyn output, although they have never been able to dispose of more than 1% of their total waste in this way. Other quarries have long had, at least a minor trade in it, with varying degrees of success. In 1919 the North Wales Development Company was set up at Bethesda to make powder at Pantdreinog. Although they processed some 100 tons per week, some as 'Myrtox' for metal cleaning, by the end of 1922 they were insolvent. Hafodlas when it was reactivated in 1919 included a pulverising plant, but the quarry closed ten years later.

In south Wales Cefn and Glogue made respectively blocks and bricks with limited success. In 1947 Penrhyn did some cement-block making but like the 1949 plant at Porthmadog to make tiles from Nantlle tips, failed to meet expectations. Dinorwig's 1954 brick and tile plant initially produced, with two-shift working, some 50,000 bricks per day, but failed to recoup the large investment. Likewise the unsuccessful brick making plant at Llwyngwern and the abortive Corris Fillers, pulverising plant at Braich Goch.

Pulverised slate has been used for cement making, such as the Solite plant at Bwlchgwyn, Wrexham in the 1960s, which used tip material from the Oernant quarries. Also as an abrasive, for compacting into insulators etc., as a filler for linoleum and plastics, as source of mineral wool and for glass making, even for face powder. Yet more bizarre than the suggestion that it might be processed to extract its Alumina content was the idea that Blaenau tips could be a handy source of Uranium to fuel Trawsfynydd nuclear power station! The pulverising plant at Blaenau, supplying the 'artificial Slate' industry has been successful, but the difficulties and using anything but fresh waste does little to reduce the existing tips.

A more promising outlet for slate waste is bulk-fill. Only a fraction of the several hundreds of millions of tons of slate waste generated by the industry is economically recoverable, but the fiscal regime is making such activity increasingly attractive. In fact there are ambitious plans to work the Blaenau tips on a big scale. On addition, the availability of portable crushing plant means that comparatively small and relatively inaccessible tips can now be economically worked, providing the potential for a widely spread industry.

There is a perception of slate quarrying in Wales sentimentally clinging to an obsolete way of life. This is far from the truth; it is run by businessmen, who are too busy calculating cash flows, returns on employed capital and bottom-line margins, to have time for sentiment. They employ hard-working and ambitious young men (and women) with skills more allied to the microchip than the chipping tool.

However no matter how state-of-the-art the equipment, Welsh slate will meet increasing competitive pressure from other materials in mainstream usages so will need to seek niche markets for this precious and finite resource.

Realistically, the slate industry of the future must follow three routes.

1. **The 'Swiss Watch'** approach where a small quantity of raw material is converted into a valuable product. One may scoff at wine coasters, house names and knick-knacks but these retail at 20 –30 times the price per ton of dearest roofing slate and often waste can serve as raw material. They also serve a social purpose in being much more labour intensive than 'mainstream' products and so help keep skills alive. Furthermore making such items calls for little capital investment and can be profitable on a modest scale, encouraging start-up business. With works by such as Lucy

Sweeney and Richard Boulton, this category spills into the second –

2. **The Artistic.** Following the tradition of slatemen engraving their chimneypieces and of making skill-displaying curios, slate is increasingly being used as an artistic medium. There are the juxtaposed colours of William Rice, the bold, uncompromising carvings of John Cleal, the bas-reliefs of Meic Watts and Ivor Richards, the light relief carvings of Diana Hoare, sculptures by Reg Beach and William Roberts and indeed jewellery by Sara Humphries and other eminent artists. A number derive their sympathy for and understanding of the rock, from inbred skills. Others artists are incomers who, merely by dwelling among the slate, seem to acquire by a curious osmosis a similar empathy with the material. Slate gravestones are, despite the use of computer technology and mechanical cutting, regaining for monumental masons their 19th century eminence. The 800 R.A.F. squadron plaques in Welsh slate in St Clement Danes church must be surely categorised as art. Commemorative tablets are also now *bona-fide* artistic works its 'calligraphic superstars' such as John Williams, Ieuan Rees or the late Jonah Jones. Again this category impinges on the next.

3. **The Prestige Artefact.** Present day costs debar slate slab from its old utilitarian role, but with a growing worldwide affluence there is a growing demand for and appreciation of the best. Firms such as Cerrig, Inigo Jones, Snowdon Slate and Clean Slate Design, appreciate that Ford makes the most cars, but Ferrari makes the most money. Hence merging creative design with the latest technology, they apply skills inbred over generations to produce, aspirational products to the highest standard.

Whilst not all these confine themselves to Welsh slate, they do ensure that the skills that have grown over the centuries are not only nurtured but are developed to embrace the latest technologies. No longer do the quarries and works quaintly cling to 19th century methods, Penrhyn has combined 21st century engineering with 'lateral thinking' to use sawing to eliminate splitting and simulate the traditional product with mechanical edge-deckling and surface flame-treatment. At least two manufacturers use high presssure waterjet profiling. Wales is again a world leader in the working of slate. This augurs well for the survival of the unique social fabric of places such as Bethesda or Blaenau Ffestiniog.

Admittedly the culture of the Caban no longer exists, if indeed it ever did quite to the extent that historians would have us believe. Nor does the industry have poets of the stature of Eifion Wyn, (a clerk to the Croesor quarry), or prose writers to match Kate Roberts (daughter of an Alexandra quarryman) nor bibliophiles such as Bob Owen (another Croesor clerk), literary giants of the 20th century. Yet who is to say that their peers may not appear at some time in the 21st?

But in any case, like everywhere else, the visual image is displacing the written word, and scions of slate working dynasties are already prominent on the national scene in drama and television.

It is in music that the old traditions are most manifest. Brass bands and choirs are fewer and are no longer chapel-driven nor quarry based, but both are still central to the communities. The Deiniolen Band for instance, which is headquartered in an old writing-slate factory, is the centrepiece of village life. The Moelwyn Male Voice Choir probably has a stronger following in Blaenau Ffestiniog than even the Rugby team. The magnificent Faenol Festival held in the grounds of the erstwhile Dinorwig quarry owner's house has obvious slate associations. That centre of musical and artistic excellence, Y Tabernacl at Machynlleth draws on a cultural tradition forged in the slate workings of southern Meirionnydd.

Whilst these follow the more classical musical tradition, the slate regions are in the forefront of developments in modern music. 'Pesda Roc' places Bethesda firmly in the national scene, leading Wales if not the UK in the production of recordings, its only rival being Blaenau Ffestiniog.

Happily the tradition of Welsh slate is being made accessible to the wider world by such initiatives as the Welsh Slate Museum. Thanks to the energy (and guile) of the late Mr D. Morgan Rees part of Dinorwig Quarry site and much equipment was secured to form the basis, of the present museum housed in the old quarry workshops.

At much the same time the resourcefulness of Mr Hefin Davies resulted in the setting up Quarry Tours at Llechwedd quarry, Blaenau Ffestiniog that preserved machinery and unprecedentedly took visitors underground, by train and by a passenger incline. More modest underground visits are also provided at Llanfair Quarries near Harlech. Inigo Jones offers a unique opportunity to see slate machinery actually in operation.

Such initiatives have also developed an interest in old skills and past activities and created recognition of the need to conserve the physical remains of them – hence for instance the work done by the Snowdonia National Park in stabilising the unique Cwm Ystrallyn slate mill.

FFESTINIOG ROADS
(With acknowledgments to Mr. G. R. Jones)

Until the early 19th century the Vale of Ffestiniog like many other places in upland Wales, was almost inaccessible to wheeled vehicles. Such roads as there were, were scarcely passable in summer and totally impassable in winter. So slate and any other industry was largely dependent on pack-animals. It was only the quarry-built and the turnpike roads that gave wheeled carts anything like a free passage.

1801 Diffwys. Built present road from quarry to Tan y Manod (SH708452) and along line of present main road to join a pre-existing road to Llan Ffestiniog just beyond Congl y Wal (SH705442). This latter road is still the main road although it then went though Pen y Bont (SH706429). (Still readily traceable).

1802 Bowydd (Lord) built road directly down to Four Crosses (SH704458), now defined by a street. There it picked a pre-existing route over the river at Pont Fron Goch (SH703453) then on to Congl y Wal. (Still readily traceable).

1804 Graig Ddu/Manod This well engineered road almost continuously traceable from the quarry to where it joined the Blaenau-Llan road near SH706433 (at some time it may have been diverted (SH721459) to join the pre-existing Cwm Teigl road (SH724435)

1820s Rhiwbryfdir. Followed present street to the now main road (SH698463) and on to Four Crosses where it picked up the 1802 route. All these routes went from Llan Ffestiniog to Tâl y Bont (SH685416) via the existing road, which had been rebuilt in the later 18th century to ease the gradient (The old road is traceable immediately to the south). The present bridge at Tâl y Bont dates from the 1860s, before that traffic took the present 'back road' to Maentwrog, crossing the river to join the present road by a bridge that still exists at

SH684416 (It can be seen how this bridge was widened, possibly when the abovementioned road down from Llan was re-routed.

The difficulties were illustrated by the fact that to reach Congol y Wal it typically took two prodded and beaten horses in tandem harness to move a mere half ton (500Kg). At Congol y Wal the lead horse could be unhitched and the load augmented from a roadside dump to some 13cwt (650Kg) and at Llan Ffestiniog, the laod coule be increased to the full one ton. for the journey to the Dwyryd wharf.

Late 1820s Diffwys. Built the 'Hen Ffordd Casson' that is defined by the present road from Congol y Wal to Rhyd y Sarn (SH690421) via Cwmerau (SH695432). A road of sorts already existed from Maentwrog to Rhyd y Sarn, where their sawing facilities had been established. This road and a road down to Cwmerau from the Orthin valley formed the Ffestiniog turnpike. With the increasing volume of traffic the formation of the Ffestiniog Turnpike Trust must have seemed a good idea at the time but it soon lost much of its traffic to the Ffestiniog Railway.

There was no road from Blaenau Ffestiniog to Tanygrisiau until the mid 1850s when the present (back) road developed along the line of the Ffestiniog Railway

Any quarrying to the east of Llan Ffestiniog had to make do with the roughest of tracks to Llan Ffestiniog until 1818 when the Ffestiniog-Bala turnpike was built. This (now forming the present road) instead of going straight up onto the mountain from Llan, turned left to ease the gradient.

SELECTED BIBLIOGRAPHY

Baddley & Ward *Through Guide, North Wales, Vol1* Dulau & Co 1892

Bennett, G. J. *Pedestrian's Guide Through N Wales* Colburn 1838

Bingley, W. *A Tour Round Wales (1stEd)* Bingley 1800

Boyd, J. I .C. *The Festiniog Railway* Oakwood 1975

Carrington, D. C. *Delving in Dinorwi*g Carreg Gwalch 1994

Davies, D. C. *Slate & Slate Quarrying* Crosby, L'wood 1878

Davies, D. L. *The Glyn Valley Tramroad* Oakwood 1966

Davies, J. *A History Wales* of Allen Lane 1993

Dodd, A. H. *The Ind. Revolution in N. Wales* U of W Press 1971

Eames, A. & Hughes *Porthmadog Ships* Gwynedd A.S. 1975

Eames, A. *Heb Long Wrth y Cei* Carreg Gwalch 1991

Holmes, A. *Slates from Abergynolwyn* Gwynedd A S 1986

Hughes, J. E.& B. *Chwarel y Penrhyn* Penrhyn Quarry Ltd 1979

Isherwood, G. *Cwmorthin Slate Quarry* Merioneth Field Study 1982

Isherwood, G. *Slate* A. B. Publishing 1988

Jenkinson, H. I. *North Wales* Stanford 1878

Jones, E., *Bargen Dinorwig* Tŷ a'r Graig 1980

Jones, G. R., *Chwarel Blaenycwm* Ff P T B 1992

Jones, G. R., *Hafodlas* Jones 1998

Jones, G. R., *Rhiwbach* Jones 2005

Jones, I. W. *Eagles Do Not Catch Flies* J. W. Greaves 1986

Jones, I. W. *The Llechwedd Strike 1893* Llechwedd 1993

Jones, R. M. *North Wales Quarrymen 1874-1922* U of W Press 1982

Lewis, M. J. T. (Ed) *The Slate Quarries of N Wales 1873* S N P Study Centre 1987

Lewis, M. J. T. *Blaen y Cwm – Cwt y Bugail* Adit 2003

Lewis & Denton *Rhosydd Slate Quarry* Cottage Press 1974

Lindsay, J. *History of the N.Wales Slate Ind.* David & Charles 1974

Lindsay, J. *The Great Strike 1900-1903* David & Charles 1987

Lloyd, L. *The Unity of Barmouth* Gwynedd A S 1977

Lloyd, L. *The Port of Caernarfon 1793-1900* Lloyd 1989

Lloyd, L. *Pwllheli The Port and Mart of Llŷn* Lloyd 1991

Lloyd, L. *Wherever Freights May Offer* Lloyd 1993

North, F. J. *Slates of Wales* Nat. Mus Wales 1925

Owen, R. *Diwdiannau Col*

Parry, B. R. (Ed) *Chwareli a Charwelwyr* Gwynedd A S 1977

Pennant, T. *A Tour of Wales MDCCLXIII (1st Ed)* T Hughes 1778

Rees, D. M. *The Industrial Archaeology of Wales* David & Charles 1975

Pritchard, D. D. *The Slate Industry of North Wales* Gwasg Gee 1946

Tomos, D. *Llechi Lleu* Agraffdy Arfon 1980

Williams, G. J. *Hanes Plwyf Ffestiniog* Hughes & Son 1880

Williams, M. *The Slate Industry* Shire 1991

Williams, M. Elis *Bangor, Port of Beaumaris* Gwynedd A S 1988

Williams & Lewis *Pioneers of Ffestiniog Slate* Plas Tan y Bwlch 1987

Williams & Lewis *Gwydir Slate Quarries* Plas Tan y Bwlch 1989

OTHER SOURCES
Public Reports

Report of the Departmental Committee upon Merionethshire Slate Mines 1895
Inspector of Mines Reports 1875 on.

Journals
The Mining Journal, 1846 – 1891.
Quarry Manager's Journal, Vols 14 on.
The Slate Trades Gazette 1912 – 1926
Transactions of the Caernarfonshire Historical Society Various
Transactions of the Merioneth Historical Society Various

Archive Material
J.S. Wilkinson & other deposits Gwynedd County Archives Caernafon

Various deposits	Gwynedd County Archives Dollgellau
'	Ynys Môn County Archives Llangefni
'	Pembroke County Archives Haverfordwest
'	Carmarthen County Archives Carmarthen
'	Ceredigion ArchivesAberystwyth
'	National Library of Wales Aberystwyth
Field Reports	Plas Tan y Bwlch Maentwrog

Home Office lists of Mines, various dates.

SIGNIFICANT SLATE SITES MENTIONED

Aber	SH977594	Denbigh
Abereiddi	SM798314	Fishguard
Abercorris	SH754089	Corris
Abercwmeiddaw	SH746093	'
Aberdunant	SH583420	Tremadog
Aberllefenni	SH768103	Corris
Alexandra	SH519562	Penygroes
Allt Ddu	SH591610	Llanberis
Alltgoch	SN620964	Aberdyfi
Arthog	SH652152	Dolgellau
Berthlwyd	SH629481	Beddgelert
Berwyn	See Clogau	
Blaen y Cae	SH498535	Penygroes
Blaen y Cwm	SH735459	Bl'au Fest.
Bowydd	SH708464	'
Braich	SH510552	Penygroes
Braich Ddu	SH718384	M'ntwrog
Braich Goch	SH748078	Corris
Braich Rhyd	SH512548	Penygroes
Brondanw Isaf	SH616421	Llanfr'then
Brondanw Uchaf	SH619426	' '
Bronyfoel	SH544390	P'madog
Bryneglwys	SH695054	Towyn
Brynfferam	SH519558	Penygroes
Brynglas	SH732423	Ffestiniog
Bryngwyn	SH627133	Fairbourne
Brynmawr	SH555595	Llanberis
Bryn H' y Wern	SH631693	Bethesda
Bwlch Cwm Llan	SH600521	Beddgelert
Bwlch Gwyn	SH767558	Bet's y c'd B'ch y
Dd'y Elor	SH557500	Caernarfon
Bwlch y Slaters	SH732455	Bl'au Ffest
Cae Abaty	SH846136	D'ns M'dy
Cae Madoc	SH825654	Llanwrst
Cae'n y Coed	SH681408	Ffestiniog
Cae'r Defaid	SH784233	Towyn
Caermenciau	SH562601	Llanberis
Cambergi	SH765108	Corris
Cambrian	SH566603	Llanberis
Cambrian (Glyn)	SJ189378	Chirk
Cedryn	SH719635	Dolgarrog
Cefn	SN209429	Cilgerran
Cefn Ddu	SH555604	Llanberis
Cefn Gam	SH680256	Dolgellau Cesail
	SH690466	Bl'au Ffest
Chwarel Ddu	SH721521	Dolwyd'an
Chwarel Fawr	SH552600	Llanberis
Cilgwyn	SH500540	Penygro's
Cletwr	SH985348	Bala
Cloddfa'r Coed	SH493532	Penygroes
Cloddfa'r Lon	See Pen y Bryn	
Clogau	SJ185463	Llangollen
Clo'wn y Fuwch	SH759618	Trefriw 1
Coed Madog	SH490530	Penygroes
Conglog	SH670467	Bl'au Fest
Cook & Ddol	SH560605	Llanberis
Craig Rhiwarth	SJ053262	Llangynog
Craig Wynnstay	SJ202473	Llangollen
Craig y Cribin	SJ047262	Llangynog
Craig y Glem	SJ171478	Llangollen
Craig y Orin	SJ234362	Gl'nCeir'g
Croesor	SH657457	Llanfr'th'n
Cr's y Dd'y Af'n	SH754424	Ffestiniog
Cwm Bach	SH564406	Tremadog
Cwm Brechiau	SH708043	Abergy'l'n
Cwm Bychan	SH683655	Bethesda
Cwm Caeth	SH605466	Beddgelert
Cwm Du	SH831125	Dinas M
Cwm Dwyfor	SH541505	Tremadocl
Cwm Ebol	SH689017	Pennal
Cwm Eigiau	SH701634	Dolgarrog
Cwm Gloddfa	SH766062	Corris
Cwm Machno	SH750471	B's y Coed
Cwm'ngwynedd	SJ075326	Llangynog
Cwmorthin	SH681459	Bl'au Fest.
Cwm Teigl	SH736446	Ffestiniog
Cwt y Bugail	SH734468	Bl'au ffest
Cyfannedd	SH631125	Fairb'ne
Cymerau	SH777106	Corris
Daren	SH721058	Corris
Deeside	SJ138404	Corwen
Dolbadau	SN198429	Cardigan
Dinorwig	SH595603	Llanberis
Diphwys	SH712463	Bl'auFf'st.
Dolfriog	SH611458	Beddgelert
Dolgarth	SH538495	Tremadoc
Dorothea	SH500532	Penygroes
Drum	SH735431	Ffestiniog
Egryn	SH605205	Aberdyfi
Era	SH760064	Corris
Faenol, Fachwen	SH578615	Llanberis
Foel	SH717556	Capel C'ig
Foelgron	SH744428	Ffestiniog
Fforest	SN190450	Cardigan
Foel Gron	SH744428	Ffestiniogl
Fotty	SH706465	Bl'au f'st.
Fridd	SH573526	Rhyd Ddu
Fron	SH515548	Penygroes
Fronlog	SH489517	Penygroes
Fronboeth	SH652448	Llanfr'then
Fron Goch	SH664972	Pennal
Fronheulog	SN600998	Towyn
Fronlog	SH489517	Penygroes
Gaewern	SH745086	Corris
Gallt y Fedw	SH499535	Penygroes
Gallt y Llan	SH601583	Llanberis Garreg

Fawr	SH538582	Caern'rfon	
Gartheiniog	SH822117	Dinas M'y	
Gelli	SH637463	Llanfr'then	
Gerynt	SH631484	Beddgelert	
Golfach	SN128271	Whitland	
Glandyfi	SN698961	Mach'lleth	
Glanrafon	SH581540	Beddgelert	
Gloddfa Coed	SH493532	Penygroes	
Gloddfa Ganol	See Mathew's		
Gloddfa Glai	See Coed Madoc		
Glogue	SN220327	Cardigan	
Glynrh'wy Uppr	SH565607	Llanberis	
Glynrh'wy Low'r	SH570610	Llanberis	
Golwern	SH621122	Fairbourne	
Goodman's	SH572606	Llanberis	
Gorseddau	SH573453	Tremadoc	
Graig Ddu	SH724458	Bl'au Ff't.	
Gwanas	SH798160	Dolgellau	
Gwastadfryn	SH678098	Aberdyfi	
Gwernor	SH510526	Penygroes	
Hafodboeth	SH638418	Llanfr'then	
Hafod Las	SH489540	Penygroes	
Hafodlas	SH779562	B's y Co'd	
Hafod Uchaf	SH643434	Llanf'then	
Hafod y Llan	SH613524	Beddgelert	
Hafod y Wern	SH530571	Caernarfon	
Hafoty	SH632436	Beddgelert	
Henddol	SH619122	Fairbourne	
Hendre	SH698512	Dolw'dlan	
Hendre Ddu	SH519444	P'thmadog	
Hendre Ddu	SH799125	Di's M'wy	
Hollands	See Cesail		
Llangolman	SN130271	Fishguard	
Llaneilian	SH481932	Amlwch	
Llanfair	SH580288	Harlech	
Llanfflewyn	SH347892	Amlwch	
Llechan	SH756757	Conwy	
Llechwedd	SH700470	Bl' Ffest	
Llidiart y Arian	SH633433	Llanfr'then	
Llwyngwern	SH757045	Corris	
Llwydcoed	SH470508	Penygroes	
Llwynpiod	SN433299	Carmar'en	
Llyn Lagai	SH651485	Llanfr'then	
Llyn y Gadair	SH564519	Beddgelert	
Maenofferen	SH714465	Bl'au Fest.	
Maes y Gamfa	SH818127	Dinas	M'y
Manod	SH725452	Bl'au Ffest	
Marchlyn	SH602628	Llanberis	
Mathew's	SH694470	Bl' Ffest.	
Melynllyn	SH705654	Dolgarrog	
Minllyn	SH852139	D's M'y	
Moel Faban	SH626678	Bethesdal	
Moelfre	SH521451	Tremadoc	
Moelfferna	SJ125399	Corwen	
Moel Tryfan	SH515559	Penygroes	
Moelwyn	SH661442	Bl'au Ff's.	
Moel y Faen	SJ185477	Llangollen	
Morben	SN716992	Machll'th	
Nantglyn	SH978598	Denbigh	
Nantlle Vale	SH497524	Penygroes	
Nant y Fron	SH486518	Penygroes	
New Crown	SH513556	Penygroes	
Nantyr	SJ166384	Chirk	
Nyth y Gigfran	SH689462	Bl'au Ffes.	
Oakeley = Rhiwbrifidr Cesail & Mathew's			
Oernant	SJ185469	Llangollen	
Old Pen y Bryn	SH502535	Penygroes	
Pantdreiniog	SH623671	Bethesda	
Pantmawr	SH658446	Llanfr'then	
Pantglas	SJ215478	Llangollen	
Parc	SH626436	Llanfr'then	
Parc (Slab)	SH632444	Llanfr'then	
Penarth	SJ107424	Corwen	
Penlan	SN207284	Cardigan	
Penllyn	SH746522	Dolwydd'n	
Penrhiw	SH722540	' '	
Penrhyn	SH620650	Bethesda	
Penrhyngwyn	SH704149	Dolgellau	
Pen y Bryn	SH504538	Penygroes	
Pen y Ffridd	SH776612	Trefriw	
Pen yr Orsedd	SH510538	Penygroes	
Plas y Nant	SH552562	Caernarfon	
Porthgain	SM813325	Fishguard	
Portreuddyn	SH573409	Tremadoc	
Powys	SJ074294	Llangynog	
Prince of Wales	SH549498	Tremadoc	
Prince Llywelyn	SH744528	Dolwydd'n	
Princess	SH553495	Tremadoc	
Ratgoed	SH787119	Corris	
Rhaeadr	SH682012	Pennal	
Rhiwbrifdir	SH693473	Bl'au Ffes.	
Rhiwbach	SH740462	Bl'au Ffes	
Rhiwgoch	SH749537	Dolwydd'n	
Rhos	SH729564	Capel Cu'g Rhos	
Clogwyn	SH576530	Beddgelert	
Rhosydd	SH664461	Bl'au Ffes.	
Rosebush	SN079300	Fishguard	
Sealyham	SM960275	Hav'dw'st	
South Dorothea	SH496531	Penygroes	
Talymeiryn	SH825119	Dinas M'y	
Tal y Sarn	SH495535	Penygroes	
Tan yr Allt	SH491523	Penygroes	
Tan y Bwlch	SH628683	Bethesda	
Treflan	SH539584	Caernarfon	
Trwynllwyd	SM832329	Fishguard	
Twrch	SN145294	Cardigan	
Tyddyn Shieffre	SH630135	Fairbourne	
Tŷ Mawr East	SH497524	Penygroes	
Tŷ Mawr West	SH496524	Penygroes	
Tŷ'n y Berth	SH738087	Corris	
Tyn y Bryn	SH742521	Dolwydd'n	
Tŷ'n y Ceunant	SH744088	Corris	

Tŷ'n y Coed	SH649148	Dolgellau
Tyn y Garth	SN691945	Mach'n'llt
Tŷ'n y Weirglodd	SH494523	Penygroes
Vivian	SH586604	Llanberis
Votty	SH706465	Bl'au Ffes.
Welsh Slate	See Rhiwbrifidr	
Westminster	See Craig y Glem	
West Llangynog	SJ049259	Llangynog
Wrysgan	SH676458	Bl'au Ffes.
Wynne	SJ199379	Chirk
Ystrad Ffin	SN787461	Lland'very

SOME 'OFF SITE' QUARRY MILLS

Escairgeiliog	SH759059	Mill for Cwm Gloddfa & Era (In reuse)
Glandŵr	SH501559	Mill for Moeltryfan (Vestiges)
Glandŵr	SH676427	Mill for Mathews's & Nyth y Gigfran ??? (No trace)
Nant y Pandy	SJ148417	Mill for Deeside (Ruins)
Pant yr Ynn	SH708454	Early mill for Diffwys (In reuse)
Pentrefelin	SJ218436	Mill for Moel y Faen etc. (In reuse)
Pont Cyfyng	SH734570	Additional Mill for Foel (Ruins)
Rhyd y Sarn	SH691422	Putative Sawing mill for Diphwys 11 (Later buildings)
Ynysypandy	SH550433	Mill for Gorseddau (Conserved)

SIGNIFICANT INDEPENDENT FACTORY SITES
SITES IN TOWNS OR AT PORTS NOT INCLUDED

Britannia	SH530710	Vestiges
Bryngwyn	SH494562	?
Crawia	SH536643/ 540641	Ruins & reuse
Glan Dinorwig	SH572632etc	Various buildings in re use
Glanmorfa	SH484615	In reuse
Groeslon	SH470551	Still active
Llifon	SH482562?	No trace?
Matthews Mill	SH768091	House on site
Peblig Mill	SH491620	Factory on site
Pont Rug	SH512630	?